BEYOND DOUBT

Vivek Nityananda grew up in Bangalore, India, where he trained as a biologist. A scientist and a science communicator, Nityananda is currently a BBSRC David Phillips Fellow at the Centre for Behaviour and Evolution and the Biosciences Institute at Newcastle University, UK. He has several publications in the fields of evolutionary biology, animal behaviour and psychology. Nityananda is also an illustrator and has published short stories, including in Penguin India's new-writing anthology, *First Proof 7*.

Find him at viveknityananda.com.

Praise for Beyond Doubt

'How do you rate yourself? A fantastic look at the natural history of those who are smarter than average, and also of those who just think they are.

From the threads of many different research areas, Vivek Nityananda weaves together a coherent and entertaining account of overconfidence, where it comes from, and the worrying places it may yet lead us. Illustrated with fascinating anecdotes from history, contemporary India and the rest of the world, this book provides a field guide to some of humanity's most perplexing features. In so doing it helps us understand why everyone is suddenly an expert, and real expertise isn't valued as much as it was.

An illuminating account of the Who? What? Where? When? And especially Why people are prone to overconfidence, to lying to themselves and to making catastrophic errors in judgement. If you thought you knew already, you may have been suffering from overconfidence yourself. I found the book replete with subtleties, surprises, a grounding in rich examples—both familiar and unexpected—and, most of all, mountains of wonderful scientific research.'

ROB BROOKS, evolutionary biologist and author of, most recently, *Artificial Intimacy: Virtual Friends, Digital Lovers, and Algorithmic Matchmakers*

'Fascinating and sobering. An essential reminder to be wary of confidence in others—and also in oneself.'

OLIVIA JUDSON, author of *Dr Tatiana's Sex Advice to All Creation: The Definitive Guide to the Evolutionary Biology of Sex*

BEYOND DOUBT

Overconfidence and What It Means for Modern Society

VIVEK NITYANANDA

cntxt

cntxt

Published by Context, an imprint of Westland Books, a division of Nasadiya Technologies Private Limited, in 2024

No. 269/2B, First Floor, 'Irai Arul', Vimalraj Street, Nethaji Nagar, Alapakkam Main Road, Maduravoyal, Chennai 600095

Westland, the Westland logo, Context and the Context logo are the trademarks of Nasadiya Technologies Private Limited, or its affiliates.

ISBN: 9789360459710

10 9 8 7 6 5 4 3 2 1

Typeset by Jojy Philip
Printed at Parksons Graphics Pvt. Ltd

Contents

ONE

An Entomologist on Mars

THIS IS AN EXERCISE IN OVERCONFIDENCE. I'M WRITING A BOOK about human psychology. I research insects. Besides, I've never written a book before. I usually write scientific papers about the different ways insects—and other animals—sense information about the world and make decisions with that information. Comparing different animals helps us figure out when evolution selects for common strategies, and when different. That's what my research tries to do, drawing inspiration from both human psychology and animal behaviour. I have investigated how and why katydids call in synchrony. I've studied frogs and asked how they find their mates in noisy ponds. For a while now, my research has focused on how insects see and think. How do bees choose between flowers? And how do praying mantises calculate the distance to their prey?

So what's an insect biologist doing in a whole other world—an entomologist on Mars, if you will?

My ticket to Mars comes from a collaboration with my friend Shakti Lamba, now at the University of Exeter. Back when I was doing my PhD, we were both studying insects at the Indian Institute of Science in Bengaluru. She was studying cooperation among wasps and I was studying communication in katydids. Later, when we ended up with postdoctoral stints in London, however, she was doing fascinating work on the evolution of human cooperation. We had been discussing some ideas we could work on together, and decided we wanted to test a theory about the evolution of self-deception. The theory, put forward by the evolutionary biologist Robert Trivers,[1, 2] proposed that self-deception evolves because it helps individuals deceive others. He had first proposed this idea decades before, but nobody had tested it experimentally, so that's what we set out to do. After the rush of activity running the experiment, we sat down to write the paper,[3] sending drafts back and forth. It was then, while we were writing up the results, that I realised there was a lot that I didn't know about self-deception—especially about a specific form of self-deception: overconfidence.

How widespread is overconfidence? How do people become overconfident? Most importantly, why does overconfidence persist? My fascination with these questions is what led to this book. Part of my interest was (and still is) about whether we would find overconfidence in other animals. How would we measure overconfidence in a crow? In a bee? Under what conditions does overconfidence evolve, and are those conditions unique to humans? These are all interesting questions, but I do not have all the answers yet. This book, instead, focuses on humans and what others have already figured out about our own overconfidence. I dove into research by psychologists, evolutionary biologists, economists and political scientists. I read hundreds of papers, books and articles. I tried to link the material I read to the world around me. The results have in turn inspired me to run more studies which I currently have underway. What this book presents is the story of everything I have learnt—the perils and profits of our overconfidence. Does this book manage to make a convincing case? Or have I clearly taken on more than I could handle? You, dear reader, will have to pass the verdict on my overconfidence.

I am no stranger to overconfidence. In 2017, I was selected to interview for an important research fellowship. Getting the fellowship would mean I could begin my own independent research career. Without it, it was highly likely that I would be in no position to continue my research. The stakes couldn't be higher for my career. I was enthusiastic about the interview as I boarded the train from Newcastle to London—it felt like my career had built up enough momentum. In retrospect, the interview was not all smooth sailing. There were clearly questions I could have prepared for better or answered more clearly. Yet, after the interview, I thought it had gone well. I remember feeling confident, texting friends from the train that I was optimistic about my chances. I did not make it. And so, I had to face up to my overconfidence. For the next interview, if there was to be one, I would have to prepare better.

I could cite several other examples of my own overconfidence, but I'll resist the urge to self-flagellate here—the negative consequences of overconfidence are obvious. Besides, overconfidence isn't unique to me. There are any number of examples of overconfidence everywhere. A friend doesn't pack enough winter clothing for a trek in the Himalayas and faces bitterly cold nights that can lead to serious health consequences. Your cousin stakes all his savings on a business he thought was a sure bet and is left struggling to keep afloat. Once you're looking out for it, there are ever more examples—from celebrities to business magnates to politicians.

Vijay Mallya, one of the three 'bad boy billionaires' of India, featured in the Netflix series of that name, hails from my hometown, Bengaluru. In the episode that features him, there is some pre-2016 footage I found particularly entertaining. Mallya is asked by a reporter what he thinks about the frequent comparison with Donald Trump. Mallya breezily replies that he, at least, is not bankrupt. I burst out laughing—Mallya, of all people, throwing shade at Trump. The moment is even more fascinating because, while Mallya would go on to face his own financial woes, Trump's overconfidence might well have helped land him the presidency of the US. We'll return to both Mallya and Trump later in the book, but that exchange perfectly captures two symbols of overconfidence, the CEO and the politician, and demonstrates both sides of the trait: some people profit from overconfidence, while others are laid low.

The effects of overconfidence are felt around the world and at every level, from our individual lives to the leaders of companies and countries. Speculative bubbles leave the world economy in tatters. A country that doesn't take swift action in the face of a pandemic risks people's lives. If overconfidence is all-pervasive, is it a danger that we haven't reckoned with yet? One that we might urgently need to tackle to stop us lurching from one disaster to the next?

Looked at like this, it might seem obvious that overconfidence is overwhelmingly negative. Something to avoid for oneself and resist in others. But what if that was the wrong way to look at it? What if overconfidence helped us and was an essential aspect of getting through our lives? Those advantages would explain why it persists.

Remember the evolutionary argument made by Robert Trivers—overconfidence could help deceive others about our capabilities. If there are strong reasons like this for overconfidence to persist, does it not then become all the more dangerous? How bad could it get? One way to look for an answer is to begin outlining a worst-case scenario. We'll see in later chapters that there is at least some evidence for each piece of this scenario, so let's first assume the worst and see where that leads us. Let's start, as I did, with a scene from Charlie Chaplin.

As Chaplin's *Modern Times* opens, we cut from a shot of sheep jostling against each other to people pouring out of a subway, pushing their way forward on their way to work. The metaphor is not a subtle one. Humans, says the film, do as the group does. We move blindly with the flock, living out our ovine lives. Chaplin's metaphor might be a bit on the nose, but our decisions and lives are clearly influenced by the norms of our societies. We learn from the majority and follow the actions of others. Our norms, our ways of living and our habits are easily picked up through social learning. But we don't learn from everybody around us. Much as we flock together in woolly groups, some sheep are more equal than others. We pick our bellwethers and trust in them.

When faced with a decision, individuals have very different approaches. Ask ten people for advice and you might well get eleven different suggestions. How would you filter out the opinions that aren't useful? One way to do this is to rely on other people's confidence. In our daily lives, we use confidence to rapidly gauge our peers and our rivals, we make hiring (and firing) decisions based on confidence, confidence smooths the course of romance, and political discussions are perpetually scrutinising the strength and confidence of our leaders and our nations. Perhaps this isn't just a runaway trick of the mind. Humans could have evolved this tendency because it's actually useful. Trusting in someone else's confidence saves an individual time and effort, especially when dealing with difficult tasks or uncertain situations. This would give them an advantage over others who might want to work everything out for themselves every single time. If trusting confidence is so useful, perhaps they would follow a confident person's lead again without a second thought. That provides us with the first piece in our scenario: trusting confidence because we assume it signals competence can prove dangerous.

Our trust in confidence makes us vulnerable to the charms of this book's protagonist: overconfidence. Is that something we need to worry about, though? Why should anyone be overconfident? Surely it makes sense for every one of us to know what we're capable of and choose our challenges accordingly? Almost certainly, some forms of overconfidence should naturally fade out of the population. People with a tendency to overestimate their mountain-climbing abilities would soon find themselves falling down cliffs and drowning in the waters below. Getting into a fight with a much stronger opponent would bring about another sort of unhappy end. The ancient Tamil text, the Thirukural, has an apt verse stating that one who reaches the end of a branch and ventures further will not survive. It would appear that not all of us have learnt that lesson. In a wide range of situations, from driving to academic achievement, we tend to overestimate our abilities. We consistently have an exaggerated sense of ourselves and often think we are better than others. What's worse, it looks like we are particularly susceptible to overconfidence during tasks about which we are most ignorant. This might seem surprising. Surely, we should be able to recognise our shortcomings most clearly when they are most glaring? Yet, the evidence says otherwise. The more ignorant we are about a particular topic, the less knowledge we have to form a judgement even about how much we know. If you've never studied architecture and have no idea how complicated designing a building is, you might well believe that anyone can do it, including you. It's only when someone is stupid enough to let you design their dream home that you might gradually discover the heights of your ignorance.

Where does this overconfidence come from? For one, this is a trait that involves a series of psychological biases that come naturally to humans—some reflecting our innate limitations and others driven by our motivations. We seek out information that confirms our own self-serving views. If I wanted to support the notion that I am a good person (which I typically do), I would only remember the incidents which show that I am such a person and ignore all the times when my behaviour has been less than ideal. Our minds are expert spin doctors constantly enhancing our self-images. They also find the right arguments to support our points of view while ignoring evidence to the contrary. Think of how this might play out on a societal scale. It isn't hard to imagine how this is hard at work in our brave new world of fake news and alternative facts. If there is fake evidence out there that supports our claims, our minds might be constantly telling us to believe it and use it.

Are we then doomed to overconfidence? Why wouldn't we try to overcome it? In fact, there are actually multiple benefits to overconfidence. It can motivate us to seek out opportunities or persist in our actions. Overconfidence can help us achieve better mental health. And of course, it can help us deceive others about our capabilities. Imagine you're in an interview and they're asking you about your interpersonal skills. Rather than reveal your full awkwardness to the panel, you decide to provide them with fabricated accounts of your social savvy. As you lie, you're holding in mind the clear knowledge of your social ineptitude alongside the new unfolding legend of your expertise at teamwork. This isn't an easy task. The conflict in your mind increases your levels of stress. As a result, the effort you're making to hold these two contradictory ideas shows. Sweat trickles down the side of your head, your voice wavers. The panel is going to see through your lies. Instead, if you were self-deceived and truly overconfident about your abilities, you wouldn't be stressed and your deception would be more difficult to discover. This argues for an evolutionary advantage to overconfidence: it gives us the power of influence over others and all the benefits that come with that. These benefits provide us with the central piece in our worst-case scenario; they are an answer to the question of why overconfidence exists and a warning that it might be here to stay.

We are then left with the idea that people who are self-deceived might be precisely the ones who are going to influence us the most. That can't end well. Overconfident people are more likely to be risk-takers. Financial markets and companies where risk plays a prominent role should then be particularly vulnerable to the ill effects of overconfidence. Sure enough, overconfidence has been implicated in financial meltdowns and in the poorer management of companies. If overconfidence helps companies and CEOs profit (remember Vijay Mallya?), then perhaps economic crashes will keep recurring. Now that *is* a scary prospect. Overconfidence also plays out on a national and global scale, most strikingly in wars, emergencies and elections. Only a foolish country charges into conflict believing that it would lose. It would be far more reasonable for countries to assess each other's relative strengths and reach a deal rather than actually head into a war. Wars and financial crashes could be the disastrous consequences of overconfidence, with massive human and economic costs. Yet again, perhaps the reason wars still persist is due to the personal advantages they convey to overconfident people, regardless of the cost to everyone else.

Does this call to mind politicians bluffing their way to power? Political humour and analysis constantly highlight the long lists of broken promises made by politicians. Some of these failures no doubt reflect very intentional deceit. Yet, it is possible that politicians do believe their lies more often than not. If overconfidence helps politicians convince other people that they are right, then it should hardly be surprising that they convince themselves of both their greatness and their righteousness. This would also help explain how politicians sway people into voting for them and their policies, even in the light of failures. From the politicians' point of view, their very jobs would therefore rely on being overconfident. Their confirmation biases must operate on turbo charge, reframing reality to fit their worldview.

But this is not peculiar to politicians. We are all more likely to justify and defend our own decisions once we have made them, with our commitment escalating if it wins us approval from the partisan social groups we are part of. So, rather than realising our voting errors in the face of tanking economies and national discord, we are more likely to stand by the politicians we voted for and cite other reasons to explain the chaotic state of the nation. Masters of self-deception could thus get voted in time and again. We clearly need to find ways to prevent ourselves from being swayed by self-deceit and overconfidence if we want effective leaders and peaceful, thriving nations.

Building in checks and balances should avert the disasters that overconfidence could lead to. Allowing independent or opposing views to influence decisions could block biases from reinforcing each other. You might think that reading widely from a variety of sources—with openness and scepticism—could combat our confirmation biases. Perhaps it could also give us a more nuanced perspective that reduces our own overconfidence. Potentially, if we gain a clear picture of the facts, we could then make more reasoned, accurate decisions. Yet, there is evidence that facts alone don't always change minds. Sometimes a reasoned argument can even reinforce someone's prejudice. The more well informed I am, the better I will be at using facts to justify my position.

Could we be doomed to staying overconfident, each in our biased worlds? There is also a price to pay for reducing our own overconfidence. Having a more well-rounded argument seems to make for a less convincing argument. So, while you might be less deceived, you could also have a reduced ability to convince others of your argument. This is the choice we are left with: which superpower would you rather have? The ability to deceive others at the cost of losing touch with reality, or the ability to see reality at the cost of failing to convince others. The fate of our societies might lie on which of these two we choose.

So, this is our worst-case scenario. Our trust in confidence is useful and instinctive, but may not be justified, especially at crucial points. After all, it is confidence that puts the con in the con game and gives the con artist their advantage. If we are all sheep following our trusted bellwethers, then overconfidence is our Judas goat. We must learn to break its spell if we don't want to be led to the slaughter.

How well does this doom-mongering case hold up? Let's start finding out together.

TWO

Trust in Me

SUSHIL KUMAR HAD A CHOICE TO MAKE: SHOULD HE RELY ON THE advice of other people or not?

Here was a small-town boy, on prime-time television with a chance to earn millions. If he made the correct choice.

Sushil had grown up in Motihari, Bihar, and that's where he went to school. When the mega-quiz show *Kaun Banega Crorepati* (*KBC*) launched in July 2000, he was sixteen. His family didn't have a TV at home, but he watched the show every week at a neighbour's house. He was fascinated with it and always ready to test himself alongside the participant on screen. Episode after episode, he watched the joy and despair of the chosen few who got to participate on the show. It was thrilling when they won fabulous fortunes, but gut-wrenching when they made a gamble at a winning answer and lost. Across India, millions of others were just as fascinated. Millions registered to see if their knowledge—and luck—would somehow help them earn the top prize of Rs 1 crore (later Rs 2.5 crore), a prize that could change their lives.

Eleven years later, when Sushil Kumar got the call to participate in the show, he was working as a computer operator in a government office. The show was in its fifth season. In the first four seasons, the top prize had been won only three times. Based on his mock-playing as he watched the show, Sushil didn't expect to win more than Rs 50 lakh. He would have been happy to go home with that much. Yet, on the third question in the game—for only Rs 20,000—he found himself in trouble. He didn't know which part of the computer was associated with the slogan 'Intel Inside'. But he was sure what to do next. The question was barely finished when he requested the audience poll lifeline. This could go different ways. Sometimes the poll could be evenly or near evenly split between answers. This was not one of those times. The audience gave Sushil a clear answer: 72 per cent of them went for option D: the processor. Now Sushil had a choice to make. Should he go with their confident consensus or risk choosing another answer altogether? Sushil made the obvious choice and decided to go with their answer. Was he right to do that?

All of us face questions like this on an almost daily basis. How we respond determines the first piece in our worst-case scenario: do we trust other people and why? We might trust in people for all kinds of reasons—perhaps they seem friendly or we trust their expertise. But time after time we also trust people because they seem confident. We use what has been called a 'confidence heuristic'. The word heuristic is just a fancy way of describing any quick-and-dirty rule of thumb that deals with the task at hand. Typically, this rule of thumb is efficient, if not always accurate.

Let's take a look at the evidence for this. A natural first idea is simply to see whose opinions people trust—someone with confidence or someone without. To do this, psychologists Paul Price and Eric Stone asked participants to choose between two stock analysts.[1] Both analysts had the same accuracy of predictions on average. The event they predicted occurred 50 per cent of the time. They differed, however, in how closely they tracked the outcome. One of them had predictions that moderately tracked the outcome. So, if the event had a 40 per cent chance of occurring, the analyst might say it had a 50 per cent chance of occurring. The other analyst was more extreme, saying that the same event had a 65 per cent chance of occurring. All of the extreme analyst's predictions tracked the moderate analyst's predictions, but were shifted away from 50 per cent towards the extremes by an extra 15 percentage points. This extreme analyst was, therefore, clearly more confident and certain in their predictions than the first one. The key question was which analyst the participants preferred. The answer? The majority of the participants preferred the certainty of the extreme advisor. In addition, all participants thought the advisor that they had chosen was more knowledgeable and more confident. This was despite the fact that the accuracy of the event occurring was the same for both advisors—although admittedly the participants weren't told so explicitly. The advisor who was more overconfident was the preferred choice. Besides, participants even overestimated the percentage of correct predictions for the extreme advisor and underestimated the percentage for the less extreme one.

This result has been replicated using scenarios from financial predictions to weather forecasting—people place greater value on opinions that are more confident.[2, 3, 4] Take interviews. You can ask people to rate interview performance and then look at what factors correlate with these ratings. The best predictor of the ratings is self-presentation, including factors like appearance and impression management.[5] That's not a comforting thought. Our external show-and-tell is all it takes to max those interviews. But wait a minute—perhaps having self-presentation skills is a good indication of how good we really are. If that were so, there's no problem here; our ratings would actually lead to the right hires. No such luck. Self-presentation cues are more strongly associated with performance during interviews than performance on the job.[6] Similarly, another correlate of confidence, self-esteem, predicts interview evaluations and the number of jobs a candidate is offered during a job search.[7]

Let's consider another example: dating. You could ask people to rate how desirable dating profiles are, and then go back and see how ratings on other traits correlate with this rating of desirability. What predicts how desirable profiles are rated? Perceived confidence.[8] Now imagine the dating profiles of your rivals. Which of them would you choose to share a table with when talking to a potential date? People tend to choose another table rather than compete with the profiles perceived to be more confident. There's more data like this. Traits like mental speed that are linked to confidence also create an impression of charisma.[9] Advice by confident people is more likely to be followed,[10] and confident people are more likely to be believed.[11, 12] Unsurprisingly then, confidence influences who we choose as leaders[13, 14, 15] and romantic partners.[16] How do confident people manage to convince us? The most likely possibility is that their consistent defence of their positions and self-representations makes them more persuasive.[17] Another possibility is that they might just be more resistant to other people's opinions, and so others in a group might eventually cave in and go with the most confident (or stubborn) person.[18]

Either way, the evidence is clear: we trust confidence. Well then, how do we know who's confident? What are the telltale cues that convince us to trust people? We've touched on appearance and mental speed as examples of this. Unsurprisingly, other cues include the usual suspects—eye contact, hand gestures and poise also do the job.[19] The speed with which people make their decisions is arguably the best indicator of confidence. Observers rate people in videos as confident if they are quick in two different ways—quick to make a decision but also physically quick in terms of moving to make the decision. That is, the speed of their movements appears to convey confidence.[20] That's pretty shocking when you think about it. Simply by being quicker, plunging into action, perhaps talking more rapidly, we can create this impression of confidence. And then this impression, this image that we've projected, can help us ace an interview or get that first date or, well, get us elected prime minister.

So far, it seems like Chaplin might not have been far wrong. Going only by these studies, it appears that people are trusting—perhaps trusting enough to be vulnerable to overconfident scamsters. Yet, surely we don't rely on confidence so absolutely? Surely it can't be that simple, I hear you say. Sure, many of us do fall prey to smooth-talking salespeople and a variety of scamsters, but is this really our default mode of being? Why would we trust in confidence if it was such an unreliable indicator of things to come? There are two ways of answering that question. First, perhaps trusting in confidence and trusting others more generally is actually a good thing. Maybe we should explore the benefits of doing so. Second, perhaps rather than unthinkingly falling for people's confidence, we are sensible about how we trust people. Let's look at each of these in turn.

Let's start wide as we look at the benefits of trust. We make decisions gathering inputs from a variety of sources. We form opinions and estimates based on the facts we have but often enough we also need to ask others for advice. And how would a larger group work to make the right decision? The simplest way might be a poll like the one in *KBC*. Surprisingly, this vote often ends up being more accurate than any individual decision. This is true in a wide variety of groups, from fish schools or bees making a consensus decision to humans guessing the number of marbles in a glass jar.[21, 22] Audiences in *Who Wants to Be a Millionaire*, *KBC*'s parent show, are no exception. When they've been asked, the audience gets the answer correct impressively often.[23] Sushil Kumar had it right, the answer his audience chose was correct. This flock of sheep was the correct one to follow.

Seeking information by yourself is rewarding, of course. The information is potentially more reliable and you know exactly where to find resources or food. But the process of arriving at that information has its costs, even if only in time and effort. Exploring the world could have more serious consequences. An animal or a human adrift in *Jurassic Park* would find themselves vulnerable to predators.

On the other hand, relying on others often saves these costs and has the added benefit of providing new information that an individual might not have encountered. For the first two years after moving to Newcastle, I followed a complicated cycling route to get to work. Then a couple of friends at work pointed out another route I could take—one that saved me time and took me through a green area of town. Almost everyone would recall instances where they learnt about a new restaurant from others or about a particularly useful site on the internet. Listening to others can certainly help. It's no surprise then that humans are very good at learning from others. Social learning is our thing: individuals choose to learn from specific model teachers, from what the majority are doing around them and from those who have had success before.[24]

If the sum of people's votes is a highly accurate tracker of reality, then going with the majority opinion makes perfect sense. The big question is if this is true in all situations. It turns out this isn't even equally true for all questions in *Who Wants to Be a Millionaire*. The astonishingly high success rate audiences have for getting answers right seems to apply only for the first ten questions in the game and not for the remaining, harder questions.[25] The wisdom of the crowd works for easy questions, but you need the real experts for the harder ones. There are clear situations when relying on others helps: when we aren't certain of our own information, when finding things out is costly or when our usual way of doing things isn't leading to results.

When groups make decisions, the rule of totting up equal votes works well in simple situations, but there's an underlying flaw in its logic when applied to other situations. The rule assumes everyone is more or less similar to each other. Yet, people differ in their capabilities and in the level of information they have at any given point in time. You don't construct a skyscraper by consensus, you talk to builders and architects. For more involved projects like that one, you need some way of giving greater weight to the opinions of people who know what they're talking about. It's easy if you know you're choosing between a builder and, say, a biologist. But what do you do when you don't know what each person knows or what the quality of that information is? You could use a simple trick, something most of us do instinctively. We could trust the voices that seem the most confident.[26]

The simplest experiment to test if this works involves not an entire group, but just two people. In these kinds of experiments, we can compare the performance of people when they perform a task individually to when two people are allowed to discuss their decisions and reach a joint result. For instance, they could be asked to find a visual odd one out in a set of figures. Who spots the odd one out better, individuals or pairs? Such experiments have had a consistent result: two heads are better than one.[27, 28] In fact, a simple rule that often works well is to simply choose the decision of the person who had the greatest confidence in their decision.

So, trusting others and trusting confidence have actual benefits. But how sensibly do people employ this trust?

On his twelfth question, Sushil Kumar used a second helpline. He called upon an expert. The question asked was: what did former prime minister Lal Bahadur Shastri receive as dowry apart from a few yards of khadi? Kumar played his cards perfectly. This wasn't one of the first ten questions; it was in the later, more difficult category. The ideal thing to do here was to ask not the audience but an expert. When asked, the expert suggested that the answer was a charkha. Sushil now trusted in the confidence of a single other person and once again got the answer right, earning Rs 1 crore. This second helpline points to one of the conditions in which you should rely on another's confidence—when you lack the knowledge yourself. Conversely, when you have the knowledge relevant to a situation, or think you do, you should be less trusting in another's confidence.

There is evidence that this is actually how people behave. A study that neatly demonstrates this[29] asked people to make estimates of the dates of historical events. They were then given an advisor's estimate on the same events and given a chance to revise their estimates. The findings were clear. Those who were initially less accurate revised their estimates to be closer to the advisor's. Those who were initially more accurate were less influenced by the advisor's estimate.

Yet, studies arguing for a confidence heuristic—the tendency to rely on people's judgements based on their confidence—highlight the fact that people are easily swayed by overconfident and inaccurate advice. This view has been criticised by psychologists who argue that we aren't blindly following confidence, we are actually well calibrated to reality.[30] From this perspective, previous studies with analysts and experts can be explained by the fact that participants had no information of their own about the fictional stock market or weather fronts they were seeking advice about. What happens, for example, if you provide participants with additional information, especially information about how accurate the advisor really is?

One context in which this has been studied is eyewitness testimony. The confidence of witnesses has an important role to play in judging cases. But the correlation between the confidence of an eyewitness and their accuracy can be poor.[31, 32] The correlation is a bit better for positive identifications from line-ups compared to failures to recognise anyone in a line-up.[33] Even so, in general, the link between confidence and accuracy is never very strong for eyewitnesses. It would, therefore, be crucial for people on juries to take note of both the confidence and the accuracy of a witness.

Participants in mock jury studies have been asked to take on the role of jurors listening to witnesses about accidents or robberies. In some studies,[34] they then encountered something that could well happen in real life—two contradictory statements about the accident from different witnesses. One witness was confident about their testimony, while the other wasn't. Predictably, in these experiments, the mock jurors were much more likely to believe the confident witness. After all, they knew nothing about the accident apart from what the two witnesses had told them. That's the confidence heuristic saying hello once again.

Subsequently, however, following further research by 'lawyers', the jurors were provided additional information from sources that were deemed credible. This was information that either confirmed or contradicted smaller details in the statements of one or the other witness. The details had nothing to do with the actual accident. They were about another activity the witness was involved in on the same day.

In *Mera Saaya*, Sadhana is asked in court to prove that she really is the wife whom Sunil Dutt believes to be dead. She responds by giving us the devastating evidence that she knows about the mole on Dutt's back. So far, so impressive. Imagine if she then went on to say he had jalebis for breakfast, while all other witnesses swear it was poha.

When new information like this contradicts minor details in the witness statements, learning about even these peripheral errors changes the juror's views of the witnesses.[35] When the confident witness makes errors, witnesses switch to believing the less confident one.[36] This only occurs, however, if the less confident witness is correct about their assertions. If not, the trust in the confident witness goes down but there is no benefit to the less confident one. When similar experiments are run with children, they also pay attention to both confidence and errors, but not to how they relate to each other.[37] It is only adults who lose trust in people who make confident errors. However, if people are performing another demanding task simultaneously, they too are less likely to take into account the errors,[38] suggesting that relying on confidence might be a quick and easy default strategy if you don't have the time to consider all the factors involved.

The conclusion here is that people don't seem to believe in confidence uncritically. Interestingly, not all errors are equal in this context. Jurors don't change their beliefs if the errors made by the witnesses are explained by something beyond their knowledge[39]—for instance, the accident wasn't caused by the person they thought was responsible, but by his identical twin. Witnesses don't bear the cost of such an error, even if they were confident in their initial statements.

Our trust in people is not absolute. Start out based on confidence, then reassess and trust the most accurate people—that sounds like a sound strategy. Perhaps we might go even further. Do we actually 'punish' inaccurate advisors if we find out they were overconfident? Some psychologists argue that this is true. They view confidence as a signal to others of our commitment to our statements.[40] The higher the confidence, the greater the commitment we are signalling. If this is so, and our commitment is utterly misplaced, anyone who followed us in good faith has reason to be disappointed with us. There would then be costs to our reputation. Here's how they tested this. Advisors in one set of experiments gave participants directions to a location. In another, they gave them estimates of how long a typing task would take. In both cases, there was a confident advisor and a less certain one. Again, the large majority of the participants typically trusted and took the advice of the more confident one. Subsequently, both advisors were shown to be wrong. The important question then was whether the participants were willing to punish either of the advisors (or both) for their error. For instance, they were asked which of the two they would assign to a rewarding task and which one to a demeaning, boring task. In some conditions, they were asked which of the two they would prevent from getting a bonus. Despite the fact that both advisors were wrong, participants largely chose to punish only the one who was confident and wrong, not the less confident one who was also wrong. Confidence appears to only get you so far. When it's revealed to be misplaced, there's a reckoning to be had.

There's also a difference in which kinds of tasks lead to a greater trust in confidence. Some psychologists distinguish between what are called intellective and judgemental tasks.[41] The former are tasks where the answers can be worked out given enough information, and the accuracy of the answers can be unambiguously assessed. Judgemental tasks, on the other hand, have more subjective answers and can't be worked out from the information given. These tasks exist on a spectrum. Examples could range from maths problems and logical analogies (more intellective) to uninformed forecasts of the future or decisions on which was the most deserving winner of the Oscar for best picture (more judgemental). It turns out that confidence seems to have a greater influence when groups are solving an intellective task. These are exactly the kind of tasks where confidence is also a greater indicator of accuracy. For the judgemental tasks, confidence isn't as influential. That would explain the interminable arguments I've sat through about which is the best song ever or who was India's greatest cricket captain. When there isn't a clear answer, confidence is not going to resolve the issue. Group size also seems to matter for these tasks. The larger the group, the more overconfident people can be—at least on judgemental tasks.

These qualifications about our trust in confidence make perfect sense. The pattern is the same. Where confidence doesn't reflect accuracy, we are less likely to trust it. In fact, the psychologist Hugo Mercier makes a strong case that we are nothing like gullible sheep in his fascinating book *Not Born Yesterday*.[42] The central argument of the book is that we are fundamentally vigilant rather than trusting. The book convincingly argues that we scrutinise sources of information for how intuitive their arguments are, how reliable and consistent they are and whether they want what's best for us. Where confident sources are untrustworthy, they lose our trust and we might even go so far as to punish them. As we can gain more information about an issue, we tend to trust ourselves more than an external advisor, discounting their confidence more.

Our contestant Sushil Kumar played the game perfectly according to these principles. When he didn't know an answer, he asked for help—trusting the confidence of the audience for the easy questions and the confidence of an expert for the difficult question. On the very last question, when asked which colonial power sold rights to the Nicobar Islands to the British, he wasn't exactly the picture of confidence. He agonised over the answer, phoned a friend and eventually chose Denmark as the answer. That answer proved correct. He leapt out of his seat to embrace Amitabh Bachchan in celebration, knowing that he had won a whopping Rs 5 crore!

If confident advice forms a series of signposts, we follow their path strategically, trusting in our GPS when we can, ignoring the signs if they have been wrong before. Our picture then is reassuring—the very first piece in our worst-case scenario doesn't hold up quite as strongly as we thought. Time to relax then? Not quite. The very strategies we use while evaluating confidence indicate where things might go wrong. In what situations might our trust in confidence lead us astray?

To begin with, there are several situations where we have incomplete information. When starting out on anything, whether interviewing a candidate, meeting someone on a first date or even hearing a witness in a trial, we don't know enough to make accurate decisions ourselves. In other situations, we might have difficulty acquiring information—we might be under stress from other tasks, for instance—and trusting confidence could be the easier route to arrive at a plan of action. Alternatively, if information comes at an economic cost, we might trust another, more confident person's advice rather than spending money finding things out for ourselves.[43] We depend on online reviews of laptops and restaurants because we'd rather trust them than spend all our money on a range of computers and dining joints to figure out which one is best.

The problem is that we often do not know if information about a particular advisor or source is credible. Unlike the mock jury experiments, there are no handy lawyers who are guaranteed to provide us true information. Given the proliferation of opinions on the internet, we constantly have to decide who is credible and whom to potentially punish for giving us wrong advice. This is especially true when we can't keep track of every person's position and its validity—in larger groups, for instance.

There's also a difference in who faces the reckoning when the information is wrong. People are particularly likely to lose their trust when sources are inaccurate about information that is relevant to them.[44] It seems possible that people might trust exaggerated claims if they aren't affected by them. We're more likely to check a rumour about a work colleague or a family member than about whether or not aliens landed in Roswell. It's, therefore, more likely that it's the second type of rumour that will persist. A persistent rumour in the 1990s declared that Bobby McFerrin the singer of 'Don't Worry Be Happy' had gone on to commit suicide. I saw no reason to disbelieve this, and I think I confidently spread the rumour. It wasn't something that affected me. The irony and storyworthiness of the rumour probably helped its spread too.[45] The story was of course untrue. I can confirm that wholeheartedly, having seen the brilliant artist live in concert since. The idea that exaggerated claims persist amongst people who have no incentive to check them is an exciting—and urgent—idea that needs more investigation. It certainly could explain the long shelf life of a variety of strange ideas.

Finally, and perhaps most dangerously, people are more prone to trusting confidence when it suits their interests. Hugo Mercier makes this point in his book, calling it an asymmetry of trust, that is, 'we trust people deemed to be on our side much more than those deemed to be on the other side'.[46] This might be someone full of praise for our performance or a politician promising to give us a grand future.

The important thing here is that their motivations match our own—believing the implausible is easier when that helps us keep our social status or take over someone else's property. In the end, despite our best strategies, trust in confidence could be pointing us in the wrong direction in several situations.

But is it the wrong direction? Our trust is misplaced only if the confidence of others is inaccurate. It is only when the gusts of overconfidence have blown the signpost away from the real route that we end up lost in the wilderness. What matters is how commonplace overconfidence is, where it occurs and why it survives despite a world of scrutiny.

THREE

Smarter Than the Average Bear

DO YOU THINK YOU'RE SMARTER THAN AVERAGE?

Yogi Bear does. He's the title character in the classic 1960s Hannah-Barbera cartoon, *The Yogi Bear Show*. Yogi is a resourceful bear, harnessing all his smarts to steal picnic baskets in (the fictional) Jellystone National Park. He is smart enough to successfully forage for himself and there's no doubt that he's aware of it. That's announced to us loud and clear with his catchphrase, 'smarter than the average bear'. By the 1980s, this signature phrase even crept into the title song of the show. The phrase has since taken on a life of its own. People proudly use it to describe themselves. 'Smarter than the average bear' goes the dating profile or Twitter bio. It's become a humorous but effective bit of self-promotion.

This isn't a claim unique to cartoons. If you've travelled in Rajasthan, you might recall towns with the term 'Sawai' in their names. Sawai Madhopur is perhaps the most famous example, the gateway to Ranthambore National Park. Sawai in those names refers to a historical title of honour that literally credits a person as having one-and-a-quarter times more intelligence or strength than the average person. To begin with, it was a title conferred upon a person, and gradually it went on to become a hereditary title. In effect, rulers began proclaiming themselves—like Yogi Bear does—to be smarter than average.

Rulers in our modern age do this too. Here's Donald Trump:[1] 'Nobody knows more about taxes than I do and income than I do', 'Nobody knows more about construction than I do', 'Nobody knows more about technology than me'. Infrastructure, campaign finance, environmental impact statements, renewables, courts, banks, trade—he's made similar claims about every one of those topics. Overblown claims are part of his act. Trump is easily one of the most egregious examples of self-proclaimed expertise. But what about the rest of us?

I'd bet you think you're smarter than the average bear. When faced with questions like that, the majority of people inevitably say yes. Most of us think of ourselves as smarter than the average person. Also more beautiful. And more moral. This effect is so consistent that there's a name for it: the better-than-average effect.[2] It seems a natural enough thing to believe, but pause to think about it. The very definition of an average, however you calculate it, is that it lies somewhere in the middle of the population. The average salary earner earns something between the vast majority who earn more or less than her. The average consumer buys less than a lot of people, but more than a similarly large number of people. By definition, we can't all of us be better than average—whether in looks, talent or smarts. So, logically, several people who think of themselves as better than average have to be wrong.

The key point is that, when we are wrong, we are all wrong in the same direction. It's not like some of us think we are worse and the others think we are better. In that case, the effects could cancel out and there wouldn't be a better-than-average effect. We would just find a 'people have no clue' effect, perhaps not very surprising. Most people are systematically wrong in a way that enhances their self-image. In other words, human bias is very much towards overconfidence.

The previous chapter explored the idea that people can be trusting, but they are usually sensible about whom to trust. There are circumstances, however, where we are more ready to trust in others.[3, 4] For instance, in the absence of enough information, we can look to the confidence of others. However, this trust in confidence hinges on one crucial assumption: that confidence is a sign of true competence.

What if this wasn't true? What if, when we hire people, fall in love or elect our leaders on the basis of their confidence, we might be making some big mistakes. Far from rewarding the best at their work, we would merely be promoting the ones who could impress us the most with their claims and their behaviour. We would have untrustworthy romantic partners and politicians who never deliver on their promises, mostly because they don't know how. These fears only matter if overconfidence were widespread. That's why the better-than-average effect is important. If it is anything to go by, overconfidence could very much be the norm. Let's drill down a bit deeper.

To search for evidence of overconfidence, we first need to define it. As it turns out, a foundational paper by two behavioural scientists have captured three different ways to be overconfident.[5] The first is Don Moore, a professor in Leadership and Communication at the University of Berkeley, and an expert on all things overconfidence. His name and research will keep appearing throughout this book. The second is Paul Healy, a professor of Economics at Ohio State University. What do they say are the three ways of being overconfident?

First off, what you're doing when you think you're better than average is thinking that you're better compared to other people. That's what they would call 'overplacement'. Every time we decide we could do a better job than the professional on TV or think we're better than the person who got that promotion, we're likely guilty of overplacement. Luckily for us, we aren't often called upon to do their jobs and reveal our inadequacies.

The second form of overconfidence is 'overclaiming' or 'overestimation', the claiming of an ability beyond one's actual capacity. This could be the general assuring the nation that they will win the war before going on to suffer a huge defeat. It could also be the colleague who fails to deliver to a deadline they were confident about. Where overplacement is measured relative to other people, overestimation is a mistake of judgement in absolute terms.

The third form of overconfidence is called 'overprecision', a measure of being overly certain. You're a beginner at poker and you see a path to a winning hand. Sure of your victory, you hold on to your cards and keep playing far longer than you should have, certain that you will win. It is this excessive certainty that is called overprecision.

To recap, when you claim you're smarter than the average bear, you're probably showing overplacement. When you declare you could easily run a marathon without practice, you're most probably overclaiming. And when you are 100 per cent confident that your next attempt at the lottery will finally deliver you your millions, you're being overprecise—unless you've rigged the lottery.

Back in *The Yogi Bear Show*, we don't always get a good comparison with other bears to prove Yogi's relative smarts. But like all classic cartoon characters, the humour often rests in precisely those occasions where he overestimates his cleverness and fails to outwit the ranger. If we wanted to figure out for certain whether Yogi Bear was guilty of either of the three forms of overconfidence, we first need to be able to measure them.

One approach is to use questionnaires. Psychologists love questionnaires. Some questionnaires measure proxies for overconfidence, such as scales for narcissism or social desirability. For example, Yogi Bear might face a choice between two options declaring 'Modesty doesn't become me' or 'I am essentially a modest person'. Don't ask me which one he would choose. Other questionnaires compare how we rate ourselves compared to others (as in the better-than-average effect), or how others rate us.

Some other studies don't use questionnaires at all. Instead, they try to measure how much our claims differ from our performance. For example, if you were measuring overconfidence in intelligence, you could use some kind of intelligence test. If you were measuring altruism, you could measure contributions in an experimental game or donations to charity. Of course when judging claims of a social nature, the important criterion would be how others rate you—we'll have to wait until we hear what Winnie the Pooh thinks of Yogi Bear.

A particularly ingenious approach uses a 'self-claiming' questionnaire.[6] People are asked how familiar they are with a whole range of items across different categories, perhaps items like 'Manhattan Project' or 'satellite'. But the questionnaire also contains items that don't exist, what the researchers call 'foils'. And no, I'm not revealing examples of the foils—no spoilers here. People who claim familiarity with these non-existent items more than about actual items are overclaiming. This convenient questionnaire can thus make for a solid measure of overconfidence. It's a useful tool to have. Using the questionnaire shows that our tendency to self-enhance is actually fairly malleable. When told that the questionnaire contained the foils, people were more modest. When instructed to give a more positive impression, people were more likely to overclaim. Individuals in the study also differed in their tendencies to overclaim. Narcissists (as measured by an independent questionnaire) were predictably more likely to overclaim than non-narcissists.

Now that we've got our definitions and a variety of means to get to the roots of overconfidence, what do they tell us about how widespread overconfidence really is?

Let's start by going back to the better-than-average effect. All the way back in 1976, there were students who clearly showed this effect. A full 70 per cent of them said their leadership abilities were above median, 60 per cent said so about their athletic ability and 85 per cent said so about their ability to get along with others.[7] Or consider another more recent set of students from 2011, of whom 95 per cent said they had a better sense of humour than average.[8]

You can see that this effect isn't restricted to any one particular ability. It also isn't restricted to students. When professors were asked to rate themselves in another study, we see even stronger results—94 per cent of all faculty in one study ranked their teaching as better than average.[9] Around 30–40 per cent of engineers at high-tech companies in another study said their performance was in the top 5 per cent of all engineers.[10] Even when people are given monetary incentives to be accurate, they still placed themselves higher than they really were.[11]

In fact, people overplace themselves on a whole range of positive attributes. As the psychologists Nicholas Epley and David Dunning put it: 'Researchers have repeatedly demonstrated that people on average tend to think they are more charitable, cooperative, considerate, fair, kind, loyal, and sincere than the typical person but less belligerent, deceitful, gullible, lazy, impolite, mean, and unethical.'[12]

Most satisfyingly, we show the same tendency even when considering how susceptible we are to this bias.[13] People who had just shown the better-than-average effect on a task were then informed about the better-than-average effect. We could reasonably assume this would cause them to revise their judgements. In contrast, 63 per cent of them insisted that objective measurements would find they were accurate on the task, and 13 per cent even claimed they had been too modest before. On another test focusing on social intelligence, people who had performed well rated the test as a good and valid measure, while those who had performed badly rated the test as less valid. Even more tellingly, they rated other people as being more susceptible to the bias than they themselves were. Not only are we biased in our own favour, we also think others are more biased than we are.

Closely related to overconfidence is what has been called an 'optimism bias',[14, 15] something that appears to be built into how we view our lives. It causes us to consistently overestimate the occurrence of positive events in the future and underestimate the occurrence of negative events. This bias is sometimes called 'absolute optimism' or 'absolute unrealistic optimism'. What I find most fascinating is that we also estimate our own chances differently compared to the average person, displaying comparative unrealistic optimism.[16, 17] For example, if you were thinking of how likely you are to own your home, or have your work recognised with an award or live past eighty, you would be relatively positive about your chances. When thinking of others, however, you'd think it was less likely that they would get to experience these same things. On the other hand, if you were thinking about how likely it is that you would divorce a few years after getting married, or have a heart attack before you were forty or get fired from your job, you'd think that the likelihood any of these would happen to you would be lower than for other people. Again, this relative optimism is seen for a wide variety of situations, from diseases or natural disasters to unwanted pregnancies or divorce. This sort of optimism seems to be widespread, regardless of age, sex or education. One curious correlation, though, is that the more prestigious your occupation is, the more likely you are to underestimate your risk from cancer.

Both the better-than-average effect and the optimism bias hold a mirror up to our self-absorption. It's one rule for us, another for everyone else.

There's more on that front. Our predictions about others tend to be more accurate than those about ourselves. Conversely, other people's predictions about us are more accurate than our own. For example, self-ratings of naval officers don't match those of their subordinates, but the ratings of the subordinates all agree well. In fact, ratings by the subordinates better predicted who would go on to get a promotion.[18] In a similar vein, college students could better predict which of their friends' romantic relationships would last than the friends themselves could.[19] The same is true about job performance; our peers and supervisors have matched ratings about us, but we rate ourselves as performing better.[20] Our predictions about others are more accurate than those about ourselves, *even when we make these predictions about relative strangers*.[21] It seems as though the best people to trust when we need to judge our abilities are our friends and colleagues—and potentially even people who don't know us. The one person you definitely shouldn't be relying on is yourself.

Hold on, though. There are some tasks on which we rate ourselves as worse than average.[22, 23] Here are some examples of the tasks on which we do so: juggling, unicycle riding, joke telling, computer programming, answering questions on a quiz on the indigenous vegetation of the Amazon. You've probably guessed already: tasks that we think are hard are the first ones we back away from. When we assess a task as being too tough for us or where success is rare, we lose our optimism even when others may not. Students, for example, would find making investment decisions harder than finance professionals do. They correspondingly show no comparative optimism about their investment abilities, but finance professionals definitely do.[24] In the same vein, given that marathons are harder than half-marathons, runners are more optimistic about half-marathons than about marathons.[25] It's good to see that some things can rein in our self-belief.

There are other factors that also influence overplacement,[26] and they go a long way towards explaining the origins of the better-than-average effect. Here are two of them. First: ambiguity. The more ambiguous a trait or event is, the more likely we are to interpret things to enhance ourselves. That explains why traits such as idealism or sensitivity have stronger overplacement compared to traits such as being mathematical or punctual. This holds true for negative traits too. It is easier for us to claim we are less naive and insecure than the average person than it is for us to claim the same about being less clumsy or less gossipy. Traits like these are typically independently classified by others as ambiguous or unambiguous before a test. But when individuals are allowed to form their own definitions for any given trait, we see the pattern of overplacement again—with people finding the right spin on any characteristic.

Another factor influencing overplacement is an individual's perceived control over a given trait. People are less likely to claim to be better on traits that are perceived as uncontrollable, such as, say, intellectual ability compared to traits perceived to be more controllable, such as fairness. Similarly, they would be comparatively optimistic about health risks caused by diet or alcohol compared to risks caused by pesticides or contamination.[27] Come to think of it, optimism does make sense when we believe we can influence the course of things.

Our belief in our own superiority isn't all down to self-love. At least in part, it stems from how the human brain works and the different kinds of information available to us. Even if imperfect, we have better and more information about ourselves compared to our knowledge about others. When asked about a positive trait, we can immediately bring up instances of our own good behaviour. 'Oh yes I remember when I helped out that stranger! Oh I gave up my seat on the bus yesterday. Oh I'm so kind'—a bounty of positivity. Of course several others might have been just as kind or ethical, but not having observed their actions, we automatically assume we are better. Similarly, when we find that we have so far been healthy and avoided disasters, we blithely assume that this is how it will be in the future for us. This pattern of thinking is called an 'availability bias' or 'focalism', which means that we don't consider the events occurring to other people or their internal lives, and end up assuming that we are somehow special.

If some of you have read the evidence above with a sceptical eye, you have company. Not everyone is satisfied with the better-than-average effect as a measure of overconfidence. One of the criticisms is that the effect might actually be measuring our inability to deal with averages. Rather than measuring overconfidence, perhaps we're measuring ineptitude. We're poor at figuring out what an average person is like and so we make a guess—admittedly in the direction that makes us look better. In fact, anything that removes the concept of an average with a more specific individual immediately reduces the effect. When comparing ourselves to any specific person, rather than an average, we are less likely to claim to be better.[28] This is true even if we only see a picture of the person or even the back of their head! However, the effect doesn't entirely disappear. The self still has a privileged position amongst other specific individuals. I'm the first among my equals. Individuals close to us, like friends or groups we favour, have a privileged position too—we extend the idea of being better than average to them.

Another criticism of the better-than-average effect is that, if we only compare our judgements of our own actions to our judgements about others, we're missing something crucial: objective measurements. What we need here is not just people's judgements of each other, but how this compares with actual performance. For instance, how many baskets does Yogi Bear collect and how many do the other bears? If someone claims to be more charitable than average, we could, for example, see how much they give to charity compared to everyone else. If they say they are better at maths, let's put them to that differential equations test. We could then measure how much their claims deviate from actual performance and also from the average—a far more satisfying way to approach overconfidence.

Objectively measuring overconfidence is perhaps more directly applicable to the second form of overconfidence we talked about: overestimation. How much of this type of overconfidence is out there? Is it also as prevalent as the better-than-average effect? To answer this, let's begin by considering the Sydney Opera House.

The Sydney Opera House, often described as one of the wonders of the modern world, is a UNESCO world heritage site and an instantly recognisable landmark. Yet, this iconic design by Danish designer Jørn Utzon was reportedly one of the final rejects, until it was rescued and selected.[29] The winning design was eventually announced in 1957 after a long planning and selection process beginning in the 1940s. After design selection came the costing and scheduling—the opera house would cost US$ 7 million and would be completed on 26 January 1963, six years later. So far, so good. But as the work progressed, problems began to arise—there were tensions between the architect and the client, some designs were incomplete and costs began to increase. When the opera house was eventually finished, it was a decade late and cost US$ 102 million[30]—estimated to be a massive 1,357 per cent over budget in real terms.

We are now inured to these massive discrepancies between planned and realised budgets or schedules when it comes to public works—testament to how accustomed we are to the idea of overconfidence in public life. In fact, this form of overestimation is specifically called 'the planning fallacy',[31] our inaccuracy about how long a project will take or how much it will cost. The planning fallacy has probably been around for as long as humans have been building monuments. I'm imagining a resident waiting with a towel for the Great Bath at Mohenjo-daro to be completed.

Ongoing projects still give us shining examples of this fallacy. England's high speed rail project, HS2, linking London to Birmingham, Manchester, Leeds and beyond has now gained a reputation for ballooning costs. Initially costed at UK£ 32.7 billion in 2010, the 2019 estimate had already reached UK£ 81–86 billion.[32, 33] An independent review in 2020 estimated the costs rising to UK£ 106 billion,[34] and the National Audit Office has admitted that the eventual cost might be impossible to estimate with certainty.[35] The first and second phases are scheduled for completion in 2026 and 2033, but the Public Accounts Committee has already called this schedule 'overly ambitious',[36] and the final phase is now estimated to be completed in 2043.[37] Bengaluru's public transit system, Namma Metro, has also struggled to meet its projected deadlines. The first phase of the metro system was scheduled for completion in 2010, but the deadline was pushed back nine times and the budget revised four times.[38] The first line finally opened seven years later in June 2017. Phase two was expected to be complete by 2020, but locals never forget to add at least five years to the projected inauguration dates, even without a pandemic throwing a spanner in the works. This is one domain where overconfidence isn't fooling the public, even if it fools the politicians and planners making their projections.

When is the planning fallacy especially acute? When launching new projects and entering new markets—exactly when we need to be as accurate as possible about our abilities. The planning fallacy gives us clear criteria against which to measure overconfidence, our own initial estimates of time and cost. We are of course equally guilty of this in our daily lives. We regularly underestimate task completion times, and every one of us has that friend who always turns up an hour after you were expecting them. 'I'm on my way' is the sound of the planning fallacy chalking up another successful example.

Other kinds of claims can also be measured against objective criteria. This is possible even with something relatively abstract, such as altruism. For example, researchers at Cornell University measured students' self-predictions of how much they would purchase to benefit a charity, donate to a non-profit organisation or cooperate with a partner in experimental tasks.[39] The predictions were then compared with the actual behaviour of the students when they were presented opportunities to be altruistic in all these situations. The results followed the familiar pattern. While 83 per cent of students predicted that they would make charitable purchases, only 43 per cent actually did. The students predicted they would donate more than they actually did, and were less cooperative than they predicted they would be. Once more, the predictions for their peers were more accurate than their predictions for themselves. Overestimation of our altruism makes us all feel holier-than-thou, doesn't it?

How about something potentially more difficult to measure? Do we, for example, overestimate how good-looking we are? An elegant study by Nicholas Epley and Erin Whitchurch figured out a way to measure this.[40] The researchers took photos of all the participants and morphed these photos in varying degrees with two other photos. One of those two photos had been previously rated as being very attractive and the other as being very unattractive. The morphs thus represented progressively more attractive versions of the participants or less attractive versions of the participant. When asked to find their own faces amongst several others, participants were more likely to find a slightly more attractive version of their face than a photo of their actual face. They were also quicker to spot the attractive version of themselves compared to the real version. This effect was true even when trying to find a friend's face, but wasn't true when trying to find a stranger's face. So, our skills at enhancement and overestimation appear to not be restricted only to ourselves, but get to work on others we think positively about. The tendency to prefer an attractive version of oneself was not linked to self-esteem measured using a questionnaire. It was, however, correlated with more implicit measures of self-esteem—liking one's initials more than those of others and choosing positive words when primed to think of oneself. This suggests that the bias towards overestimating the self or self-enhancement is more implicit than deliberately thought out.

Across several different areas, studies have found ways of measuring predictions against actual performance, and study and after study demonstrates our predilection for overestimation. The psychology professors David Dunning, Chip Heath and Jerry Suls make a strong case for our 'flawed self-assessment' in a variety of fields in their excellent summary of past research.[41] Students overestimate their performance on exams and assignments. Lawyers overestimate their chances of winning cases.[42] Long-distance runners overestimate how quickly they will finish races.[43] Doctors overestimate the accuracy of their diagnoses.[44] CIA analysts overestimate the accuracy of their predictions about future world events.[45]

Overestimation is everywhere—although the occasional study does show up where participants show no evidence for overconfidence and are even underconfident.[46]

Earlier, we discussed comparative optimism (good things happen to me, bad things to others) and absolute optimism (overestimating the occurrence of positive events in the future and underestimating negative events). To empirically test the latter, we could map people's predictions for future events onto the real occurrence of those events, i.e., optimism measured against an objective statistic.[47] If comparative optimism is closer to overplacement, absolute optimism is closer to overestimation. Here again, research shows misplaced absolute optimism. Here's an example: when asked to estimate whether their homes had elevated radon levels, around 27 per cent of householders in Columbus, Ohio in the US thought they might have a problem.[48] In fact, 73 per cent of the households faced the problem. Unrealistic optimism has similarly been found in a wide variety of areas ranging from estimates of the likelihood of a divorce to contracting a sexually transmitted disease.[49] It can even have a knock-on effect. A substantial number of people are unrealistically optimistic about paying off credit card debt. This is bad enough for their finances. Yet, these people are the same ones who are more likely to choose cards with lower annual fees, ignoring the fact that these cards also have higher interest rates.[50] The combined effect of the debt and the interest rates is a hard price to pay for the initial optimism. It isn't then only our relative estimates that are skewed. Even when compared to actual statistics, we make optimistic errors, sometimes with scary consequences.

But wait—are there any tasks on which we underestimate? With overplacement, studies show that, in tasks that appear more difficult, we are less likely to think we are better than others. With overestimation, we find the opposite effect. We are most likely to underestimate our performance on easy tasks, where success is likely, or ones in which we are skilled.[51] Think of any task you excel at or even take for granted: walking in a straight line or remembering your friend's names. Your performance on any of these tasks is going to be so high that it is almost impossible to overestimate your performance. If you regularly scored 100 per cent in a maths exam, it would be impossible to predict that you would score higher. So the only likelihood for making an error is going to be in the lower direction, i.e., underestimation. We are, therefore, more likely to underestimate our performance on easy tasks. The difference between overplacement and overestimation on difficult tasks leads to some curious findings. On the one hand, we think we perform worse than we really do, and on the other, we simultaneously believe we perform better than others.

Now for the third form of overconfidence: overprecision. Let's briefly return to the Audience Poll in *Kaun Banega Crorepati*. Trusting the audience when it gives you a clear answer is a sensible thing to do. But over the course of the show's history, some contestants have ignored that clear mandate and used their own answer, losing out on the money they had won thus far as a result. This excessive confidence in your knowledge and information above that of others, even in the face of objective evidence, is overprecision. I'd argue a more commonplace example is on display at family reunions—all those relatives ready to get into an argument because they know better than you, even if you are the expert on the topic.

One estimate indicates that just under a third of all psychology papers about overconfidence measure overprecision, excessive certainty in your knowledge.[52] Yet, this is perhaps the least understood form of overconfidence. It's also the form where we see the least number of interventions that reduce or mitigate overconfidence. That doesn't bode well for those family reunions or the wonderful world of beneath-the-line comments on the internet.

Some of the difficulty lies in the fact that overprecision is more difficult to, well, pin down precisely. What is the measure for how certain somebody is? One approach is to ask a person to put numbers to how confident they are about their answers. If they were accurate, their confidence and their accuracy should be well matched. So, answers that they were 90 per cent confident about should be accurate 90 per cent of the time. Predictably, tests that have used such measures have found that there was a poor link between confidence and accuracy, especially when people are the most confident. You could go further and ask people to consider the entire distribution of probabilities and then mark the interval of probability for the specific answer. For example,[53] people were asked to estimate items such as the number of eggs produced in the US in 1965. They were then asked to provide estimates of intervals that were likely to contain the right answer 98 per cent of the time. Even in these tasks, people are pretty overprecise. The actual estimates, averaged across all those people, only contained the right answer 60 per cent of the time. These tests seem to capture the idea of overprecision, but they have their limitations. We're not great at thinking about probability distributions,[54, 55] so perhaps it isn't surprising that we fail to make accurate confidence estimates.

You can see from these examples that studying overprecision often takes a particular form, usually involving numerical estimates of intervals. If you found the example tasks difficult to follow, you're not alone. These aren't the most intuitive tasks for most of us, and that's a problem for attempts to measure overprecision. I'll take a broader view and talk about overprecision as excessive certainty that is unjustified by evidence or facts. This would often be difficult to quantify, but to me, it has broader applicability. It's something we can relate to a number of situations in real life where we aren't asking people for only numerical estimates.

Where does overprecision come from? The simple answer is, we don't know, or at least there doesn't appear to be a single explanation so far. A variety of reasons have been proposed. One of these is something we just discussed: our inability to think clearly about probability distributions. Another explanation is that initial information dominates decision-making, so much so that it becomes the starting point for all future estimates. In the tasks above, for example, we might stick to our original answers, and therefore grow further confident of them. Another kind of explanation suggests it might actually be useful. We prefer to be precise and inaccurate because that provides more information.[56, 57] If you were making plans to meet someone, it isn't helpful to say you'll meet them sometime in the next two hours at the cafe. Instead, it is more useful to give them a specific time, say 11.30 a.m., even if you end up being late. Precise information allows for better coordination and decision-making even when it is inaccurate.

While the reasons overprecision might still need to be clarified, there is no doubt that, along with overplacement and overestimation, overprecision is all around us. As we toured these three forms of overconfidence, you have already seen how these biases aren't limited to things that have little consequence. Overconfidence in one form or the other has been shown to work in several important fields,[58] sometimes playing a dangerous role. In fact, perhaps the most quoted study of the better-than-average effect is about driving. Try this at the next social gathering you go to—ask people if they think they are better drivers than average. You're going to find almost everybody claiming they are better-than-average drivers. In one of the most cited studies about overconfidence,[59] most people were only too happy to say they were better than 50 per cent of other drivers. In fact, 88 per cent of American college students and 77 per cent of Swedish college students said they were in the top 50 per cent of drivers. Similar results were seen for motorcyclists and truck drivers. Even when a group of people, say younger drivers, recognise that their group is particularly susceptible to risk, they nonetheless think that they are personally less susceptible,[60, 61] demonstrating an optimism bias with respect to driving.

In fact, people rate themselves as above average on almost every trait associated with driving,[62] whether it be responsibility, wisdom, consideration, safety or relaxation. Perhaps even more striking results come from one of the earliest studies on overconfidence in driving abilities. This study[63] compared responses between people who had been hospitalised in road accidents and those who hadn't. Surprisingly—or perhaps no longer so surprising to us—even in this study, both groups were just as likely to say they were good drivers.

This was even though about 70 per cent of the people hospitalised were implicated in police reports as having caused the accidents. If we're going to need a dent in our collective overconfidence, it's evidently going to take a lot more than merely going to hospital after a road accident.

Another well-studied field where overconfidence has important implications in our lives is education.[64] Students tend to be overconfident about how well they understand the material they have just read and about newly learnt skills. People's estimates of their intelligence and academic abilities in their first year in college correlate only about 0.2–0.35 (perfectly accurate judgement would have a correlation of 1) with their actual performance on intelligence tests or marks obtained in tests.[65, 66] Combining research from several studies shows that students on average give themselves higher marks than the teachers did 68 per cent of the time.[67] Clearly, we think we learn better than independent assessments demonstrate.

Perhaps the most important area, and the one with most consequences, where overconfidence plays out in our lives is in medicine and health.[68] People rate their personal risk of a variety of health threats as being consistently below average. This includes the risk of a heart attack, of lung cancer, of food poisoning, of being infected with HIV (if uninfected so far), of catching the flu, of having high blood pressure, of contracting SARS ... the list goes on. We also overestimate our health knowledge and behaviours. Adolescent boys' estimates of their knowledge about condom use doesn't correlate well at all with their actual knowledge.[69] School students who smoke are unrealistically optimistic about their own personal risk from smoking.[70] People believe they drink and smoke less than the average person and eat less red meat and greasy food compared to this average person. Interestingly, the belief that one is better than the fictional average peer is seen more often for unhealthy behaviours than for healthy behaviours.[71] So, we are less likely to claim we eat more greens than the average person, but more likely to claim we eat less junk food than them. This changes if we are asked to consider future behaviour rather than past behaviour.[72] After all, in principle, we do have more control over our future behaviour than over our past. Thus, when it comes to next week, I'm likely to say I will eat more greens than the average person. Of this are New Year's resolutions born year after year.

What if we turn the question around and examine the overconfidence of healthcare workers? Again, ample evidence of overconfidence. In a range of studies, healthcare professionals overplace themselves above their colleagues and supervisors in several relevant skills,[73, 74] including hand hygiene, the ability to provide feedback and infection prevention skills. One telling detail is the presence of a belief that a high degree of education implies further training in hand hygiene is unnecessary—as if education is all the training you need for every professional skill. On the other hand, people definitely agree that others need training. The confidence that nurses have about their knowledge of life-support tasks correlates poorly with their actual knowledge levels.[75] Surgical residents' ratings of their skill also do not correlate well with their performance on exams.[76] Surgical trainees, physicians and clinical psychologists have all been shown to overestimate the accuracy of their diagnoses. One study demonstrated huge levels of overprecision—with doctors making diagnoses of pneumonia with 88 per cent confidence but being correct only 20 per cent of the time.[77] Self-ratings about skills and competency are clearly inaccurate. Interestingly, those who rate themselves highly also rate others in their specialisation highly, including colleagues and supervisors, but rate colleagues in other specialties poorly. Once again, the overconfidence about competence spreads in-group people.

All these forms of overconfidence have quantifiable negative outcomes. People are only motivated to seek treatment and improve their health when they perceive themselves to be vulnerable. The optimism bias specifically works against this possibility. The more people believe they are somehow uniquely invulnerable to a threat, the less likely they are to get help. For instance, believing they are uniquely shielded from risk leads to people having high-risk sex[78] and not using contraception.[79] People who underestimate the likelihood of problems with alcohol show greater alcohol-related risky behaviour, leading to more problems a year later.[80] People who think their health is superior to that of others were less likely to take swine flu shots.[81] In a study that looked at this behaviour, most people fell into the overconfident category, and only those who had recently had an experience that shook their confidence were planning to get, or had already got, the flu shot. If most people end up not getting the shot, that would increase the chance of swine flu spreading, creating a health problem for the entire community. Misplaced optimism poses a serious problem for our health and it is vital that we find ways to work against it.

We began thinking of overconfidence as a source of cartoon comedy, but the consequences of overconfidence in our daily lives can be deadly serious. Whether it's driving, education, health or a host of other important areas of our lives, overconfidence is not just an inconsequential quirk seen in a few people. Its influence goes outwards, with effects for both individuals and society as a whole. Fictional bears might get away with it, but the rest of us suffer the consequences of widespread overconfidence. That's one more link in our worst-case scenario.

FOUR

A Biased World

THE WRITER REBECCA SOLNIT DIDN'T USE THE TERM 'MANSPLAINING' in her popular essay from 2008.[1] The essay—later part of a book with that title[2]—was called 'Men Explain Things to Me' and is credited with launching the term. In her essay, she relates how a man at a party tried to introduce her own book to her. He first assumed that she didn't know what he was talking about, then ignored her when she told him she was the author. Mansplaining involves being so sure of yourself and your knowledge that you assume that others, even those with expertise, need things explained to them. Our tour of overconfidence in the last chapter should already throw up the similarities—a belief that you are more knowledgeable than others, potentially an overestimation of how much you really know, and perhaps a determined but unjustified confidence in your facts. A *New Yorker* cartoon from 2018 perfectly captures this sort of overconfidence. A bespectacled man sits across the table from a woman, both of them drinking wine. At the exact moment captured, the man is enthusiastically saying, 'Let me interrupt your expertise with my confidence.' Jason Adam Katzenstein, the cartoonist, shared this cartoon on his Twitter feed in early 2018, and it's safe to say it struck a chord—it has since been liked and retweeted thousands of times. For so many people, this cartoon perfectly illustrates mansplaining. But is overconfidence more evident in men? Or to widen the scope of the question: where exactly do we see overconfidence? Do people get more or less overconfident with age? Are current generations more overconfident than older generations? Let's begin by taking a trip around the world.

The majority of psychological studies, including a lot of those that formed the basis of the previous chapter, have a well acknowledged and serious limitation. They focus on people from countries that are Western, educated, industrialised, rich and democratic—or to use the tongue-in-cheek acronym—WEIRD countries.[3] In fact, the results are often only based on responses from undergraduates at universities in these countries, a group it's easier for researchers to recruit from for participation in studies. The unspoken assumption, of course, is that these results are representative of all humans. How representative this population is of humans in general is up for debate. Some researchers argue that people from these countries are actually complete outliers in terms of their psychology.[4] Could this mean that all the overconfidence in the last chapter is not something we see in most humans?

Confidence and optimism do seem to vary across the world. A 2016 survey by the polling company YouGov asked people from nineteen countries whether they thought their country was the best in the world.[5, 6] The results don't fit the pattern of a nationwide better-than-average (or better-than-everyone-else) effect—few countries had greater than 15 per cent of respondents agree with the statement. The USA and India had the highest percentage agree—with 41 per cent and 36 per cent respectively. One the other hand, a 2018 Ipsos Mori survey[7, 8, 9] of young people across the world found that more than 90 per cent of young people in India, Kenya, China, Mexico and Nigeria were optimistic about their future. In countries in Europe the numbers weren't as high, but more than 60 per cent of young people were still optimistic. This kind of optimism turns out to be widespread across the world, with people consistently saying that they will be better off in five years' time.[10] The gap between these predictions and actual reported well-being is less in richer countries and for older people, but for younger people, the gap persists and is large. The expectation of a better life only reverses after the age of sixty-five.

Is this optimism justified? Let's consider social mobility. People are far more optimistic than they should be when evaluating social mobility, but this varies around the world. A report from the Brookings Institution[11, 12] ranks the US in the lowest category of social mobility within the countries they looked at. US citizens were nonetheless more optimistic than others about their chances of getting ahead. In contrast, people in the UK, France and Italy actually overestimate the probability of staying poor and underestimate the probability of moving from the poorest fifth of the country to the richest.[13, 14]

In India, the story that Narendra Modi went from selling tea to becoming prime minister of the country is widespread. It is perhaps not surprising then that India topped a recent survey by the World Economic Forum asking people if it was possible to start life poor but end up rich. India was followed by Saudi Arabia, Pakistan and Egypt in the ranking.[15, 16] Actual social mobility in India—measured in one study as the change in educational attainment from generation to generation—has on average remained low since Independence.[17] There has, however, been an increase in mobility for boys from Scheduled Castes, potentially due to the affirmative action policies of the Indian government. Social mobility in India is still a little lower than even the US.

Also, 66 per cent of Indians believe that most Indians have access to quality education[18]—despite India being amongst the lower-ranked countries internationally in terms of number of schooling years. There is an aspirational aspect to Indian optimism.[19] Urban people who self-identify as middle class are 7 per cent more likely than rural people to be optimistic that their children would be better off than they were. This is not true of people who are objectively classified as middle income. The self-identification is key to the difference, hinting at the importance of aspiration. This is no small group, comprising 40–60 per cent of all Indians. In India, most people think they are middle class—a sort of better-to-be-average effect. Self-identified middle-class people were also likely to be more optimistic about the Indian economy, and rich people were much more likely to be optimistic. Perhaps both groups expect to benefit from a booming economy and the motivation of possible personal gains is what drives their optimism. This is the sort of individual optimism that helps keep people motivated even when circumstances are dire.

Despite opening up a whole range of fascinating ideas, the questions in these surveys are not real measures of overconfidence. To get at that, we could turn to what studies of overconfidence show across the world. A great example is a study of small-holder farmers in Ethiopia.[20] Not only is this study from a different part of the world, it focuses on a real-world situation far from the artificial experiments in universities. Ultimately, these are the kind of studies that can really show us if overconfidence persists in the real world. In this situation, too, we find that some farmers are clearly overconfident, falsely thinking they are more productive than their fellow farmers. They take on more risks and are more likely to choose crops with returns that had greater variation. What's interesting is that these farmers were actually more likely to have recently encountered a shock that led to losses. Could their overconfidence be a defensive response helping them find a way of recovering from these losses to forge ahead? Or were they just consistently overconfident, leading to loss after loss that they hadn't learnt from? There's more to find out there. Older farmers and poorer farmers who were more vulnerable to economic shocks were, however, less likely to be overconfident. That's telling us something. Overconfidence seems to have a weak hold on those with repeated experience and those who face harsh consequences.

Let's take another approach. What if we combined data from several countries, as a few studies have done? It isn't an easy task. A lot depends on the number of people you sample from each country and regional variation within a country. So it's worth keeping that caveat in mind when looking at the results of any such attempt.

You might want to, say, compare people from Asia with people from Europe. Researchers from Singapore and Australia came together to do exactly this. They gave people from four Asian countries (Singapore, Taiwan, Hong Kong, South Korea) and five European countries (Finland, Denmark, the Netherlands, Serbia and Latvia) a set of math problems,[21] and compared their confidence levels to their performance. Confidence levels were pretty constant across all countries, even though performance on the task varied from country to country. That gap between confidence and performance meant that people from some countries were more overconfident compared to others in this study. Which were these countries? The highest levels of overconfidence were seen in participants from Latvia and Serbia, who actually performed the lowest on the cognitive test. Overconfidence was lowest for people from the Asian countries, with people from Finland, Denmark and the Netherlands slightly more overconfident than them.

Another study went even further, testing people across thirty-three countries. Similar patterns emerged: confidence varied less across all participants compared to accuracy.[22] Once again, people from some countries were more confident of their answers than they should have been. And again, it was the people that performed the worst that showed the highest overconfidence. When grouped broadly by world regions, people from East Asian countries were the least overconfident and people from anglophone countries were also less overconfident. This was not true for all Asian countries—people from South Asia had the most overconfidence, along with people from Sub-Saharan Africa and Southeast Asia. It's interesting that, in both studies, the levels of confidence were high across the board, regardless of accuracy. It's as if the one thing we cling on to, regardless of how badly we do, is our confidence.

People have also tried to see if overconfidence maps on to what can be called an individualist–collectivist divide. Western countries, like say the US and the UK, are often taken to be examples of individualistic cultures, while Asian countries, including India, Japan, Taiwan and China, are taken to be examples of collectivistic cultures. The idea is that we might find more overconfidence in individualistic cultures and less in collectivistic cultures. Westerners seem to self-enhance more and have more self-serving biases than East Asians.[23, 24] One explanation suggested for this is a cultural difference. Perhaps Western cultures tend to encourage self-enhancement, while countries such as Japan focus more on self-criticism. But the message is not so simple. The absence of one type of bias doesn't mean that others aren't present. That's what we see when we look for overconfidence in judgements, i.e., overestimation or overprecision. For example, people from China and Taiwan can be more overprecise than Europeans or North Americans, being excessively certain of their understanding and facts.[25]

Another study found no difference in overplacement between people from cultures they called individualistic (UK and US) and collectivist (India and Hong Kong), but also found that people from Hong Kong were more overprecise. Grouping Asian countries as uniformly collectivist might, however, ignore important differences. Indian participants in that study[26] were consistently the most extreme in how confident they were, regardless of their accuracy. In fact, they were also the only ones who overestimated their abilities and were the most overly certain in their abilities. The task required participants to guess the weight of ten people based on their photos and then estimate how many they had guessed correctly (within 2 kg). Participants from the UK, US and Hong Kong all actually underestimated their performance on the task. They thought they had got about one less correct than they actually did. Indians, on average, thought they had got one more correct than they actually did. It was a small but significant difference.

An even more interesting challenge to the cultural divide over overconfidence argues that it all depends on what we are measuring. What if we see the better-than-average effect in Western cultures only because we ask questions about individualistic tasks? If, instead, we use more collectivist tasks, then perhaps we would see the same overconfidence in people from East Asian cultures as well?[27] What are these different traits? Collectivist traits would, for example, include being respectful, loyal, tolerant and modest. Individualistic traits would include being independent, free, unique and original. To look at this question, three researchers from different parts of the world came together—Lowell Gaertner from the US, Constantine Sedikedes from the UK and Yoshiyasu Toguchi from Japan. They asked people to make judgements comparing themselves to others on both individualistic and collectivist traits.[28] Participants were then asked how they rated themselves on each of these and other traits compared to a typical person in their group. The results were clear: Japanese participants self-enhanced compared to an average person on collectivist rather than individualistic traits. This was true regardless of how long the Japanese participants had stayed in Western countries. The opposite was true for people from the US. They self-enhanced on individualistic traits. Similar results were found from Taiwanese students.[29] They self-enhanced on collectivist traits and also rated these traits as important to them personally. Other large-scale studies add to the picture further by showing that, even where overconfidence or positivity biases vary in different countries, that can be dependent on the test and on the presence of incentives to be accurate.[30]

The so-called East–West divide could then perhaps not be about the presence or absence of self-enhancement, but the particular aspects on which people self-enhance. You can even take nationalities out of the picture and run the same kinds of tests with people (of any culture) who self-identify as 'independent' or 'interdependent'. Again, independent participants are overconfident on individualistic traits and interdependent ones on collectivist traits.[31] The studies, however, do not imply that self-enhancement is independent of culture. In fact, the researchers who champion this approach argue that culture and social norms are precisely what decide which traits are the ones we tend to self-enhance on. We self-enhance tactically.

Now that we've travelled the world, let's get back to mansplaining. Study after study shows that men are more confident than women. In the workplace, for example, they are more likely to negotiate job contracts to their advantage[32] and more likely to apply for promotions.[33] On IQ tests in one study, both American and Japanese men not only gave themselves higher ratings, they also rated their fathers and brothers higher than their mothers and sisters.[34] Even women in that study rated their male relatives higher than their female relatives. But how does that confidence relate to performance or knowledge? Are men also more overconfident than women? If they are, they would just be reaping the benefits of their bluster, and women's expertise would regularly be undervalued and ignored, as in Solnit's anecdote. Perhaps then the suggestion from Sheryl Sandberg, the one-time COO of Facebook, that women should 'lean in', makes sense. On the other hand, when it comes to 'leaning in', we also have evidence that, as Michelle Obama put it, 'that shit doesn't work all the time'. There are other reasons leaning in doesn't work that have nothing to do with male overconfidence. Perceptions of confidence too vary depending on gender. While male confidence is seen as a positive sign, confident women often encounter negativity or are evaluated as having less potential,[35, 36] rather than receiving the same positive outcomes. Even when they ask for a raise, they are less likely to get one than men are.[37] You can imagine how the same dynamic plays out with race or caste as well.

Given the differences in confidence between men and women, it isn't a bad starting point to assume that perhaps men might be more overconfident than women. Men and women both show overplacement, mistakenly believing they are better than others.

Men are, however, usually more overconfident. Men are also more likely to overestimate their performance or ability. This occurs on a range of tasks, including cognitive tasks or predicting what their grades will be in exams. Women in these studies actually seem to be underconfident or just more accurate. Take the case of runners in marathons and other races. To get at overestimations here, we can compare explicit predictions of timing in these races and how they differ from actual performance. There's also another measure that works just as well. An important consideration when running a race is maintaining a constant pace. Starting off with a much greater burst of speed usually results in slowing down later on and a struggle to finish. Looking at pace and measuring any changes in pace could, therefore, also serve as an indication of overestimation—runners who slow down dramatically clearly thought they were going to be able to maintain a greater speed than they managed. Both these measures yield a familiar pattern: men are overly optimistic in their initial predictions and more overconfident than women.[38] They also are the ones who are more likely to slow down in the later phases of the races.[39] Women were on average one-and-a-half times more likely to maintain their pace compared to men. While the difference in pacing could reflect different strategies for finishing or the difference in physiology and fat storage in men and women, the overestimations in predictions are clear measurements of overconfidence. These measurements correlate well with the results from studying pacing and dropouts.

Other more implicit measures in a study of a Swedish 10K race did not find a difference between men and women.[40] Here, the measures were based on which starter group men and women self-select into. Some starter groups were faster than others, so the choice of starter group forms a declaration of how fast you expect to perform in the race. Comparing this with the actual performance and the performance in the previous year's race provided two measures of overconfidence. Neither of these differed between men and women. One explanation for this is that women who self-select into competitive environments, especially male-dominated environments, are typically as confident (or overconfident) as the men. Interestingly, overconfidence helped both men and women better their performance—overconfident runners improved their timings by about 4 per cent. In general then, both men and women can be overconfident during marathons, with men often being more overconfident. Women are just less likely to be overconfident at estimation tasks ('can I do this?') in general. It's interesting to think about why this is so, given that in placement tasks ('am I better than her') they do seem to show overconfidence, even if less than that shown by men.

Relatedly, how certain are men and women about their statements or predictions (i.e. who's more overprecise)? This is perhaps the trait that best captures and explains mansplaining. Unfortunately, this is where the trail of evidence begins to run dry. Overprecision has generally been understudied in its own right, and gender differences in overprecision have not really been pinned down yet. A few studies definitely do find evidence of greater overprecision in men. Men are, for example, more likely to trust their private information than publicly available information when the two conflict.[41] Men are also more likely than women to overestimate how much a potential partner is interested in them.[42] This could even explain why a recent survey by a security firm found that men were twice as likely as women to fall for romantic fraud scams.[43] Studies with other tasks, however, fail to find a clear difference in overprecision between men and women.[44]

Here, a note of caution. There is definitely ample evidence for overconfidence being more prevalent in men than in women. However, the difference in overconfidence between men and women is often not too large. A fair number of studies also show no difference between men and women, including some studies looking at perceptions of driving skill—the classic measure of the better-than-average effect—and the early studies on optimism bias. A massive recent study[45] carried out across the world argues that when measured against actual performance, overplacement is no longer predominantly male, at least in tasks that are stereotypically thought of as male. While the study still finds evidence of greater overprecision in men, the researchers wonder if this is a strategic way of getting greater rewards, given the experimental tasks. In that case, overconfidence could in fact be a useful strategy.

The variability of overconfidence across genders seems to suggest that perhaps the differences we find are task-specific. Undoubtedly we could do with more clarity, perhaps by pooling together data from several studies and looking for patterns across all of them—what's called a meta-analysis. If gender differences were task-specific, then perhaps, as with culture, we again self-enhance tactically. Maybe we see more evidence of male overconfidence because the women in these studies just aren't as interested in trivia or cognitive tasks. We should be asking participants what skills or fields matter to them, and measure whether they are overconfident in those fields, regardless of gender.

As a final example, there is one area where women do show more overconfidence than men, and it's one with serious consequences. It's a classic finding that men are less likely to report health problems or contact a doctor early. In the case of heart-attack symptoms, however, it is women who have longer delays between the onset of symptoms and contacting the doctor.[46] Female overconfidence has been suggested as an explanation for this. Heart attacks before the age of sixty-five are more common in men than in women, and it ends up being perceived as a male disease. Consequently, when women first experience their symptoms, the excessive certainty that it isn't a heart attack causes them to seek other explanations, while men assume it is indeed a heart attack. If the same pattern plays out in other areas of our lives, we should look out for where we make gendered assumptions. That would perhaps be where we would be most likely to find overconfidence and differences between men and women.

Both gender and culture can thus inform overconfidence. What are the other individual traits that have been implicated? Age and experience is one possibility. Experienced drivers, for instance, are more likely to think they are better than average compared to beginners.[47] Overconfidence and certainty in one's knowledge also appears to increase with age and experience[48]—that image of the argumentative old uncle wasn't far off. Personality traits such as extraversion, narcissism and proactiveness have also been linked to overconfidence.[49] There might even be a link between fields of study and student overconfidence. Students of Political Science, Law, Economics and Business Administration show the highest levels of overconfidence, and students of the Humanities tend to be underconfident, at least on the trivia questions used to test them.[50]

We can only hope this changes once the former launch their careers in business and politics.

There is one final thing to consider. What has the trajectory of overconfidence been over the years? Are humans as a species or as societies getting better at self-knowledge? A consistent level of overconfidence over the generations would seem to suggest either that it was baked into our natures or that it's the result of how our societies are built. And so, perhaps we would have to learn to live with overconfidence, and manage how we deal with it. Changes in overconfidence over the years, on the other hand, might suggest that we're actually getting better or worse at dealing with it. All of these answers could have far reaching consequences on how we manage as people and as countries. But where do we begin?

It's difficult enough to measure overconfidence in the lab. Measuring it in the real world requires much more innovative approaches, and looking at how it has changed over the years seems like an almost insurmountable task. We could of course look at classic moments of overconfidence from history—ill-advised military campaigns, governmental policies that were far too ambitious or Hollywood fiascos that were predicted well in advance. There might actually be a way of compiling these to get a measure of how overconfidence has varied over time, but this is hard and we run the risk of reading too much into a string of anecdotes. What we really need are long-term studies with similar groups of people for several decades.

The bad news? We don't have that for overconfidence. The good news? We do have that for a personality trait that's well correlated with overconfidence: narcissism. Psychology professor and author Jean Twenge has documented the change in narcissism over the generations through her body of research. She argues that, at least in the US, people belonging to Generation Y (aka millennials) are different from previous generations. They have higher self-esteem and narcissism, but also have higher rates of depression and anxiety and have a lower need for social approval.[51] Her book, *Generation Me*, captures the essence of the research in its title.

In her research, Twenge employs data from a test that has been used for several decades now, the Narcissistic Personality Inventory. The test asks you to choose between pairs of questions. For example, which of the following describes you better?: a) I like being the centre of attention or b) I like to blend in with the crowd. Summing up the number of responses for which you choose the more 'narcissistic' answer gives you an index of how narcissistic you are. This particular test was invented in 1979 and has been tested on undergraduates repeatedly until the present. This means that we have data from people of the same age year after year. So, any results we find are not just an effect of age but a generational effect.

The most striking results from Twenge's research is that the average number of narcissistic items undergraduates have chosen on this test have increased year on year.[52] So, from the eighties to the noughties, people now chose about two more narcissistic items on the list than they used to. In 2006, the average student scored higher than 65 per cent of students in the 1980s, and was more likely to agree with statements like 'If I ruled the world it would be a better place', 'I think I am a special person' and 'I can live my life any way I want to'.[53] Interestingly, a lot of the change appears to be driven by changes in women's attitudes. Assertiveness in college women increased between the seventies and the nineties, and it is college women's scores of narcissism that increase over the years.[54] In general, compared to the eighties, students now have increased self-esteem and are more likely to believe that external factors, such as luck, are to blame when things go wrong. There has also been some further evidence of this from other countries. In the Netherlands, one study[55] reported smaller increases in extraversion and agreeableness in students between 1982 and 2007. A more long-term worldwide study or set of studies would be needed before we can see if this is the case around the globe or linked to particular social, cultural or economic climates.

Twenge's explanation for this change is a change in sociocultural factors in the US.[56] She points out that, over the decades, children are more likely to be given unique names, that the rates of plastic surgery have increased, that high school students have greater expectations of success, even that pop songs have more individualistic lyrics. She argues that the shift in culture creates a space where specific personality traits have been allowed to thrive—if not actively encouraged—due to constant boosts of self-esteem and affirmation regardless of actual achievement. It isn't difficult to see how that kind of environment would also be conducive to an increase in overconfidence: you might no longer be well calibrated to estimate the effort required for good performance at any task.

Several researchers have, however, disputed Twenge's argument. Some have argued that the Narcissistic Personality Inventory is more complex than it first appears, and is actually measuring a range of things, including ideas of leadership, exhibitionism and entitlement.[57] Another problem is that the studies have focused on college students, who are typically wealthier and whiter than the US population as a whole. Others have contested the pattern found by Twenge altogether.[58, 59] When a larger pool of studies and other survey data are used, they argue, there is no clear evidence for an increase in self-esteem and narcissism. In particular, when data from another long-term project—Monitoring the Future—is used instead of the Narcissistic Inventory, the pattern of increasing self-esteem or egotism is absent. This might be particularly telling for overconfidence, since the measures of overconfidence there featured questions like 'Compared with others your age around the country, how do you rate yourself on school ability?' and 'How intelligent do you think you are compared with others your age?' These aren't too different from the questions that measure overplacement in the better-than-average effect or optimism bias. The fact that responses to these questions haven't changed since the 1970s is perhaps telling us that overconfidence hasn't increased over the years. In fact, there is even some suggestion more recently that millennials are risk-averse,[60] staying away from the stock market and more likely to choose job-oriented courses at university. Perhaps there is something special that is being captured by the Narcissistic Inventory that isn't quite linked to overconfidence, and which we still need to pin down.

Across the world and over time, cutting through personality and gender, overconfidence pops up time and again. How it shows up and how tactically we use it varies. The message, however, is clear. Overconfidence is everywhere. There is one special situation which brings it to the fore. In her essay, Solnit describes it best as the 'confrontational confidence of the totally ignorant'. Overconfidence is nowhere more present than when we haven't got a clue. Which is why it could be changing our relationship with those who do have a clue—the experts.

FIVE

The Experts and Us

ON A SUNNY MARCH DAY IN THE MOJAVE DESERT, MIKE HUGHES, a sixty-one-year-old man, used a homemade steam-powered rocket to propel himself into the sky. But we can safely assume his mind was upon the earth, for the goal of his aerodynamic endeavours was not to reach the stars or to invent a new form of transport. He was confirming that the earth was flat, shaped like a frisbee, which is what he believed. There was one sure way to find out: to head out to outer space and see the shape of the earth with his own eyes. Hughes's rocket sped into the sky reaching a speed close to 350 mph. We can imagine the landscape rapidly shrinking beneath him—all tiny cars, tiny houses, tiny trees—the air buffeting the rocket relentlessly as he shot up further and further. In a few minutes, the fabulous sight of the shimmering plate of the earth would be within his reach. But things went awry. Unable to continue in his rocket, Hughes had to jump out in his parachute without conclusive proof of his beliefs. Yet, even after crashing in the desert, he was unfazed and already planning future launches.

It seems utterly baffling that someone could have such an unshakeable belief in a flat earth that they would be willing to risk their life to prove it. After all, a spherical earth is hardly a new idea.[1] In India, belief in a spherical earth potentially dates back to 300 BCE, if not earlier. Around the same time, Aristotle also listed several reasons for why the earth is a sphere: in a solar eclipse, the earth casts a round shadow on the moon; when ships sail over the horizon, their hulls disappear first; the same constellations are not visible at different latitudes. Then, in 100 BCE, the Greek scholar

Eratosthenes noticed that when the sun's rays were directly overhead at noon in the city of Syene, further north in Alexandria they were at an angle. By measuring the shadow of a rod in Alexandria, he could determine that the rays there were at an angle of seven degrees. This result again confirmed the curved nature of the earth's surface. In fact, Eratosthenes would then go on to use the distance between Syene and Alexandria to calculate the circumference of the earth. Later still, in the fifth century CE, the Indian astronomer Aryabhatta[2] also dedicated one part of his magnum opus to the spherical earth and made an estimation of its circumference.

Despite centuries of evidence, however, Mike Hughes isn't the only person who believes the earth is flat. Flat earth proponents have been around for at least two centuries, starting with the Zetetic Society in the nineteenth century. Our own online era has helped—they have had an increasing presence with annual conventions and an active presence on social media. Why would this belief in a flat earth persist in opposition to all the expert knowledge across centuries? It seems like a startling rejection of proof and common sense, a display of overconfidence that demands an explanation.

Here are two possible reasons. The first one is linked once more to trust. Who you trust to be right and who you trust to have your best interests at heart. Whether we trust the experts in their fields to tell us the truth—or to have the right motivation—has a huge influence on how much we doubt their conclusions and recommended courses of action. In the US, anti-intellectualism has been paralleled with a drop in trust in several kinds of experts, including scientists and journalists.[3] In the UK, scientists are still trusted, but other experts not so much.[4] Understanding why this trust has been lost would definitely go a long way to determining why several attitudes stand in opposition to those of the experts.

Secondly, it's easy to see how sharing non-mainstream beliefs could give people a supportive community. It is perhaps no accident that people with these beliefs form societies and hold conferences where they can form connections with each other. If claiming to believe in a flat earth helps you bond with others, we can already begin to see the attraction. After all, there are few disadvantages. Hughes notwithstanding, few of the true believers are actually risking their lives in steam-powered rockets. Psychologist Hugo Mercier argues for this explanation when discussing conspiracy theorists in his book *Not Born Yesterday*,[5] and we'll return to the idea later in this book. Mike Hughes himself was a daredevil who revelled in his stunts. Like professional BASE jumpers[6] and other thrill-seekers, his life was built around seeking risks, regardless of his beliefs. His public relations representative later claimed that tying up the stunt with his beliefs about a flat earth was only a way to gain publicity. It is possible that, even in his case, courting danger was not an outcome of deeply held beliefs.

For this chapter, however, let's focus on another kind of explanation. The majority of us lack expert knowledge in several fields. Flat-earthers are typically not students of geography, even though some of them confidently elaborate self-generated theories which confirm their beliefs. In fact, we certainly seem to be in a time when popular opinion is often at odds with the views of the experts. The overwhelming support for evolution among biologists has not prevented a long history of disbelief in the fact of its existence. A similar absolute consensus on climate change amongst climate scientists has not deterred those who deny that it is occurring or caused by humans. Also, some of the biggest box office hits of 2018 were films that critics had panned. *The Greatest Showman*, *Mamma Mia 2*, *Bohemian Rhapsody* and *Venom* all have mixed-to-unfavourable scores on the review aggregator site *metacritic.com*, but have been hugely popular with audiences. Of course, preference in films belongs in a different category to the other beliefs, one that's more subjective. And as we've already seen, it's easy to be overconfident about subjective topics. It's overconfidence in the other topics that needs explanation.

Even if you aren't a fan of any of these films and have no doubts about evolution and climate change, perhaps there are other fields where you might all too easily believe that you know better than the professionals. I often have strong opinions on economics and politics, with barely any relevant training and arguably a poor concept of all the complexities involved. A lack of knowledge doesn't stop us from staunchly defending the policies that we just know will be the best for the country. Perhaps we aren't quite behaving like flat-earthers there, but the point remains—few of us are as immune to being anti-expert as we would like to believe.

As with flat-earthers, our strong opinions no doubt also appeal to the communities that we find supportive. We also learn them from people we trust, rejecting the opinions of those we don't. But there's something more than distrust in our inexpert overconfidence. It's almost as if there's something about a lack of expertise that invites and encourages overconfidence. You've probably heard of the famous effect that explains this—it's called the Dunning-Kruger effect.

The Dunning-Kruger effect was first described in a now-classic paper published in 1999[7] by two social psychologists: Justin Kruger, now at New York University, and David Dunning, now at the University of Michigan. We've discussed some work by Dunning in earlier chapters. His body of research has given us huge insights into the errors we make in our self-perception, and of course underpins a lot of the discussion in this book. The results in Kruger and Dunning's paper have since taken on a life of their own. People all over the internet cite this effect in popular commentaries, highlighting examples of it amongst the rich and the famous. What is the effect exactly? Simply put, the Dunning-Kruger effect shows that we overestimate our knowledge or abilities most when we have the least knowledge of those abilities. I think of this sometimes when I read research papers. The results make the headlines, but the methods are often where the heart of the paper lies. When you read that researchers managed to train animals to perform a particular task or created stimuli to present to people, you could fall into the trap of thinking it would be easy to build on their experiments yourself. When I was a student, that happened often, my mind all abuzz with new ideas. I still have the ideas, but I know through years of experience the difficulties that underlie the simple statement of methodology. Those difficulties are the sum of all the things that we don't know we don't know.

Here's how Dunning and Kruger went about their study. They first put together observations from several studies showing that beginners and non-experts find it more challenging to evaluate both the difficulty of a given challenge and their own performances on these challenges. These observations had been made over years across many fields—physics problems, driving, chess, tennis, even social skills. Kruger and Dunning used these results to argue that people who were less skilled might be less able to assess themselves, and would therefore overestimate their own abilities. To test this hypothesis, they ran three studies with very different tasks: assessing humour, solving logic problems and evaluating grammatical correctness. In all the tasks, they predicted that poorer performers would be the ones who overestimated how well they had done.

To measure actual performance, you would also need an independent measure of success. In the case of logic problems or grammar, there are clear correct answers that are easy to measure. For humour, a set of jokes were assessed by professional comedians. This formed the scale against which the participants' judgements could be compared. The tasks participants performed involved rating jokes, giving answers to the problems or evaluating sentences. They then estimated how many other participants would perform worse than them if there were a total of 100 participants. In other words, which 'percentile' they would belong to. The researchers could then compare these estimates with actual measures of performance and the corresponding percentiles that each participant belonged to. You might, for example, think 80 per cent of the others were worse than you, but measures of your performance might show that actually only 70 per cent of the others were worse than you. This discrepancy between actual and estimated performance would be the measure of your overconfidence. In our example, that would be an error of 10 percentile points. Now, all that was left for the researchers to do was see who had the most overconfidence. Was it going to be the low performers or would it be more evenly distributed across all participants? They split up the participants into four groups depending on their performance and looked at the estimation errors of each of these groups from the lowest performing one to the highest.

The results gave strong support to the predictions. In all three studies, the participants on average ranked their performance as above 50 per cent (i.e., better than average). In addition, as predicted, participants in the worst performing group consistently overestimated how well they had done by a large margin. In the humour test, the poorest performers were on average wrong about their abilities by 46 percentile points—a sobering thought for the amateur comics amongst us who think we're absolutely hilarious. In the logic and grammar test, the poorest performers were on average off by 50 percentile points or over. In all cases, the estimation of performance was more accurate for the participants in the higher performing groups. Participants in the highest performing groups actually underestimated their performance by a small amount. In other words, while the non-experts were wildly optimistic about their performance, the experts were actually a bit pessimistic about their performance.

Right there is the difference between experts and non-experts. No wonder most of us smoothly transition into the role of armchair psychologist, economist or politician at the slightest provocation. Plenty of studies have shown the same effect on tasks ranging from the cognitive to the social. The pattern is especially true for beginners on different tasks—including real-world financial forecasts—who quickly gain a high degree of confidence after only a few learning opportunities. According to follow-up research by Dunning in collaboration with Carmen Sanchez[8] at the University of Illinois Urbana-Champaign, we start off less confident in several tasks, and then rapidly become overconfident thanks to a 'beginner's bubble'. It is only later, as our skills increase, that our overconfidence reduces. We seem most likely to be overconfident soon after starting new ventures, at a point when it is potentially the most dangerous. In the last chapter, we also discussed a study[9] that looked at overconfidence in several countries around the world. One of their take-home conclusions was that countries where people performed poorly on the task had the highest levels of overconfidence.

The pattern of non-expert overconfidence is evidently widespread. As Kruger and Dunning put it, when we are faced with a task which we are poor at, we face a dual burden: we are both unskilled and unaware of it.

Perhaps the most concerning area in which the Dunning-Kruger effect has been implicated is in the movement against vaccinations. Vaccines represent one of modern medicine's great tools for the prevention of disease. Once-fatal diseases, such as smallpox, measles, polio and whooping cough, have been vastly reduced—and in some cases eliminated—across the world, thanks to vaccines. I have a small dark patch on my shoulder that is testament to this success. I was part of the last generation of babies in India vaccinated against smallpox. Later generations didn't need the vaccination. The disease has disappeared.

In recent years, however, a growing number of people resist any efforts to vaccinate children. This has grown into a full-blown movement. People feel so strongly about it that it has become a badge of identity. As might be expected from this lack of vaccinations, some of the diseases where cases were previously rare are now back on the rise. In the first few months of 2019, the number of measles cases tripled compared to the same time period in 2018.[10] In the Philippines, the number of cases increased 500 per cent between 2017 and 2018.[11] In 2019, the US saw the greatest number of cases in over two decades, despite having 'eliminated' the disease in 2000.[12] The distrust of vaccines has had disastrous effects.

In as much as this distrust is growing, despite the weight of medical opinion, there is a resemblance to the Dunning-Kruger effect. People are confident enough to trust their knowledge over those of the experts, even though this could have fatal consequences. In fact, people who reject vaccines rely more on intuition, have less intellectual humility and greater distrust.[13] They are less likely to believe well-established facts and more likely to believe alternative facts. It's worth returning to the question at the heart of a previous chapter.

The important question is whether it is reasonable to trust the experts or not. For example, the past behaviour of politicians and pharmaceutical companies might make it hard to trust their current recommendations for a vaccine. Even a default distrust of introducing unknown chemicals into the body doesn't seem so unreasonable at first glance. The clear connection to the Dunning-Kruger effect, however, comes from one specific origin of the movement against vaccination in Western countries. This is often traced to a paper published in 1998 that claimed to have found a link between vaccinations and autism.[14] The paper has since been retracted and discredited, but its claims live on, and a fear of vaccine-induced autism still drives the resistance to vaccination.

One study[15] looked at this phenomenon by surveying a large group of people in the US on their knowledge about autism, and their beliefs about the links between vaccination and autism. To measure overconfidence, the researchers asked people how much they believed they knew better than doctors and scientists about autism. This measure of overconfidence is not exactly similar to other measures we have talked about—trusting one's own opinion over that of an expert perhaps best resembles overprecision, excessive certainty in one's own knowledge. The results of this study are striking. More than a third of people were overconfident, but a large proportion still trusted experts, and people were moderately knowledgeable about autism. Comparing knowledge of autism with the tendency to be overconfident did give clear evidence for the Dunning-Kruger effect. People with less knowledge about autism were more likely to be overconfident about their views, and people with more knowledge were less likely to be so. It would be interesting to see if the same effect was repeated with an assessment of people's knowledge of vaccines rather than autism. Would people who knew less about how vaccinations work be more likely to be overconfident as well?

The Dunning-Kruger effect is evidently widespread, and persists even in the face of death and disease. How do we explain this pattern? Why do we persist in trumpeting our genius despite our evident failures? The classic explanation for this is that the skills that are needed to perform a task—solving a logic puzzle, assessing grammar—are the same as those needed to assess how good we are at the task. Imagine a task where you had to listen to musical notes and assess whether a given note was a C or a D. If you were tone-deaf, you would of course be quite bad at this task. But in addition, a note that was almost at the same frequency as C or halfway between C and D would sound the same. You would be unable to tell if a given note was difficult or easy to discriminate from C or D since the tones would all sound pretty similar. You might, therefore, be fairly confident that you've done well. Psychologists call the ability to assess your own knowledge 'metacognition', knowing what you know. We could, therefore, say that our incompetence at a task means we have poor metacognition. It prevents us from correctly assessing what we know. It turns out that people who are less analytical at reasoning tasks are more likely to show poor metacognition.[16] In fact, they are also more likely to be inaccurate about how good their analytical skills are, effectively being oblivious to their own biases. Poor metacognition would thus explain why we might be bad at assessing ourselves when we have inadequate skill or knowledge. To fully explain the Dunning-Kruger effect, we have to add on another layer, that is, when we lack the skills to assess our own performance, we appear to default to believing we've done well. Perhaps this helps poor performers in particular, since they are the ones who might need to save face the most.

This lack of self-awareness means that it isn't just the difficulty of tasks that determine our overconfidence, but how difficult we *perceive* them to be. Poor performers see the tasks as being easy since they lack the skills to correctly assess the difficulty of the tasks. That's what makes them overconfident. High performers, on the other hand, possibly think that others must have also performed similarly to themselves. They, therefore, end up underestimating themselves compared to others.

There are of course different fields or tasks at which we are experts and non-experts. We might be brilliant in the narrow field of our expertise, but surely, most of us have poor knowledge about the majority of fields and domains in the world around us. Are we then fated to always be blithely overconfident in all of them? Not necessarily. The Dunning-Kruger effect occurs in specific conditions.[17] The first is that the task needs to be actually difficult—on easy tasks, we are all going to be more accurate in our performance and possibly all overestimate how well we do.[18] Second, and more importantly, only some tasks require the same set of skills for both performance and judging skill levels. In our example of judging musical tones, being tone-deaf hampers us in two ways, preventing us from doing the task as well as judging our own performance. As a counterexample, though, when you're running a race, the skills needed to succeed are physical but the ability to assess your skills is not physical. Several of us lack the skills to win races, but that doesn't hamper us in any way from knowing exactly how awful we would be if we tried to compete.

Finally, another important contribution to the effect is the role of feedback. We should expect to see the effect only on tasks that don't provide direct, immediate feedback. That's the reason why we can make grand errors in our estimations despite doing poorly. On tasks like racing, for instance, we can immediately see how poorly we perform. It would take a truly exceptional person to insist they are amongst the top racers despite consistently coming in at the rear of a group of runners. Kruger and Dunning also make the point that, for several of the tasks they studied, participants did not often receive negative feedback, and even when they did, it could be ambiguous. We might easily ascribe our poor performance to one of several other factors, rather than acknowledging our own lack of skill or knowledge.

Putting all of this together, our lack of skill leads to overconfidence in difficult tasks without clear feedback. From social relationships to managing projects, several demands on us could fit the criteria for the Dunning-Kruger effect. This confirms the next aspect of our worst-case scenario: that we lack accuracy when we need it the most, that is, when we are unskilled, incompetent beginners. At this point it seemed to me that we should perhaps start despairing about overconfidence engulfing us from all sides. But as I read about the effect further, I was heartened to discover that not only are there other explanations for the Dunning-Kruger effect, there are also ways to combat it. It needn't all be down to our poor self-knowledge or metacognition.

To understand the alternative explanations for the Dunning-Kruger effect, let's imagine ourselves taking part in a competition, say the Great British Bake-Off. You've been baking for years, and you know you should rank at least amongst the top 50 per cent of the participants. But, as with all competitions, it's your performance on the day that really matters. On that sunny first day in the bake-off tent, let's say you have other things on your mind. You end up making many more errors than you might have made, finishing amongst the lowest 20 per cent—the soggy bottom of the group. Your errors affect two things simultaneously: your performance of course, but also the error in your performance estimate. Since you think you usually do well, your estimate will be high, and so errors will make sure your real performance is further off from this estimate. The same errors that dragged your performance down also produces an increased measurement of overconfidence—in this case by at least 30 percentile points. Other errors in your performance due to external factors (the heat, the distracting judges) or random mistakes in measurements would have a similar effect. For all these cases, errors would change both performance and performance estimates in a correlated fashion.

This correlation does indeed create the kind of effect we have been talking about. More sophisticated statistical analyses have also questioned whether there is a true link between ability and estimation as seen in the Dunning-Kruger effect.[19] Even worse, the Dunning-Kruger effect has been replicated using completely random simulated data,[20] posing a formidable challenge to the idea that it has psychological roots.

Is the effect then only a statistical anomaly which doesn't reveal anything to us about our psychology? Perhaps unsurprisingly, other studies[21] have responded to these challenges and tried to see what happens when you correct for these errors.[22, 23] One way of doing that is to repeat the task more than once for each participant. You can then look at whether overconfidence on one occasion (the first day in the bake-off tent) correlates with performance on the other occasion (the next week). The idea is that random errors on any given performance would not affect overconfidence in the other performance. Any remaining correlation could not then be due to errors of confidence and performance being correlated as we discussed above.

When this correction is applied, the Dunning-Kruger effect still persists. Other more sophisticated ways of tackling this problem modelled responses correcting for errors and still found an effect. In response to the criticisms, Dunning and colleagues also ran experiments where participants were paid to be accurate and the overconfidence of low performers still persisted.

The second alternative explanation for our favourite effect makes a different kind of argument. Imagine you were amongst the best bakers, making an apple pie in the final rounds of the Bake-Off. If we're looking at getting the technique exactly right, there is only one way to pull off a perfect apple pie. As a top baker, your feedback is clear. A few things go wrong with your bake, and you can tell what you did wrong each time. Now imagine you were amongst the worst at doing this task—one of the early contestants with lots of personality but little skill. Every time you attempt to bake, you get an inedible mess. What's worse is that it's never clear exactly why you got it wrong. Was there too much fruit in the pie? Did you not set the oven to the right temperature? Was there too much water in the dough? Imagine comparing your mess to the mess that other bakers have made. You're probably better off throwing your creation in the bin in a fit of temper. How can you evaluate whether you're better or worse than them? This would be a problem even for tasks with more objective measures of performance. Did your neighbour get the maths problem wrong because they were distracted, because they read the problem wrong or do they actually have poorer maths skills than you? The problem of figuring out feedback is far worse for poor performers than for the top performers. If you bake the perfect pie or solve that maths problem, you did everything right—you weren't distracted, you read the instructions right and you executed them right. It's clear that anyone who didn't succeed has done something more wrong than you. It's easy to think you're good when you're at the top. The difference in the information available to poor and good performers means that, even if all of us had perfect capacity for self-awareness, when we perform poorly we still struggle to understand our abilities. The fault, therefore, would be external and not in the make-up of our minds.

There is evidence from both modelling[24, 25, 26] and experiments that such an explanation could hold true. One study[27] that set out to measure metacognition on a visual task found that it does not explain the poor self-estimation of the participants. Instead, it was the level of performance itself that best explained it. In other words, it was true that poorer performers had poor metacognition and self-knowledge. But the reason underlying the Dunning-Kruger effect—at least in this study—was not a psychological shortcoming, but the limitations that poor performance imposes on all of us.

These results might of course not be true for every task. But it does suggest that we need to be able to better measure different contributions to our errors on any given task, including metacognitive errors and other sources of error. Perhaps this isn't possible when we're asking how funny we are or how good our social skills are. But without thus measuring our errors, we wouldn't know which tasks really require self-knowledge and which don't. Interestingly, in different experiments, as we control for various sources of error—from random correlations to contributions from our performance levels—the strength of the Dunning-Kruger effect often decreases. In fact, in some studies, when they controlled for all these errors, it disappeared entirely.

This is, in a way, a hopeful message. The pattern of the effect remains true, and people with low skills or expertise are bound to be overconfident. But these results suggest that we aren't doomed to remain overconfident because of some innate psychological limitations. The prediction is that, if we improved our performance or knowledge, we would get better at estimating our abilities. To get better at recognising your baking skills, you need to be perfecting your brioches.

As it turns out, there is evidence of exactly that. Even in the original paper by Kruger and Dunning, there's a fourth and final study that investigated something similar. They first reran their logic experiment and reproduced the effect they had seen before. Some of the participants were then given a training pack containing similar logic puzzles with the tricks that you could use to solve them. They reran the experiment after the training to see whether there was any change. What they found was that the students who were previously the poorest performers at the logic task now performed better, and also showed the most improvement in their accuracy of self-estimation. Remember how one of the criteria for observing the Dunning-Kruger effect was unclear feedback? If you give clear, consistent feedback, people get better at predicting their performance.[28] One study[29] asked students to predict their midterm and final exam grades and looked for our by now familiar effect. The midterm exam grades provided feedback about their performance, and this resulted in predictions for the final exam being more accurate. This was especially true for those who performed the worst. For predictions of *absolute* scores, feedback completely removed the correlation between performance and prediction accuracy. There was, however, still some overconfidence amongst poor performers about their *relative* performance. Even if we realise we're poor at a task, we still seem to find a way to believe that we are better than at least some others.

Outside of psychology labs, there's some sign that improved knowledge might have an effect on real-world beliefs as well. For example, people are more likely to accept evolution if they have more detailed knowledge of it.[30, 31] This is true even amongst people who are more conservative or religious and potentially less inclined to accept evolution. This seems to suggest that, as we learn more about evolution, we might get more accepting of it because training or feedback reduces our overconfidence in our own knowledge or skills.

But let's not all launch into re-education campaigns and sneer at people without training. There's a final coda to this story. Despite all that we've read so far, a lack of training does not always mean that people lack expertise. Researchers based in the Netherlands[32] asked people to predict which experiments from social psychology would show the same results if they were repeated. This is an important concern, not only for psychology but for science in general. It's possible that a single experiment might give you a result that seems striking—for example, that people who are encouraged to think about old people walk slowly afterwards. This result might, however, be a chance occurrence or the product of the particular conditions the experiment was run in. To ensure that the results genuinely reflect a fact about the world or our minds, they should ideally be demonstrated multiple times by different researchers. In other words, *the results need to be replicated*.

Despite having no training in psychology, people were able to make successful predictions about which psychology results would be replicated. Their intuitions about other people seem to have been accurate enough to match what specialists were finding using rigorous scientific methods. Perhaps there is some scope for the idea of armchair psychology after all. We need to be careful about which fields allow for inexpert opinions to be accurate and which require a more non-intuitive expert approach, rather than assuming non-experts are always bound to be overconfident. My guess would be that our intuitions would be more accurate about aspects of life that we have evolved to deal with, such as social interactions. On the other hand, we should be far off the mark relying on our intuitions about quantum mechanics or fractal geometry.

When we compare experts and non-experts, we find that the former are typically more likely than non-experts to give correct answers to questions in their field—as we would expect.[33] So, if you ask experts to estimate an answer, they are pretty close to the actual answer, while non-experts are not. Experts, however, can also be more confident about their answers than non-experts.[34] So, if they had to specify an interval within which the correct answer lies, they choose far narrower intervals than non-experts. The result of this is that experts and non-experts end up having similar levels of overprecision—both being more confident of their answers than is warranted, even if experts are more accurate. Experts might want to bear that in mind when initiating conversations with non-experts.

How we talk to people also matters. An expert who sets out to train or provide people with knowledge to reduce their overconfidence might have the best of intentions, but the nature of the interactions makes all the difference. Amongst professional science communicators, the so-called 'deficit model' is considered outdated and unhelpful.[35] This is the model where experts assume others have a 'deficit' of knowledge that must be provided by them. These assumptions have been questioned, and the attitude this model fosters often prevents actual communication and learning. In 2014, Professor Brendan Nyhan, an American political scientist at Dartmouth College collaborated with colleagues to show that several different methods of communicating information about vaccines all failed[36] to make people who were against vaccination change their minds. Their methods included information from the Centre for Disease Control and Prevention, text about the dangers of the diseases, images of children with diseases that could be prevented by the vaccine and a narrative centred around an infant who almost died of measles. None of these were effective in changing people's minds and the latter two actually increased misperceptions about vaccines. Nyhan and colleagues state in their conclusions: 'Attempts to increase concerns about communicable diseases or correct false claims about vaccines may be especially likely to be counterproductive.' We might naively believe that providing information or training might change people's beliefs. It is, however, evident that in real-world scenarios, simply providing information doesn't have to change people's beliefs.

What does work? Having an empathy-driven dialogue with people. A study in hospitals in Quebec[37] used this approach when talking about vaccination with mothers of newborn babies. Doctors engaged mothers with open-ended questions and conversations where the mothers felt listened to. The conversations were also adapted based on how ready each mother was to vaccinate her child. As the paper put it, this formed a 'respectful partnership, helping [the mothers] change their behaviour according to their capacities'. The methods used in the study were successful—increasing the intent to vaccinate by 15 per cent and the actual immunisation by 9 per cent.

In contemporary discussions, the Dunning-Kruger effect is often used to mock the overconfident views of others, usually people we disagree with. All of us can, however, be guilty of demonstrating the same overconfidence when we are non-experts and poor performers. Mike Hughes, our daredevil flat-earther, launched another rocket in 2020. That time around, the crash of the rocket proved fatal. Yet, he knew the risks he was taking, and the Dunning-Kruger effect perhaps didn't extend to his rocket-making capabilities. Even for the rest of us, the effect isn't always a reflection of any form of psychological limitation. For several tasks it could simply be a result of the limitations faced by those of us who are less skilled or knowledgeable. Also, it is not based on an immutable characteristic of a person—training and education helps all of us calibrate our self-knowledge to better match reality. Crucially, the training has to be the right sort. Mocking flat-earthers or writing off deniers of climate change and evolution in anger can be an immediate and perhaps understandable response for experts. Yet, to make actual change and reduce the effects of poor knowledge, they (or we) will have to learn to have better, more empathetic conversations and empower people to make their own decisions.

SIX

Building a Lie

AKBAR-BIRBAL STORIES ARE AN ENDURING PART OF INDIAN FOLKLORE. I grew up devouring them, and can still recall the Amar Chitra Katha comics that first introduced me to them. If you're familiar with the stories, you know how they go: Akbar presents Birbal with a predicament, and over the course of the story, Birbal resolves the problem with his boundless store of wit and intelligence. In one of the stories I remember, Akbar tasks Birbal with the mission of finding the ten greatest fools in the city. Birbal finds an assortment of candidates on his quest—a man chasing after his own voice, two men fighting over imaginary animals, a man who trusts a cloud to be his landmark. Then, at night, he steps out for a walk to take a break from the project. On the walk, he meets perhaps the greatest fool of them all. He sees an old man searching for a missing ring at night and asks him where he dropped it. Without skipping a beat, the man points to a tree some distance away. Baffled, Birbal asks for an explanation. The man explains very reasonably that, yes, he did lose his ring by the tree, but it's dark there. Instead, he is now searching here because this is where the light is.

Of all the fools in the story, this is the one I remember best. Perhaps I find him the most amusing, perhaps he's the one most easily mocked. Or perhaps it's because it is this fool that captures the truth about us the best. Of course none of us would behave like him when searching for a ring. Yet in other cases—when we are faced with a demanding problem, when we search for facts to confirm our beliefs or when we construct our self-images—we might not be so far off from him. How else do we explain our positive illusions about ourselves? Could it be that, rather than performing the hard task of searching where we might encounter inconvenient truths, we spend our time, like Birbal's fool, only searching where the light is?

Were Birbal to return from the dead and launch an investigation into this as a kind of zombie detective, he would find that the foundations of our overconfident errors come from many sources. We can thank the irrational quirks of our minds as well as the gravitational pull of our motivations. Then there are the mechanisms that ensure our brains respond differentially to positive and negative feedback. Finally, we have to look at our societies, how they help construct our self-views and the lengths to which we will go to keep our self-esteem and social standing. Let's look at each of these in turn.

Let's say zombie Birbal wanted to measure how foolish each one of us was. Should he begin by comparing our actions against an ideal of rational behaviour? This rational ideal has been an underlying assumption about human behaviour in different fields, not least in economics. Some would even say that rationality is what differentiates humans from other animals. Yet, over the decades, this assumption hasn't held water. The psychology story that makes the headlines now is the story of our irrationality. Scratch a popular psychology book, and you'll discover how the way we think is defined by a wealth of irrational errors, or as we've come to call them, cognitive biases.

What are these biases? Simply put, they are predictable ways in which humans behave that do not conform to a rational logical framework, at least at first glance. Over the decades, psychologists have compiled an impressive catalogue of these errors. Several of them form the building blocks of overconfidence.

We've already encountered one of them before: the availability bias or availability heuristic—a contributor to the better-than-average effect and our optimism bias. Since it is easier for us to recall examples of our own behaviour compared to other people's behaviour, the availability heuristic leads to us overestimating our own capabilities compared to others.

The availability heuristic also explains a particular quirk of our judgements and how they differ for ourselves compared to others. Smokers tend to overestimate their chances of contracting lung cancer.[1] Yet, they also think they are less likely than others to get lung cancer. Similarly, soon after 9/11, Americans overestimated the chance of a terrorist attack, but still thought they were less likely than others to be in one.[2] These results are explained by the fact that people who can easily recall examples of the relevant issues (smoking, terrorism) will overestimate the frequency of them occurring. But since they haven't personally experienced the negative consequences, they will think their own personal risk is low. How easily we can recall events and personal experiences thus influences our estimates of vulnerability and risk, leading to different forms of overconfidence—and a potential place on Birbal's list of fools.

The next cognitive bias that has been implicated in overconfidence is what is called an anchoring bias. Here, we fixate on an early estimate of an answer and don't adjust future estimates or confidence intervals away from this estimate. Our initial answer thus ends up being 'sticky'. For example, when asked to estimate how long you might take on a project, you might make an initial guess of one year. In later discussions, this initial estimate biases what you think is possible, even if others insist it takes much longer, say, up to five years. You can see how this could lead to overprecision—where in spite of evidence to the contrary, we remain confident in our initial estimates.

The anchoring bias can also have a social dimension—one person's initial guess biases the guesses of others in a group. At a pub quiz I used to attend with several friends of mine, the final question for a bonus pot was always about estimating numbers. We might be asked something like how many cups of tea are drunk in the UK every year or the total number of football stadiums in the world. For the first few months at this quiz, we would all discuss possibilities and spread out our guesses based on our discussion. Yet, we rarely won the bonus prize. It was only when we decided to make our first estimates independently and then discuss how to spread out our guesses that we began winning the bonus prize. In the initial approach, one person's initial guess biased all of our subsequent guesses, often in a region far away from the actual answer. By keeping our initial guesses independent, we dramatically increased our probability of success.

One more bias bears mentioning, the sunk-cost fallacy. People have a tendency to persist in a plan of action purely because a lot of effort or money was invested in it, regardless of how rewarding or effective it actually is. You might, for example, persist in your poor career choice rather than taking up something better suited to your abilities. This could also easily contribute to the planning fallacy. The more time and money spent on a public project, the less likely governments will be to back away from it. Budgets will then balloon, even if the benefits of the project fail to surface. The constantly increasing costs involved in building a Garden Bridge across the river Thames in London led to the project being cancelled in 2017 despite the UK£ 37–50 million that had already been spent.[3] That's an example where the government bravely resisted the sunk-cost fallacy.

These illustrations demonstrate how the different tricks our minds use could lead to judgements that contribute to overconfidence. Of all the cognitive biases that we have been shown to have, however, the one that could potentially contribute the most to overconfidence is the confirmation bias. To get an idea of how this works, imagine that you believed the theory that said 'Leaving my umbrella at home causes rainy weather'. You would go out every now and then without your umbrella and see if you returned home soaking wet. If you did this repeatedly and had the right result, you might think that you've found a new cosmic law—the clouds make weather decisions based on a report from their umbrella inspector. However, what's actually going on in the country you live in is that it just rains every single day (hello, UK!). Which means that you have missed the real rule which is at play here. When the true theory is more general than your personal theory, your investigations simply confirm what you set out to find rather than uncovering anything deeper.

The critical factor here is that you set out searching only for evidence that proved your theory, not evidence that disproved it. What you needed to do was also step out with your umbrella. This comes naturally to us, and for a good reason. As a search strategy, it might actually be helpful in finding appropriate examples quickly. Let's say you wanted to test the statement 'All birds can fly'. To test this theory, what you would do is to look for examples of birds and see whether they can fly. Such an approach should lead you to discover the existence of ostriches and cassowaries, and show you that your theory was wrong. Now imagine another approach. Here, you start by looking at all the animals that can't fly and see which of them are birds. It would take far longer to sort through the lions, the goldfish and the snakes before you could reach the ostriches. Clearly, this is a less efficient way of testing your theory. Our minds, therefore, rightly favour the first, more 'positive', strategy compared to the second 'negative' strategy—a positivity bias.[4] The key feature of importance is that we are searching for the presence of a feature (flight) rather than its absence.

This positivity bias, however, obscures truth when there is a theory that a person wants to prove, leading to confirmation bias. If they only search for places where evidence for their theory is present, rather than instances where evidence might be absent, they could make important mistakes. The information could all be from sources that fit a proposed theory. Unless one actively looks for examples that negate a proposed theory, one could end up with an incomplete, and often false, picture of the facts—this is the confirmation bias.[5,6]

This bias could be reinforced in many ways. We are experts at finding patterns. Yet, the patterns we find are usually the ones we are already looking for, whether we are searching for a bird in the woods or sorting through evidence. We tend to believe evidence that supports our theory and tend to be more sceptical about evidence that does not.[7] As a result, when presented with the same evidence, people with opposing theories will use it to reinforce their beliefs and end up further apart than before.[8] Our beliefs can bias our behaviour even at the level of smaller details—for example, people are quicker to spot grammatical mistakes in a sentence that conform to their opinions than ones that don't.[9] Confirmation biases even bias our visual attention towards evidence that confirms our theories.[10] Importantly, the confirmation bias works in favour of our theories regardless of the truth or falsehood of the theory. This could contribute to overconfidence. When it reinforces our false beliefs about our own capabilities, it could lead to overestimation and overplacement. When it reinforces other theories, even in the face of evidence to the contrary, it could lead to overprecision. In fact, potentially the more evidence we face, the more our confirmation biases can selectively use it to bolster our pet theories.

The internet amplifies all these worries. As Jeff Bezos, CEO of Amazon, once put it: 'The Internet is a confirmation bias machine.'[11] It is easy to see why. Social media, where you can follow people you agree with and block the ones you don't agree with, forms a perfect virtual illustration of how confirmation bias works. Even when accessing information on the internet outside our social media accounts, we tend to get what we're looking for. The internet relies on us typing the search term into a search engine or visiting a particular website. Previously, we might have been more likely to encounter an unlooked-for article while flipping the pages of a newspaper. Nowadays, that's less likely to happen unless we make a concerted effort to visit sites that we usually tend not to.

The internet could be an able handmaiden to our confirmation bias, and there is evidence for this. Greater access to broadband internet increases polarisation of opinion,[12] and the use of emotional language on social media increases diffusion of messages within but not across our social media bubbles.[13] There is also evidence that people spend more time on sites that are consistent with their prior attitudes, demonstrating a confirmation bias.[14] This bias is also influenced by how important people think a topic is. Yes, people do spend more time on articles from credible sources, but only on those that confirm their views. The results are especially strong for people with higher education. They show a greater confirmation bias when the sources are credible. Clearly education is no barrier to our ability to fool ourselves; it even seems to contribute. Needless to say, we don't need the internet for our confirmation bias. We naturally operate in this manner. But what studies suggest is that the internet becomes another tool that exacerbates our biases. If Birbal logged on to Twitter, he would undoubtedly be shocked that we not only search where the light is, we actively cast light only where we've searched before, rather than where we might find the truth. In this, we are worse even than Birbal's last fool.

So far, we've talked about the confirmation bias as simply a characteristic of our psychology. But we can ask a further question: are all the factors that contribute to overconfidence just products of how we process information—a cognitive limitation, if you like? Or are we systematically biased towards our preferred goals? These competing explanations have been a long-standing debate amongst psychologists, with different studies arguing the case for what have been called 'cognitive' and 'motivational' explanations.

Previously we discussed two possible explanations for the beliefs of flat-earthers—one to do with limited knowledge and another to do with community. Arguably, it's the same debate that plays out there. Almost all the explanations we've discussed, from the availability bias to confirmation biases, would be classified as cognitive explanations. An overarching idea underlying all these explanations is that they reflect the fact that we have a limited amount of brainpower, i.e., cognitive resources. So, rather than thinking through every decision, we rely on quick rules of thumb. In fact, we are less likely to show the resultant errors—for example, believe in fake news—if we use or are trained to adopt a more analytical approach.[15] But this is a more effortful and time-consuming approach, and would be hard to sustain consistently. In fact, when we are forced to respond more quickly, we are more likely to have optimistic predictions of our future and our health—but not about those of others.[16] Our default low-resource assumptions seem to differ for ourselves and for others.

In a hugely influential review,[17] the social psychologist Ziva Kunda argues that motivations have a large role to play in how people think. She argues that there are two kinds of goals people might have: accuracy goals and directional goals. Both of these goals could drive what Kunda called 'motivated cognition'. When people are motivated to be more accurate, they tend to consider information more carefully. This does not always lead to perfectly accurate processing, though. On the other hand, when they are motivated towards a particular goal, they bias information processing to support the goal. It's best summarised in that famous Upton Sinclair quote: 'It is difficult to get a man to understand something when his salary depends on his not understanding it.'

We might, for example, be biased in how we access beliefs about ourselves, selectively using memories of our own actions to bolster our characteristics and actions in a way that fits our motivations and self-concepts. In one study,[18] people who are told that extraversion is good for academic success were more likely to see themselves as being highly extroverted compared to people who were not given the same incentive. If people are instead told that introversion was what was needed, people are more likely to see themselves as being introverted. Similar manipulations in other studies[19] changed people's views of their social skills, skills on tasks, caffeine consumption and even brushing habits. You can imagine how this increases our overconfidence when we are motivated to believe we have what it takes to do something. In what might be an interesting example from a recent study, a substantial proportion of middle-class British people identify as working class,[20] but this is higher amongst actors. The authors of the study argue that this is because downplaying your privilege and presenting a story of humble origins might be of particular value amongst actors.[21]

We might equally have biased beliefs about others when we rely on them for any sort of expected outcome. Here's an example: in one study,[22] participants were randomly assigned people to date over five weeks. Since the participants didn't choose the people to date themselves, you would expect some of them to like their dates and some not, a mixed bag really. However, despite the fact that these prospective dates were randomly assigned, most participants rated them as more likeable from the outset and were more confident of those ratings compared to ratings for people whom they don't expect to date. They were biasing their beliefs to construct an optimistic future.

This is something we do for other future events too. When asked in a study[23] to evaluate which traits led to the stability of other people's marriages, people chose a variety of different attributes. You might think that these attributes would be independent of the evaluators. But, no: what these attributes had in common is that those evaluating also possessed the attributes that they rated highly. Importantly, this only occurred if marriage was important to them. A similar pattern was seen when people were asked to evaluate traits that led to educational achievement.[24]

In general, people tend to view events that have desirable outcomes as more likely to occur.[25] For instance, we question the accuracy of tests that give us unfavourable results even in fictional medical scenarios. And we are more likely to find the right statistics to support our goals and question the evidence contradicting them. Smokers, for example, are more difficult to convince about the health risks of smoking compared to non-smokers.[26] Another classic example deals with the risks of caffeine. Suppose there was a medical claim like this one (though there isn't): 'Caffeine poses a serious health risk for women.' Now imagine there was a whole article backing up that claim. Let's see how this could play out. We might all, whether we are men or women, have some ideas about the risks of caffeine even before we hear the claim. These ideas would influence how we scrutinise the claim. That's understandable. When a study[27] presented people with such an article, telling them it was a genuine claim, there was, however, a different pattern. The article was less persuasive to women who consumed more caffeine compared to women who consumed less. Tellingly, this effect wasn't seen in men (irrespective of their caffeine consumption) who read the article, presumably since there were no implications for them. This means that it was only the women who consumed more caffeine—for whom the implications of the article would be serious—who were sceptical of it. When faced with important issues, our motivations lead us to evaluate evidence in ways that serve ourselves.

Across studies, there are some consistent features. The extent to which we change our views is often still anchored in reality—we don't immediately believe we are introverted rather than extroverted just because a researcher motivates us to do so. Rather, we just believe we are less extroverted than we might have done without the motivation. Our predictions often track reality, but they are optimistically biased.[28] Another recurring feature is that motivational effects are best seen on traits that are more ambiguously defined. The more we are asked about specific details, the less effect our motivations seem to have, and if performance is clearly measured and objective rather than ambiguous, increased motivation need not lead to overconfidence.[29]

Another big idea is that our accuracy goals and our directional goals are not in contradiction to each other. At first glance, you might think that's a relief—even when we have other motivations, we can still strive for accuracy. It doesn't turn out that way. Our desire to be more accurate often ends up helping our directional goals. Priming accuracy goals can get us to look for more detailed information, but only in support of our directional goals. As a result, having more information often leads to a greater effect of motivation rather than a more accurate picture.

The mechanisms underlying motivated cognition have particular relevance to other aspects of psychology. One of these is the idea of cognitive dissonance, a response to situations when actions don't match our perceptions of ourselves or others. For example, you might think of yourself as an honest, ethical person but then go on to cheat on an exam paper. This contradiction is hard to deal with, providing a strong motivation to reduce the emotions you are feeling. Motivated cognition then often ends up finding reasons to justify and strengthen the original belief[30]—by finding more evidence that confirms that you are honest and ethical or by finding reasons why what you did doesn't really count as cheating. I'm also thinking of all the times we ardently defend our favourite actors, colleagues or politicians when they are hit by scandals.

If we can be so scared of facing the truth, could we even go further and deceive ourselves? True overconfidence is a form of self-deception. It isn't just about overselling yourself or putting up displays of bravado, but a genuine error in self-assessment. Could motivated cognition lead us down that route? In fact, the mechanisms of self-deception proposed by the evolutionary biologist Robert Trivers and psychologist William von Hippel[31, 32, 33] are not so far from those of motivated cognition. In their review of the evolutionary causes for, and the psychological mechanisms underlying, self-deception, they lay out the information biases that form the basis of various kinds of self-deception. Some of these clearly match the discussion of motivated cognition, including biased information search, biased interpretation and misremembering. Self-deception could of course lead to both underconfidence and overconfidence—you could fool yourself into believing you were unskilled or you could fool yourself into believing that you could take on any job.

As with motivated cognition, self-deception is also particularly evident when the feedback we receive about our performance is ambiguous.[34] That is when we can best deceive ourselves and develop inflated ideas about our abilities. One context in which this is neatly illustrated is when competitors can win a competition through bluffing.[35] When the bluff deters others from entering the competition, those who bluff increase confidence in their abilities as if they had actually won in the competition. Despite not actually competing and knowing that they bluffed their way to success, these competitors grow steadily more overconfident. Those who choose not to enter a competition, on the other hand, lose out on chances for competing and winning, which could have boosted their confidence in their very real abilities. A similar result comes from experiments where some participants taking a general knowledge or IQ test had the opportunity to see the answers while completing the test.[36] Predictably, this helped them perform better than others, but it also led them to make higher predictions about their performance on a subsequent test. This tendency persisted even when they were offered monetary incentives to be correct in their self-assessments. The tendency to increase self-belief despite their success being the result of prior access to answers rose when people were given public certificates for their performance. Adding a social context increases our tendency to self-deceive. It is important to note that there is a contrast here with other findings where students given monetary incentives to be accurate were less overconfident about their grades on tests.[37]

What this means is that even if you use help from computers and others to beat Vishwanathan Anand in a chess game, you're still going to think of the win as on your own merit. I'm reminded of my own confidence at solving cryptic crosswords. When I do these online, I inevitably find myself stuck on some clues and—because the app allows me to do so—I check if the letters I've filled in are correct. Occasionally, I guess at a letter without knowing the word and check that as well. Even more rarely, I give up and reveal an entire word. On Saturday Prize crosswords, where none of these options are available, I struggle and take days to complete the crossword. My performance on these crosswords is the true measure of my ability. Yet, if someone were to ask me how good I am, and I don't really think about it, I can easily see myself basing my judgement on my performances on the weekday crosswords instead. After all, I do complete the crossword every day, or so I tell myself. As I write this though, I can feel the cold dead hand of Birbal gripping my shoulder, claiming me for his list.

Other researchers focus on how processes very similar to motivated cognition and self-deception help fuel information avoidance[38] or denialism—our tendency to avoid information strategically, particularly when it's information that we don't like to hear. Sometimes this is news about our health, other times it could be stock market prices. Surely gathering more information will only help us make better decisions? It seems irrational not to want to know relevant information. Yet, when it doesn't suit us, we tend to avoid information in many different ways. Some of these include biasing our attention to particular facts or interpretations of those facts, forgetting facts selectively and even sometimes physically avoiding results we think might be negative. Think of a politician not wanting to know all the facts, and thus avoiding having to take necessary action while still maintaining plausible deniability.

Situations where you are afraid of social penalties can also lead to similar behaviour.[39, 40] For instance, an individual might feel that her decision to deny or avoid information about climate change has almost no effect on political decisions about the issue. In other words, the personal benefits from accepting that climate change is real may not seem substantial for an individual. On the other hand, accepting that it is real can have strong effects on how people perceive her, depending on the communities she belongs to and what their beliefs are. In this case, ignoring information about climate change or biasing how you look for information is positively rational. A similar argument could possibly be made for the belief in a flat earth. All of these mechanisms are akin to those discussed for self-deception and motivated cognition. Motivated cognition, self-deception or information avoidance, however you phrase it, these processes can be well laid out paths to overconfidence. It's almost as if the way our brains work fates us to be overly optimistic about ourselves and our futures. Given how many examples of this we find in different fields, we might well ask if it isn't actually a good thing after all.

The debate about whether optimism is the correct approach to life is not a new one. Optimism was the subject of heated debate in eighteenth-century Europe. Early in the century, the German mathematician and philosopher Gottfried Leibniz—in between inventing calculus and the mechanical calculator—gained fame for his philosophy of optimism. In his metaphysical work, *Monadology*, he argued that everything that exists has to have a sufficient reason to do so. As a result, he concluded that we live in the best of all possible worlds—a decidedly optimistic take. Forty-one years after its publication, this notion was challenged by a large-scale disaster, the Lisbon earthquake of 1755. This disaster is still estimated to be one of the worst earthquakes in history, with an estimated 10,000–100,000 deaths in Lisbon alone. Shocked by the death and devastation caused by this earthquake, another philosopher, Voltaire, wrote his satirical masterwork, *Candide, or the Optimist*. In it, he lays into the Leibnizian notion of the best of all possible worlds to devastating effect. One of the chief targets of his satire is a character in the book called Pangloss who consistently defends the doctrine of optimism in ridiculous ways, even in the face of the worst disasters. Pangloss's student Candide attempts to live his life according to his teachings, but in the face of the brutal realities of his life, eventually abandons the doctrine of optimism.

Candide is a much-acclaimed and venerated novel. Yet, one wonders which character in the novel better captures human nature—Candide, who rejects optimism, or his ever-hopeful teacher, Pangloss. Despite Voltaire's wit and virtuousity, it might well be Pangloss who is having the last laugh. Our brain's psychological mechanisms appear to be distinctly Panglossian. To go a step further: is there a way in which we can actually get at the signatures of optimism in our brains? Cognitive psychologist Tali Sharot does exactly this in her book, *The Optimism Bias*,[41] and her body of research.

Sharot's book points out the various ways in which the optimism bias could have implications for us, both in our daily lives and for our health. On the one hand, it allows us to persist in our endeavours and stay positive as we work towards our goals. Optimists are more likely to exercise more and eat low-fat diets, and end up leading longer lives. On the other hand, optimists could also be less likely to seek help for medical conditions and engage in risky behaviour. Either way, this bias towards optimism is a defining characteristic for many of us. Yet, every one of us faces unpleasantness and misfortune; disease and failure fall upon us all. What are the mechanisms by which we still somehow cling to optimism? Could the answer lie in how our brains work? Work by Sharot and others sheds light on this puzzle.

One key finding is that most of us process positive and negative information differently. When faced with information that is worse than expected, we are less likely to update our beliefs and self-views. On the other hand, when faced with information that is better than expected, we are perfectly happy to update our beliefs about ourselves and the world. We become overconfident even if we just encounter an unexpected gift.[42] This difference in processing good and bad news could be implemented early on in how we filter information about the world, or alternatively, it could involve a network of brain structures that directs the way our attention is deployed in the world.[43] In order to see how this plays out in the brain, one study[44] imaged the brain activity of participants while they thought about events in their lives. To this end, the researchers used a technique called functional magnetic resonance imaging. This technique visualises which brain regions are active during a task by imaging which regions have changes in blood flow. By comparing the activity during different tasks or a neutral activity, researchers are able to identify the brain regions that are specially involved in the task they are interested in.

In the study, people thought about events that were either positive (winning an award) or negative (ending a relationship) and either in the past or in the future. The first result was that most people imagined positive future events as being closer in time than both future negative events or past events. The intensity of positive events was also felt more strongly than that of negative events. The authors suggest that the special nature of future events could be explained by the idea that the future remains ambiguous. We can, therefore, make of it what we like. The past, however, is fixed and it isn't as easy to feel positive about its shortcomings.

Two different brain regions were involved, both of which had previously been suggested to be linked to emotional or motivational functions. Both regions had less activity when negative future events were imagined compared to positive future events or past events—suggesting that these regions reduce the emotional impact of negative events while allowing positive events to have a greater impact.

In another similar study,[45] people's brains were imaged while they estimated the probability of adverse events like robbery or Alzheimer's disease. They were then provided the actual average probability of each event occurring to someone of their socio-cultural background. The idea was that people would readjust their estimate once they were faced with the actual facts. In a second session, the participants were once more asked to estimate the probability of the events, having now seen these average probabilities. Most people, in fact, did update their answers when the average probabilities were more optimistic than they previously thought. Yet, when the probabilities they were given were less optimistic than their own estimates, they were less likely to do so. They remembered both kinds of information perfectly well, but used them differently. In this study too, when the errors were related to positive or desirable information, some brain regions increased their activity. When the people encountered undesirable information, it led to a reduction in activity in a separate set of brain regions—ones that had previously been implicated in tracking errors in predictions or responses. This was especially so for people who were highly optimistic, bearing out the idea that positive and negative errors have different effects on us. Another recent study[46] used a different technique to track neural activity, by looking at people's confidence when performing a visual task. The results showed that a high degree of confidence modified neural processing so that responses to evidence that contradicted the original decision were suppressed, effectively demonstrating a neural signature for the confirmation bias.

Neuroscientists have more tools at their disposal, including ones that go beyond visualising brain activity. A technique called transcranial magnetic stimulation uses a coil to deliver magnetic pulses that change brain activity in specific regions. Scientists can then observe the effect of this change. The prediction was that, when the stimulation interfered with the brain area that failed to update in response to negative information, we should be able to remove the differential effect of positive and negative information. Sure enough, this is what the scientists found.[47] Disrupting activity in that area meant that people updated their beliefs in response to both good and bad news. Disrupting activity in other areas, however, didn't change the classic pattern of optimism we've been talking about so far. Yet another way of modulating how we update our beliefs is through drugs that enhance specific functions in our nervous systems. In particular, increasing the activity of a neurochemical called dopamine further decreases our responses to negative information,[48] biasing us more towards positive information, i.e., towards becoming overly optimistic. This seems appropriate since dopamine is the chemical that links our predictions to outcomes and is commonly linked to learning about rewards.

The picture that all these studies draw up is one of a Panglossian brain. Not only do we preferentially imagine positive futures, when we encounter information that supports or contradicts these futures, we preferentially take on board the supportive information. The workings of our brains ensure that we retain our optimism and remain overconfident about ourselves and the world. Once again, we are only searching where the light is.

The final bricks in our sky-scraping tower of overconfidence are the means by which we construct views of ourselves and the roles that societies play in that process. When assessing ourselves, we attend to the positives and ignore the negatives, favouring our best selves over a realistic estimate of our failures and successes. In an earlier chapter, we talked about a study where people were faster to identify photos of themselves tweaked to look more attractive compared to realistic photos of themselves. There's also evidence that shows people prefer the letters contained in their names compared to the letters that aren't.[49] Even just priming us to think about ourselves increases our ability to spot positive words compared to negative words.[50]

There's another cognitive bias that has been seen time and again: the self-serving bias.[51] We attribute any positive event in our lives to our own efforts and any negative event to other causes. So, succeeding on an exam is thanks to my hard work and genius, but failing my driving test was because of the bad weather, the noisy pedestrians, the surprise seagull, the list goes on. This pattern of ignoring failures means that we lose out on valuable feedback about our own abilities. It's easy then to believe that we are better at different tasks than we actually are.

Self-serving biases lead to us overvaluing our successes even when they arise from random factors. Initial success could lead to later failures due to overconfidence, especially in tasks that depend on performance in non-social domains. We'll see in a later chapter that there's evidence for this in finance, and potentially during wars and politics too. In social domains, however, overconfidence might well not lead to failure. Availability heuristics, which we discussed as individual biases, have the potential to lead to availability cascades. Let me explain that. In fields where the only measure of success is fame or popularity, a person who manages to gain some initial popularity through chance could quickly gain a reputation for being successful. That is, the initial reputation would become more 'available' to entire social networks, contributing further to the person's popularity, and leading to further availability of the reputation and further success.[52] Ultimately, popularity could breed further popularity by becoming intuitive self-evident facts to others—if there is no requirement for ability.

What both the optimism bias and the self-serving bias highlight is that optimism and overconfidence can persist even in the face of negative feedback. Our ability to take on board feedback is linked to whether we view a trait as being fixed or changeable. For example, do you think our intelligence is completely determined by our genes or can we do something to improve it? Which of these views could we expect to boost our overconfidence? Testing the effect of these beliefs on overconfidence gives us a clear answer.[53] People who have a fixed view of intelligence are also more overconfident. People who read an article in favour of such a view also tended to allocate less attention to difficult problems compared to those who encountered a viewpoint stating that intelligence was malleable. By not engaging with difficult tasks, the people primed with a fixed view of intelligence don't get a chance to learn about their abilities on the task, which explains why they became more overconfident. When these people were manipulated into attending to the difficult problems, their overconfidence reduced to the same level as the other participants. Our beliefs could thus distract us from the very details that give us accurate estimates of our abilities.

We don't all experience the same levels and types of feedback, of course. A host of social and other factors determine how often we encounter praise or criticism for our performance. Repeated negative stereotypes about our abilities reinforce negative self-views without necessarily reflecting actual ability. On the flipside, some of us might receive less negative feedback about our abilities, and combined with our biased information processing, this could lead to overconfidence. It's easy to imagine how a host of other factors (class, gender, caste) would influence the degree of praise and criticism we receive over our lives, even on very specific topics, from logical thinking to business sense to empathy. For example, a paper based on a study of undergraduates from the University of Delhi shows evidence for caste-based differences in confidence.[54] The researchers defined the broad categories of Upper Caste (UC), Other Backward Caste (OBC) and Scheduled Caste/Scheduled Tribes (SC/ST). They then assessed the confidence of the students in each of these categories by asking them if they would perform better than other students at a task. They found that SC/ST students (but not OBC students) were significantly less confident by this measure than UC students. UC students were also more likely to be competitive than others, although there was no difference across categories in risk preference—two other traits that might be linked to overconfidence.

Self-views and the confidence they generate certainly influence whether we overestimate or underestimate our performance.[55, 56] This can have real world consequences. Women in one study performed as well as men in a science quiz, but underestimated how well they did. Later, when given a chance to participate in an external science competition, they were less likely to do so because they wrongly viewed themselves as poorer at science reasoning. Another study shows that young people from higher socio-economic backgrounds are more likely to overclaim.[57] Perhaps this could explain why, in the UK, teachers are more likely to underestimate final exam grades for students from disadvantaged backgrounds compared to richer ones.[58, 59] This could have important consequences, as university admissions are still initially issued on the basis of predicted grades before the real results are known. These biased interactions with the world would also then have a feedback effect, reinforcing our self-views and how confident or overconfident we feel.

People in power might be an extreme example of how this works. The luxury afforded to the powerful of being able to fail and not only bounce back but go on to better positions ensures that they remain buffered from negative feedback—a gateway to overconfidence. This phenomenon of 'failing upward' has even been characterised as leading to a 'glass-floor'[60] effect. Just as a glass-ceiling effect prevents certain people, typically women, from rising to the top of their professions despite their abilities, a glass floor keeps the rich and powerful in charge despite their ineptness. There's corresponding evidence that even feeling powerful influences overconfidence,[61] especially in combination with narcissism.[62] We'll go into this in more detail in a later chapter on politics.

Overconfidence is thus also a social bias. It can be influenced by how others view us and our views of others. For instance, people are more confident of their performance when others are present.[63]

Overconfidence in our abilities and believing that our successes are due to how brilliant we are also goes hand-in-hand with in-group favouritism.[64] People with higher confidence in their abilities even tend to hire people similar to themselves, at least in an experimental scenario.[65] In-group biases are particularly prominent when overconfident people experience successes. Self-serving biases ensure that they attribute their successes to themselves, and consequently have less support for policies of redistribution that could help others.[66] In general, having more overconfidence in their own abilities leads to men having less support for redistribution than women (at least in the US and some European countries).[67] Experiences of failure could increase support for these policies, but the evidence isn't as clear.[68] Overconfidence would then be expected to perpetuate forms of elitism, preventing a more performance-based evaluation.

Another way in which group identity and overconfidence could interact is through information biases. We've thought about information biases leading to self-deception and inflated self-views. But, it is argued, they also promote a defence of group-level identity, a form of socially adaptive belief.[69] Our overconfidence helps signal to our groups that we hold the same beliefs that they do, allowing us to avoid the costs that might arise from disagreeing with the people who support us. We could have beliefs about our identities that go beyond the evidence, leading to overprecision. We could even believe that our groups are capable of achieving more than they really can, leading to overestimation. There's evidence that those who are the most prejudiced are least likely to recognise their biases,[70] a pattern that resembles the Dunning-Kruger Effect, leaving such people robbed of the self-awareness needed to begin changing themselves. Clearly, overconfidence can be both fuelled by and exacerbate different forms of prejudice—a subject we will return to in more depth.

The very last piece we need to understand our responses to failure and negative feedback is self-esteem. Inflated estimates of our own performance (or that of our in-group) clearly make us feel better about ourselves, suppressing that sinking feeling that we are not up to any task at hand. There are multiple strategies that help us preserve our self-esteem even in the face of poor performance. We question the validity of the very tests that measure our performance or the statistics used to evaluate ourselves and the groups we belong to. This is why, when faced with failure, people are more likely to think they have the attributes necessary for success and view people similar to themselves more positively.[71] Performing badly changes not only our views of ourselves, but also our views of others. People exaggerate the performance of those who outperform them, allowing them to make greater claims about their own performance. In one study that examined this,[72] people were given the chance to either rate people who outperformed them or not. People chose to rate, and ranked those who outperformed them higher, and in addition, rated their own intelligence higher.

Alternatively, self-esteem can be reaffirmed by being derogatory about competitors. In an influential experiment,[73] students who had been told they had performed poorly on an IQ test negatively rated the personality traits of a student who appeared visibly to be of another religion in a video. This did not occur if the original students had performed well or if the other student seemed to be of the same religion. Prejudice can, therefore, possibly help us ignore our own failures, allowing us to persist with a more rose-tinted picture of ourselves even in the face of negative feedback. Steven Fine and Steven J. Spence, the authors of the study, state in the paper that 'stereotyping or derogation of a member of a stereotyped group can provide such situational opportunities to restore a threatened self-image', and that 'stereotyping and prejudice may be common reactions to self-image threat'.

A similar argument explains our self-serving judgements, where we think more favourably of ourselves than others.[74] These judgements make us feel better and are especially prevalent under threat. Some psychologists have argued that such an approach actually helps us stay vigilant to new threats. By making us feel better, self-serving attitudes rapidly stabilise our emotional state and we are then better at dealing with new challenges. So, for instance, if you've just heard that you haven't been selected for a job, your mind could kick in to convince you that you are actually good at what you do and that it wasn't your fault. This makes you better prepared to head out for another interview. The alternative would be to continue feeling depressed about it and not actually be prepared to deal with either the next interview or any new problem. Importantly, the opposite approach isn't necessary when we've done well and are feeling happy about ourselves. In such a situation, we don't need to be reminded of our limitations in order to be ready for new challenges. It's easy to see how this asymmetry might explain why our brain mechanisms update more on the basis of positive rather than negative feedback, leading to the optimism bias.

The maintenance of self-esteem thus gives us an answer to an important question we haven't yet explicitly asked: why do our brains work the way they do? Could the strategy of Birbal's fool actually have its benefits? What do we gain when we search where the light is?

We've touched on this a little bit when talking about how positivity biases and confirmation biases often end up being more efficient ways of testing the theories we have about the world. Our other biased strategies of information search, from motivated cognition to self-deception, could also have evolved to serve useful functions. In their book, *The Enigma of Reason*,[75] cognitive scientists Dan Sperber and Hugo Mercier make a deeper case: that our reasoning powers are fundamentally not about discovering the truth. They argue that the evolutionary function of reasoning is instead a social one. We use intuitions to come to conclusions about the world around us, and then use our reasoning powers to convince others of our conclusions. In light of this argumentative theory of reasoning, motivated cognition, confirmation biases and information avoidance all make much more sense. While none of them leads us closer to the objective truth, they could all help us make stronger arguments to other people.

The cognitive biases that we've been talking about don't in themselves constitute an explanation for our behaviour. They are more like descriptions of how we behave. However, just as with the argumentative theory of reason, we could expect them to have evolutionarily beneficial functions. This is a case made by Martie Haselton, Damian Murray and a former colleague of mine at Newcastle, Daniel Nettle.[76, 77] They argue that, rather than thinking of these biases as flaws, we should think of them as design features, laying out three reasons why we might have these biases.

The first of these is that a bias might serve as a shortcut to decision-making—a shortcut that makes the most efficient use of our brain resources and directs them to where they might be most gainful. The economist Daniel Kahneman also makes the same point in his book *Thinking Fast and Slow*.[78] Our cognitive heuristics can be very useful to make quick and often correct decisions when we need them. This is especially true when we are loaded with other tasks we must perform. A neat example Haselton and her co-authors give of this is the fact that people in power are more likely to use stereotypes than people with low levels of power. The argument is that powerful people can afford to make social mistakes, while less powerful people can't. Powerful people can therefore use quick but potentially inaccurate judgements and direct their cognitive efforts elsewhere. Similar considerations of efficiency could apply to some of the biases we've discussed, such as the availability heuristic or the anchoring bias.

To understand their second explanation for cognitive biases, consider how engineers approach errors. Think of a fire alarm. There are two ways in which a fire alarm could make a mistake. It could either sound an alarm when there is no fire or stay quiet when there really is a fire. Clearly the second error is more costly. So, if you were designing a fire alarm, you would choose a setting that minimised the chances of this error, even if it increased the chances of the opposite error. Similarly, while cognitive biases lead to us making certain kinds of errors, they might actually be helping us avoid other kinds of mistakes. They could, for example, allow us to be more decisive and lead to action where inaction might on average have worse consequences. This kind of approach could also help us understand the optimism bias that leads to us focusing our brains on positive information (and leading to action) and not negative information (and giving up).

We began this chapter with the story of Birbal's fool. At the end of the story, Birbal returns to court with only eight fools. When the emperor Akbar asks him where the other two fools are, Birbal says the ninth one is the emperor for assigning him the task and the tenth one is himself for carrying out such a task.

At the end of his walk through the world of biases, Zombie Birbal would agree that we could all be fools. Searching where the light is has been a good metaphor for how we construct the truth of our worlds. Yet, being this kind of a fool helps us survive and deal with the challenges we face every day. Defining cognitive biases and the other behaviours we have discussed as errors is perhaps itself an error. If deviating from the most logical way to behave is actually useful, then we shouldn't be surprised that we have evolved brains to do exactly that. However, if this idea about cognitive biases is true, it should also apply to their outcomes—including overconfidence. Overconfidence then would not be a misjudgement we make, but a useful trait that brings us evolutionary advantages. This is what we explore in the next chapter: what are the advantages of being ignorant of your own capabilities?

SEVEN

The Advantages of Ignorance

IN AUGUST 2017, BOXING FANS ACROSS THE WORLD HAD THEIR EYES glued to screens. Excitement ran high, the prices of the tickets were even higher—reaching US$ 10,000 for a ringside seat. Even on TV, fans were charged close to US$ 100 to see the most anticipated fight of the year—the much-publicised professional boxing match between Floyd Mayweather and Connor McGregor.[1, 2] Mayweather was an eleven-time five-division boxing champion. He was undefeated, with a record of forty-nine continuous victories. Twenty-six of these had been knockouts. He was so reliable in his victories that his nickname simply reflected why he was such a good bet—'Money'. Connor McGregor hadn't played a single professional boxing match.

Boxing can be a brutal business.[3] In December 2012, Kieran Farrel had to retire from professional boxing aged twenty-two after a match landed him in a coma. Since then, two other British boxers have died from head injuries. To enter a boxing ring requires a high degree of confidence. But to challenge an undefeated champion to a match when you are not a boxer would be the very definition of overconfidence. Connor McGregor spent months baiting Mayweather before the fight was even on the cards. Perhaps he never expected to actually fight Mayweather and was only trying to create a news story. We don't know what went through his mind when the fight materialised. On fight night, he appeared as confident as ever. The two fighters sparred for a full ten rounds, but in the tenth round, it was all over for McGregor. Mayweather had triumphed again, taking his tally to fifty consecutive undefeated victories. McGregor went down to another knockout, albeit a technical one.

If that sounds like a textbook example of overconfidence, it's because I've exaggerated the case against McGregor. He wasn't an entire stranger to fighting in the ring. He was a champion in his own right—twice champion of mixed martial arts—which includes some boxing training and experience. He had twenty-one wins from twenty-four fights, and he was a twenty-eight-year-old taking on someone more than ten years his senior. Nonetheless, it was overconfidence. Mayweather methodically picked apart his defences. While McGregor sprinted out and spent energy getting his jabs in from the beginning, Mayweather simply waited until McGregor started flagging twenty minutes in. He then launched into McGregor and rapidly finished the fight in the next four rounds. The total fight time of a mixed martial arts fight? Twenty-five minutes.

McGregor's own words after the fight make the point clearly: 'He's a lot better than I thought he would be.' Why would anybody take on one of the greatest boxers ever in his own sport without any history of boxing? We are all suckers for an underdog story. The world cheered when the unknown Boris Becker won his first ever Wimbledon on a wild card entry. McGregor had his strong fan base too. Yet, boxing isn't tennis—Becker could walk away unscathed from even a first round defeat. In times before there were boxing rules, players were severely wounded, even died. Evolutionary logic would then argue that people who were this overconfident would die out. If there is any genetic component to overconfidence, we should, as a species be far more accurate, at least about our fighting abilities. And yet, so many of us remain overconfident even there. The question is, why? McGregor certainly had a lot to gain from his overconfidence. It brought him opportunities, celebrity and earned him a cool minimum purse of US$ 30 million in just thirty-six minutes. There is much here that points towards why being ignorant of one's own limitations—while seemingly undesirable—could actually be an advantage. This paradox (if you want to call it that) has been discussed in different ways amongst psychologists and evolutionary biologists.

We can group their explanations into three main categories: Social Signals, Motivation and Health.

ROUND 1: SOCIAL SIGNALS

Let's suppose you were a feisty young person itching for all the fame and glory—and money—that McGregor garnered. You might remember McGregor discussing the fight saying: 'We do foolish things sometimes, but I'm not a damn fool. If I see an opportunity to make $300m in 36 minutes, why not?'[4] But to make that money, you would need to convince a whole range of people of your abilities, whether or not you had them. They would include your agent, the organisers of the fight, the sponsors and eventually the crowds of people paying US$ 100 on pay-per-view TV who wouldn't be bothered with a one-sided slugfest.

If you knew you weren't in the same league as Mayweather, you could try to fool everyone you meet with bluster and fighting words. But there's a problem with this approach. Trying to say one thing about yourself while believing another has consequences. Maintaining these two views simultaneously increases your mental load. It also means the signs of the effort you put in to do this end up showing. So keen-eyed folks—as long as there are enough of them—will pick up on the fact that you're just another blowhard. Eventually, this approach will lead nowhere.

Evolutionary biologist Robert Trivers proposed a theory, and developed it along with psychologist William von Hippel, suggesting a solution to this dilemma.[5, 6] Trivers and von Hippel argue that it is precisely in situations like McGregor's where being ignorant or self-deceived is an advantage. When a person is self-deceived, they no longer have to deal with the mental load of believing two things simultaneously. Nor do they show those tell-tale signs of stress[7] that would give the game given away. They become much better deceivers and reap all the advantages that this might bring, from job promotions to lucrative fighting contracts. This advantage overcomes any disadvantage that comes with overconfidence and allows it to persist amongst so many of us. The theory certainly rings true, but what evidence do we have that this theory works?

The theory has been around for many decades and has been much debated, even modelled mathematically.[8, 9] It is only recently, however, that experiments have actually tested it. Part of the problem is, of course, that measuring something like self-deception is always going to be tricky. You need both a person's judgement of themselves, and also an independent measurement of their abilities that isn't influenced by the first judgement. A study[10] I carried out with friend and collaborator Shakti Lamba set out to solve this problem. We asked undergraduate students in the first week of their first course at university to predict their grades on the next assignment they would be given. This would be their self-assessment. To obtain our independent assessment, we obtained their grades (with their consent) after. The assignments were marked blind to the identity of the student, and so were truly independent of the self-assessment. Now that we had our two assessments, we could ask which students were overconfident and which were underconfident. According to the Social Signalling theory, those who were overconfident should be able to better fool others about their abilities. To measure this, we also asked all the students to predict the grades of the other students in the same assignment. If the theory was right, we expected that the mistakes others made about a student would reflect the mistakes the student themselves made in self-assessment. This is exactly the pattern we found—people's self-deception correlated with how much others were deceived by them. In other words, the more overconfident they were, the more people overrated them.

How do we reconcile results like this with findings we discussed earlier, showing that people are generally wary and not too trusting? Part of the answer is that these results come from brief initial interactions. As people gain more knowledge about each other, you should expect the social effect to wear off. That is what we saw in our study too. After six weeks, the errors in self-estimation no longer correlated with the errors in estimation made by other students, at least when estimating absolute grades. We should also expect the charms of overconfidence to be particularly convincing where our wariness has a weak spot, such as in one-off encounters, when facts are less verifiable, when the consequences to us are trivial, when we believe people are helping us or when they tell us what we want to hear.

Further studies have teased apart this phenomenon in more detail. For instance, when people need to deceive others, they grow more overconfident and increased confidence makes people more persuasive.[11] Psychologist Megan Smith in collaboration with von Hippel and Trivers looked at how information-seeking, or the lack of it, influences our ability to persuade others.[12] The researchers made use of a fictional character called Mark. Participants were tasked with writing an essay arguing either that Mark was a good person or that he was a bad person, or to make neither case but just describe him. In the first two instances, the participants were paid more if their essay was amongst the most convincing ones about Mark as rated by independent readers online. What evidence could they use to describe Mark? The were presented with a series of positive and negative videos of Mark. They didn't have to watch all the videos though. If they thought they had enough evidence to write their essay, they could decide to stop watching.

Participants who were incentivised to paint a positive picture of Mark to others themselves formed a positive opinion of Mark, and the reverse was true for those who needed to make a negative case—all this with the same evidence on offer. Participants who initially saw videos that supported their position were more likely not to persist and watch videos against their position. Whether or not they saw the later contradictory videos formed a measure of bias. The next step was to see if this biased view of Mark convinced others. This is exactly what the researchers found. Amongst participants who saw initial videos supporting their assigned task, it was the ones who stopped earlier who wrote essays that were rated as more convincing. Those who evaluated the evidence in all the videos had essays that were rated less convincing. Once again, being overconfident about your views helped convince others better.

Being able to convince others of your arguments and abilities obviously could lead to a lot of opportunities and an increase in social status. This was explicitly tested by psychologists Jessica Kennedy and Cameron Anderson along with their collaborators.[13] They measured overconfidence in a series of tasks, including geography knowledge, familiarity with items in different domains (including some items that didn't exist), personality judgements, weight estimations and arithmetic ability. Some of these tasks were performed with unfamiliar people, while others were with groups that had worked together on projects. In addition, some tasks were performed individually, some in pairs and some in groups. Across all the tasks, though, it was clear that people who were overconfident about their performance were thought to be more influential and have higher status. They were also rated as more competent than non-overconfident participants.

When the researchers followed up on these results,[14] they found that people didn't lose their status if their overconfidence was revealed to others, at least not immediately. Another study by Hui Jing Lu and Lei Chang at the Chinese University of Hong Kong found that people were most self-deceived when they needed to deceive others with higher status rather than those with the same status as their own.[15] Given these results, perhaps we should expect people who want to improve their social status to be the most overconfident.

There is some evidence for this. A paper by John Jerrim, Phil Parker and Nikki Shure looked at what kinds of people were more likely to claim they know a concept that doesn't exist. They used a cross-national survey from nine Anglophone countries, and focused on the response to one question. The question asked participants which of a list of mathematical concepts they were familiar with. Crucially, it included three fake concepts, and the researchers used positive responses to these concepts as their measure of overclaiming. They found that young men and immigrants were most likely to overclaim—all potentially groups that want to improve their standing in society.[16] However, they also found that socio-economically advantaged teenagers were more likely to overclaim. That's not a group that needs to improve their social status.

The other way overconfidence can serve us socially is to signal our commitment,[17] perhaps to a theory or a social group. It is easy to laugh at people's unshakeable beliefs that the rapture is arriving or that the moon landing was a hoax. Yet, public declarations of confidence in even the most absurd ideas could show others in your social networks how committed you are to these ideas, and therefore to the beliefs of the group. On the other hand, the costs of doubting can be high, especially for beliefs that are strongly held by all your friends and family.[18]

The same logic plays out in beliefs about considerably less absurd ideas, such as climate change or nuclear waste disposal. Our political identities influence how we view these topics. This phenomenon of being selective about evidence in support of the cultural groups we are part of has been called identity-protective cognition.[19, 20] It isn't that we hold these beliefs because of misconceptions, but rather that they link us to a community, and there are real costs to holding different beliefs. The political scientist Francis Fukuyama has talked about the consequence of changing his mind and expressing regret about his earlier support of the war in Iraq.[21, 22] He lost a lot of friends when he did so. At the same time, he didn't gain support from those who were against the war in the first place. Changing your mind can be a lonely experience.

As the evidence has come in over the last few years, multiple studies across different domains hold up the Social Signalling theory surprisingly well. A related idea is also put forward in a mathematical model by political scientists Dominic Johnson and James Fowler.[23, 24] They imagine a situation where two individuals contest for a common resource. Each contestant has knowledge of their own capabilities but not of the other's. Since there is a cost to fighting for the resource, they would benefit from staying away if they think they're outmatched. On the other hand, given the uncertainty about capabilities, even when they are less capable, if they can bluff their way to causing the opponent to stay away, they can gain access to more resources. It, therefore, makes sense for individuals to overstate their abilities, and indeed, to even believe they are better than they are so that they can signal this to the competition. The maths shows that, when the costs of fighting are substantially lower than the benefits of gaining the resource, overconfidence should evolve. In such situations, an accurate person is at a loss because they will be ceding more resources compared to the overconfident person.

Other models too have shown that bluffing and overconfidence evolve together, especially in larger populations.[25] Overconfidence is predicted to be less dominant in smaller groups, where it is more difficult to persistently fool people with your bluffing.[26] Overconfidence thus can play a potent social role—at least in larger groups—helping us appear more competent, more convincing and more capable opponents as well as giving us higher influence and status. That sounds like enough incentive to ignore all reality and build up your ignorance. Small wonder then that, after ten exhausting rounds in the ring and losing in a knockout, McGregor still said of Mayweather: 'He's a tough competitor, but I was the better man tonight.'

ROUND 2: MOTIVATION

For most of us, life is strewn with setbacks, with the odd success thrown in from time to time. To take in all the failures and still keep striving for success is no mean task. Yet, this is precisely what we need to be able to do in order to get on with our lives. This is why several psychologists have argued that the human bias towards optimism and overconfidence plays a vital psychological role. This view posits that overconfidence helps people remain motivated and to work towards goals, whether these are day-to-day tasks or dreams of becoming impossibly wealthy. From this perspective, even when such overconfidence leads to a false sense of control—say over a disease—it could still make people more likely to commit to healthy behaviour. In fact, people do harness the motivating power of optimism, believing it will enhance performance.[27] This only happens when they believe they can influence the outcome of an event. And of course, predictably, people are too optimistic about the effect of beliefs on their performance.

The nub of the motivational argument is well captured in the saying 'nothing ventured, nothing gained'. A more evocative phrasing of the same statement is local to where I live in the northeast of England, 'shy bairns get nowt'. And indeed, a good example of the motivational benefits of overconfidence comes from work on child psychology. If you think we have to deal with setbacks as adults, imagine a child's world. Almost every new thing a child attempts is going to lead to failure. If this led to children giving up at every point, they would quite possibly not get up on two feet and start walking, never learn a language or master any skill that mattered. Children need to be the most overconfident humans on the planet. We owe our adult selves to our infantile overconfidence.

As adults, we might be overconfident about our general capacities, but we do take on board feedback based on our performance on particular tasks. Say, your resident psychologist asks you how many items in a display you're likely to remember. On the first iteration of this task, you boldly say you'll remember all of them and you quite likely fail to do so. You might moderate yourself a bit more on the next round and yet more on the one after. Eventually, you unlearn your confidence and get more accurate about your claims. This has been dubbed 'underconfidence with practice', and you can see how it's a rather useful trait for us to have if we want our self-knowledge to be in line with reality. This trait, however, is something that younger kids completely lack.[28]

Children up to the age of ten consistently overestimate their own abilities.[29, 30] This is true whether they are asked how far they can throw a ball or how many words they can remember from a list. When faced with their mistakes after performing the task, they are undaunted. On the next round of predictions, they are blithely overconfident all over again. There are several interesting facets to this overconfidence. First, it isn't just inaccuracy. The children know how well they have performed each time, and their 'postdictions' don't show the overconfidence of their predictions.[31] Secondly, this overconfidence changes with age. Older children take on board their mistakes in predicting performance and correct for their errors, closer to how adults behave. Finally, and most interestingly, children reserve their overconfidence for themselves. When asked to make predictions about the performance of their peers, even young children are relatively accurate. Their overconfidence seems to be centred around their own performance. How exactly is this overconfidence useful? Children who were the highest overestimators went on to have the best performance.[32] Overconfident children spent more time with the task. As a result they had the most practice, and eventually were better at it than the others. Their very overconfidence allowed them to persist, to learn and to improve themselves. The persistence of overconfidence in children is possibly because of the fact that they confuse effort with ability. Even if they underperform on a task, they can believe that their effort the next time will make all the difference. There might be something to learn here for adults too.

Overconfidence thus seems to enable persistence and motivation, at least in children. How about adults? In experimental tests, overconfident people are more likely to be motivated and put in increased effort.[33] In fact, reducing overconfidence even makes people less productive. While we do learn to temper our overconfidence based on experience, perhaps there are certain aspects of our lives or work where we still believe that, if we put in all our effort, we are going to make a change. This might be especially true in the areas that we have identified as our current goals, where we want to achieve success or status. We see such an effect for optimism at least. Optimistic MBA students are quicker to get job offers and promotions compared to similarly skilled pessimistic students.[34] Perhaps these are precisely the areas where we might expect to find the most overconfidence too. We should also expect people who need more motivation to be more overconfident. This might explain why younger people have unrealistic expectations of how much better their future is going to be compared to their current situation.

Let's look at my own career as a researcher. When I was first curious about a PhD, I talked to a researcher in my field and asked her for advice. She suggested several people I could work with, but also gave me a warning. While she now had a position at a very good university, she almost didn't get one at all, she said. She was ready to try her hand at becoming a baker when things didn't work out in science. Her advice was that I ought to brace for years of uncertainty with no guarantee of an academic position at the end. I listened, but was smugly confident that things would work out. Now, after my many years of job-hunting and moving from country to country, I can see my younger self had no idea what he was letting himself in for. Thirteen years after I received my PhD, I still hadn't got an open-ended or tenured academic position. I was still ever optimistic about getting one.

As an industry, academia relies on the work of early-career researchers, either PhD students or skilled researchers on temporary contracts (often called postdocs). However, the number of permanent positions eventually available for these researchers is meagre. About 3–4 per cent of PhD students obtain a permanent position—that's only a little better than the odds of a young person at a football academy becoming a professional footballer.[35] The number of new PhD students has, however, consistently increased. In the OECD countries, the proportion of young people completing doctorates has doubled over the last two decades,[36] and the number of US biomedical PhD graduates increased 60 per cent between 1980 and 2015.[37] Fifty-one per cent of early career researchers also said that their careers got in the way of having a successful relationship,[38] and 12 per cent have sought help for work-related anxiety or depression.[39] Nonetheless, despite the difficulties, a large proportion of early career researchers report high levels of satisfaction with their jobs. Most importantly, the majority of them aim to get jobs in academia, displaying clear overconfidence despite the statistics staring them in their face. In fact, in 2017, around 60 per cent of PhD students in one poll believed they would get a permanent position within three years of completing their degree.[40] A 2019 survey showed that on average researchers had spent seven years as postdocs before starting their own group.[41]

This overconfidence seems unreasonable. Yet, if we view this in terms of a motivational account, it makes more sense. To continue working in academia despite the poor job prospects, it is perhaps essential to delude ourselves into believing that we are going to make it; that each one of us will be the exception to the rule. The perceived rewards of gaining a position—freedom of thought, assured job security, the pursuit of one's interests—seem so attractive that they increase our motivation to continue in the face of all odds.

In this, the motivational account could also have connections to the competitive model discussed before, where overconfidence is predicted to evolve when the rewards are high compared to the cost. Therefore, the highest levels of overconfidence are potentially seen in precisely those fields where the perceived rewards are high and the chances of succeeding slim, whether it be academia, football or showbiz. It is also what we would probably see in another group where the balance of powerful successful individuals to precarious outsiders has been compared to the levels seen in academia—the drug gang.[42]

ROUND 3: HEALTH

A third take on the advantages of our overconfidence comes from a different group of psychologists. In a classic paper,[43] psychologists Shelley Taylor and Jonathon Brown address the importance of 'positive illusions', that is, unrealistically favourable notions about the self or others. Taylor and Brown argue that these positive illusions are advantageous because they predict a range of desirable outcomes, including confidence, high self-esteem and social adjustment. The classic attributes of psychological health typically include a positive view of the self, autonomy, the ability to grow and having agency at work and in social relationships. Several of these correlate well with positive illusions. Positive illusions are associated with a stronger self-image, some aspects of social bonding and—as we saw above—motivation to persist in tasks. In fact, even being a narcissist could be linked to good health because it comes with high self-esteem.[44]

Optimism is also linked with increased life expectancy, including the chances of exceptional longevity.[45]

In her book, *The Optimism Bias*, psychologist Tali Sharot[46] makes the case that this bias is beneficial because it reduces stress and anxiety about the future, paving the way for better mental health. There is also evidence that self-deception has different effects on mental health, depending on one's socio-economic background.[47] It is linked to lower depression and better perceptions of housing conditions, but only for people from lower socio-economic backgrounds. It is tempting to interpret this as self-deceptive optimism being most useful exactly when one is faced with difficult circumstances.

There's an interesting corollary to this observation. While the majority of people are overly optimistic, one group of people stands out as being more balanced about future prospects. These are people with depression,[48, 49] who engage more equally with positive and negative feedback.[50] As a result, their estimate of the likelihood of future events is not biased towards overestimation of positive events, but is rather more accurate compared to the general public. This varies with the degree of depression—people with mild depression show no bias either way and people with severe depression expect things to turn out worse than they do.

These then are three explanations for the persistence of overconfidence: social signalling, motivation and mental health. The three explanations are not mutually exclusive, of course. If anything, in combination, they reinforce the importance of overconfidence. But which of these is most important for the evolution of overconfidence? On the face of it, all three explanations give an individual potent advantages to potentially outcompete or outlive a less overconfident person. Proponents of the social signalling theory, however, have brought up an important argument. No one doubts that motivation or mental happiness are important traits. Yet, these in themselves do not require overconfidence. Human beings could just as easily have evolved to be motivated despite perceiving things as they really are. Such an evolutionary strategy would seem to be more advantageous than our current inaccurate evaluation of ourselves and the world around us.

The social signalling theory explains why we don't have this strategy. Whether it is for status or to ward off competition over resources, misjudging our own capabilities or the state of the world can be evolutionarily beneficial—as long as the rewards are large enough. Therefore, it makes sense that our motivational levels and happiness are subsequently linked to this false assessment of reality.

Researchers at the Universities of Melbourne and Queensland[51] brought all these different explanations together to ask which of these can be seen in a cohort of schoolchildren aged between twelve and seventeen. Evolutionary psychologist William von Hippel and colleagues followed the progress of about 900 schoolchildren in a private school. The objective was to test the three functions of overconfidence we talked about above—motivation, mental health and social influence (which they measured as popularity). Crucially, they monitored the children over three years, focusing on evaluations of their intelligence and sporting success. The students made self-assessments on both these fronts, judging how good they were relative to others. These assessments were compared to actual grades or measures of athletic performance. The difference revealed where children were overconfident and where they were not.

Parallelly, the researchers measured each of the three possible functions of overconfidence: motivation, mental health and popularity. To measure motivation, they asked the teachers to grade each student on the effort they put into academics or sports. To evaluate mental health, they used the self-reports of children in surveys typically used to assess mental health and positivity. Finally, to measure popularity, they asked each child to name their ten closest friends and built a social network based on their responses. Analysing this network allowed them to determine the popularity of each individual. Once they had these measures, they could look at each of these measures over time, directly asking if overconfidence related to changes in any of them.

What did they find? Overconfident students did not show any changes in effort—meaning that there was no increase in motivation. Students who were overconfident about their intelligence showed increases in their self-esteem, but no other changes in mental health were linked to overconfidence in either sport or intelligence. There was also no effect on popularity for students who were overconfident about their intelligence. Every high-school nerd can probably testify to the accuracy of that observation. Overconfidence in sport, however, was clearly linked to an increase in popularity.

The evidence thus largely supports the social signalling function of overconfidence, but this is limited to specific domains—sporting ability, in this case. The authors also make an important point about how the influence of overconfidence works. It happens over a period of time, with several small, confident actions and mannerisms adding up to create an impression. This stands in contrast to what we might typically think of when we picture an overconfident person, brash and boastful, always talking about themselves. It's easy for us to congratulate ourselves on spotting the failings of the populist politician or beloved film actor. The people we should be watching out for, though, are the ones we think are genuinely accomplished because they have convinced us with their confidence.

Where does this leave us in our quest for the advantages of overconfidence? Certainly there are links between overconfidence and both mental health and motivation. There is, however, a strong and potentially understudied role for overconfidence in social settings. It's interesting to note that the study with schoolchildren found advantages in a sporting domain, while my own study on undergraduates showed advantages in terms of academic reputation. This suggests that overconfidence is deployed strategically, depending on where each individual sees their competitive ground. There is some evidence for this from artificial competitive settings. When deterring people from entering a competition is advantageous, men at least seem to inflate their declared confidence.[52] Conversely, when attracting people to a competition is advantageous, people decrease their declared confidence. Audience effects also change how we evaluate ourselves. When reporting their performance on quiz questions to an audience, people are more likely to claim to be better than average compared to when they evaluate themselves privately.[53] It seems likely that we use confidence strategically, depending on the social situation.

This raises the interesting question of whether some of the effects we see with overconfidence in children persist in adults. When your job requires you to show excellence in a certain skill, do you stop showing underconfidence on tasks related to that skill even when you don't manage to perform them successfully? In other words, do we show the characteristics of children on these important tasks—assuming that, if we put in effort, we will end up with success. Certainly, several researchers or aspiring footballers appear to behave in this way.

Another thread that would tie in well here are the results showing that overconfidence is linked to status in a peer group. This would also be particularly important in the fields in which we want to succeed, where our status would matter the most to us. We should, therefore, expect to see people being the most overconfident and most resistant to learning from their mistakes in these areas. If we view life as a series of fights in a boxing ring, we will keep seeing the same claims and attitudes, where our self-deceiving bluster also convinces others of our impending victory. Perhaps in the things that matter most to each of us—our careers, our friendships and our public images—we might each, on occasion, behave not so differently from Frank O'Connor, insisting in the face of all evidence that we are better than our colleagues, our friends and most people we meet.

Now, given all the advantages of overconfidence, how should we see it? If we are gaining from a strategy that human beings have evolved to develop, should it not been seen simply as a rational selfish strategy?[54, 55] If you think of the fire alarm example from the previous chapter, surely setting our self-perceptions to avoid huge costs or to make huge gains is a useful thing to do?[56]

To me, overconfidence is a cognitive bias (or a product of other cognitive biases) that doesn't have to lead to negative life outcomes. If your belief about a given task is overblown or overcertain, that is a biased view of the task. The social, motivational or mental health benefits such an attitude brings might well give you a better life, but they won't make that task any easier. It is this consistent bias in someone's actions or self-perceptions that I would call overconfidence, while accepting that the biased attitude could well be rational in terms of selfish gains.

Motivation, mental health and popularity. With advantages like these, overconfidence seems like a magic elixir. If you stumbled onto it in bottled form glowing in the dark woods, you'd gulp it down and change your life. Yet, like every fairy tale fix-it-all, overconfidence has its downsides. What are the limits and costs of overconfidence? There are two different ways to think about this. One, the immediate costs to individuals, their daily lives, their social interactions. Two, the costs that society pays. These costs are often dramatic, and stretch across different domains, from finance to war to politics. That's what we turn to in later chapters. For now, let's focus on the consequences of overconfidence for the individual.

The first limits on overconfidence are perhaps obvious. Overconfidence persists even in areas such as driving and extreme sport, where its dangers are stark and potentially fatal. But we should expect to see that there are limits to overconfidence in most people when it comes to these areas—so, the increase would only be to the extent that it falls short of the genuinely catastrophic. This would also be true in other fields, where the costs might not be physical but social. Consistently taking on difficult tasks and failing would cause you to lose the trust of your colleagues or potential funders. Recall the studies that showed how people punish misplaced confidence. We should, therefore, expect to see overconfidence potentially still tracking reality, just forming an enhanced version of it.

But there could be large deviations from reality in situations where the rewards for being overconfident are the greatest. So, while most drivers might actually end up being just a little bit inaccurate about their driving capabilities, perhaps F-1 drivers whose livelihood, rankings and earnings depend on being the fastest drivers would be expected to be far more overconfident than the rest of us. We should see higher risk-taking during their driving and greater belief in their ability to avoid accidents. We should see a similar imperviousness to risk in professional BASE jumpers[57] or presenters who court dangerous animals and other thrills in exchange for TV ratings.

Another kind of cost is how others view you. Recall that overconfident people appear to be better adjusted socially—one of the contributors to their better mental health. Some researchers have, however, questioned whether this is true over the long term.[58] Their research shows that overconfident individuals are actually perceived to be narcissistic and less liked. Conversely, knowing yourself helps with better relationships.[59] Perhaps this isn't so surprising. Nobody likes that colleague who goes on about how brilliant they are and can't stop talking about themselves. However, this perception occurs for a specific type of overconfidence. That bragging colleague is most unbearable when they are making clear boasts without subtlety. In fact, it is particularly unappealing when people explicitly enhance themselves in comparison to others, resembling the form of overconfidence which we earlier called overplacement.[60]

So, overt denigration of others to make yourself look good leads to a poor social reputation. One imagines that this form of behaviour is eminently dislikeable, whether it is from someone who is genuinely competent or someone who is just pretending to be. When we don't have enough information, we might default to taking claims of competence at face value.[61] However, when we do gain information, not only do our ratings change, but our moral judgements lead us to punish people for overclaiming. That's where the costs of overconfidence come in. This fits perfectly with the results we discussed earlier, showing that confident people can get punished if they are inaccurate.

Limited overconfidence could perhaps still give us gains, as long as we are competent, but too much would then carry a cost when we are discovered. If you compare the protagonists of *Mad Men* and *Breaking Bad*, both are badly behaved and cross moral boundaries of one sort or the other. Yet, both Don Draper and Walter White hold power and influence as well as arguably the sympathies of the viewers. This is because they are shown to be so good at what they do, whether that is coming up with ideas for advertisements or perfecting the production of methamphetamine. It is only when Don fails to dazzle with his genius at work that his colleagues push him out. Walter White never suffers a similar moment of reckoning because his expertise never falters.

There also seems to be a subtler cost to overconfidence. Overconfidence could be built in two ways. One could see a task accurately but still be mistaken about one's own abilities. Alternatively, the task could be perceived as easier than it is, even though there's no mistake about one's own abilities. In the second scenario, by believing the challenges are easier than they really are, our self-delusion helps us deceive others. However, the corollary to this is that everybody else would also appear to be better at the task than they really are. So, while we do deceive others, we are also more likely to be deceived by others. Is there evidence of this?

In my study with Shakti Lamba,[62] we looked at the data where students rated each other on their performance on a future assignment. If overconfident people were deluded about the difficulty of the assignment and thought it was easier than it really was, we predicted that they would then also be inaccurate in their predictions of how their peers perform. This is the exact pattern that their ratings showed. Students who overrated themselves also overrated others, and students who underrated themselves tended to rate others lower. So, it looks like there is another cost to overconfidence. By fooling ourselves about tasks and challenges, we open ourselves up to being deceived by others. Other results also show that the more frequently people bullshit to persuade others, the more susceptible they are to misleading information.[63] This can also be linked to other findings about deception. When people are asked to lie about a scene they have witnessed, they tend to incorporate these lies into their memories and forget some of the actual details of the scene.[64, 65] This effect is sometimes amplified if they are initially given confirmatory, positive feedback about their lies. With this additional feedback, people recall their false memories even months later. Deceiving yourself changes your view of the world, even if you're only doing it to deceive others. In other words, the maxim that 'you can't bullshit a bullshitter' doesn't hold up. In fact, if you want to bullshit someone, you're probably best off finding a good old bullshitter.

These then are the constraints to our overconfidence at a personal level. We risk losing touch with reality, we court social negativity and we are likely to be fooled by others. Of course, depending on the tasks we face and the circumstances we find ourselves in, the many benefits of overconfidence and potential rewards that they might bring could well outweigh these costs. Overconfidence could still persist to varying degrees, but its contours would be defined by these costs paid by individuals. These costs might, however, be important to understand the inverse of overconfidence. Let's spend a short while considering underconfidence.

EIGHT

Underdogs and Impostors

If overconfidence is the thriving, bustling world of a megacity, each building vying to be taller than the next, then underconfidence must surely be the quiet woods next door. And if the showy world of overconfidence has all the advantages and grows from strength to strength, can the silence of underconfidence survive? Let's take a break from overconfidence for just one chapter and look at what might be a far more interesting phenomenon: underconfidence. If there are strong reasons why overconfidence persists, the question we should be asking is: why does underconfidence exist at all?

Let's begin with a reminder that there are different forms of overconfidence. So, as absurd as it sounds, you could be underconfident and overconfident at the same time. You might think you are worse than others when you are not. Or perhaps that you will perform worse on a test than you do. These are forms of underconfidence that are the reverse of overplacement and overestimation. At the same time, you might hold these negative self-views with more confidence than is justified, which would be a form of overprecision. This is where looking at the different forms of overconfidence—and underconfidence—helps. And underconfidence, in terms of underplacement or underestimation, is not uncommon at all. Studies around the world typically find about 20–30 per cent of participants are underconfident.[1, 2, 3]

When are people underconfident? We've talked about some of this before. People underplace themselves on difficult tasks, thinking they are worse than average on these tasks.[4, 5, 6] Those who perform the best at a task also underestimate their performance, partly because at near-peak performance you can't really overestimate yourself. People are also not always optimistic, tending to exaggerate the probability of some negative events, especially low-probability events that are often in the news or are on our minds. Shortly after 9/11, American citizens dramatically overestimated the possibility of a terrorist attack.[7] Soon after SARS broke, it was found that people in China overestimated their chances of falling ill.[8] Smokers overestimate their chances of contracting lung cancer[9] and women overestimate their chances of contracting breast cancer.[10] Part of the explanation for these results is psychological, stemming from the availability bias we're now familiar with. Our best bet at the true frequency of events depends on how often we hear about them or encounter them. If these are negative events, our beliefs are pessimistic.

Some other instances of underconfidence have different explanations. Let's consider the worse-than-average effect, the inverse of the better-than-average effect. This effect shows up when we're facing difficult tasks. Imagine a situation where you don't do as well as you thought you would on a task, but you aren't sure how others have performed. Since you don't have information about other people, a natural assumption is that they perform closer to the average. That means you are going to think you had a difficult time, but the others perhaps didn't do as badly. In other words, you think you performed worse than average. That's where this brand of underconfidence comes from.[11] We will always have more information about ourselves than about others. The other-shaped gap in our knowledge is best filled with a guess at the average or something close to it. Funnily, the situation is exactly reversed on simple tasks. On these tasks, the same explanation works to explain the better-than-average effect. Underconfidence thus seems to stem from both psychological biases and informational asymmetries—just as we saw with overconfidence.

Perhaps the most striking and widely discussed example of underconfidence is what has been called the Impostor Phenomenon, or sometimes the Impostor Syndrome. In 1978, clinical psychologists at Georgia State University, Pauline Clance and Suzanne Imes first described a recurring phenomenon they observed while working in therapy with highly successful women.[12] These were over 150 women who were well respected and recognised for their excellence. Despite all the accolades they had received, they did not consider themselves intelligent. Instead, they considered themselves impostors in their position, managing to deceive others about their intelligence. Since Clance and Imes's publication, the phenomenon has been widely studied and reported in a wide variety of fields, including medicine, academia and marketing. As research into the impostor phenomenon has grown, it has turned up in many more places. It has been found in men as well as women, and studies of students around the world from Romania[13] to Nigeria[14] also show evidence for the phenomenon. In an interview from 2002, even multi-Oscar winner Meryl Streep confessed that she feels like she doesn't know how to act.[15]

Clance and Imes identify multiple psychological factors contributing to the phenomenon. One of these is the expectation that perfection must come easily, potentially internalised in childhood from parental or family expectations. This means that any achievement that is the result of hard work is discounted. Imagine that for a second. You have a vision of being a successful businesswoman, say. You work hard, and when you achieve your dreams, it doesn't feel like success. Paradoxically, this feeling is precisely because you put in the hard work that got you there. You think it would only count if you had sailed through to the top, something that is rarely going to be true for anyone. Another contributing factor to the Impostor Phenomenon is the need for approval, particularly from a mentor or authority figure, instead of relying on internal confidence in one's abilities. People scoring high on measures of the phenomenon report greater negative emotions, and often also score high on measures of depression and anxiety. The general picture that forms is that feelings of self-doubt and anxiety lead to the 'impostors' striving for perfection and achievement in order to gain approval,[16, 17] rather than to reach their own goals. Achievement itself, when it occurs, is written off as due to personal charm or luck. They might also feel guilt about success, and fear that they will be found out to be impostors.[18] Success then leads to a self-reinforcing cycle that saps confidence. The elation of success is combined with a fear that allowing oneself to imagine success would only lead to future failures. This triggers further anxieties and overpreparation for the next task. Overpreparation then means that the next achievement is also undervalued as *only* due to effort.

Another way of looking at the impostor phenomenon is through the prism of cognitive biases. Think back to the discussion on the building blocks of overconfidence. One of the same suspects is implicated in this example of underconfidence—but as its inverted reflection. The self-serving bias leads to overconfidence, thanks to people attributing their successes to themselves and their failures to external factors. The impostor phenomenon stems from the opposite. Self-described impostors are ingenious at finding external or undervalued reasons to explain away their successes, including effort and luck.[19] This bias seems to be linked to low self-esteem.[20, 21] In an exact inversion of the self-serving bias, people with lower self-esteem predict future performance based on their failures rather than their successes. In fact, one assignment that helps work against the impostor phenomenon requires self-declared impostors to keep track of positive feedback and how they respond, training themselves to accept positive feedback instead of denying it. Another approach is to have a group interaction between several 'impostors' who share their fears. This helps people recognise in others the same processes they deploy, and observe how they differ from reality.

In the popular imagination, the impostor phenomenon is often associated with women, as in Clance and Imes's original study. However, research over the years has shown no strong evidence that it is more likely to occur in women than in men.[22] What about underconfidence more generally? Overconfidence is typically greater in men, but are women more often underconfident? They could, for example, simply be more accurate, rather than underconfident. Several studies show that women are also often overconfident, just less so than men.

However, there are occasionally examples where women are underconfident, while men are overconfident. Some evidence for this comes from school and university students. For example, school students from both Sweden[23] and El Salvador[24] showed a pattern where girls were underconfident about their grades in a mathematics test, while boys were overconfident. Swedish university students show a similar pattern on tests of macroeconomics.[25] The type of test was important—no difference in confidence was found on a social science test. Other studies also show no differences between men and women on questions about learning, memory or experimental design.[26] This suggests that it is the gender stereotypes about maths and some other related fields that lead to confidence differences. Tasks that are perceived to be more masculine seem to lead to differences in confidence, but not tasks that are perceived to be more feminine or neutral.[27] Interestingly, men are less well calibrated in their predictions compared to women. So, when they are wrong, men can be highly overconfident, while women have more doubts when they are wrong.

The environment also influences confidence. One study we discussed pointed out that women who self-select into competitive environments are just as overconfident as the men who do so. This could hold up in other situations too. For example, both business and non-business students show gender differences in overconfidence as measured on a scale. Amongst professional auditors, however, there were no differences between men and women on these measures of overconfidence.[28] The implication is that those who choose competitive professional environments and succeed end up having similar levels of confidence. Students who haven't yet made the same choice still show differences. Given that a lot of psychological results come from the tests of students, perhaps we should then be more cautious about them. Results from different walks of life, ideally with tasks that have real-world relevance, would ultimately reveal how generalisable these findings are.

Another good way of getting at large-scale patterns of gender differences in confidence is to combine results from several studies and see what analysing them all together can tell. These kinds of meta-analyses do show that men—across cultures and continents—usually provide higher self-estimates than women about their general intelligence, mathematical and spatial knowledge, but not about their verbal ability.[29] What's crucial is how this compares with actual measured performance. In spatial tests, the estimates seem to be close to actual performance. In mathematical tests, however, the performance difference between men and women is much smaller than the difference between their self-estimates. In general intelligence tests, women estimate themselves to be much lower than men estimate themselves to be, even when they perform equally well. In verbal intelligence tasks, women outperform men, but their self-estimates are similar to men. The results seem to point towards more underconfidence in women, at least on specific tasks.

It is worth noting though that, in Uganda, Zambia and Zimbabwe, women provide self-estimates of intelligence that are higher than those of men. The researchers who describe this result suggest that intelligence might be more broadly defined in these countries and include social and interpersonal skills. How intelligence and related tasks are perceived in different countries seems to matter. Perhaps, in the end, this is what drives the confidence levels of men and women.

Underconfidence can have serious consequences. In a now-classic experiment,[30] economics professors Muriel Niederle and Lise Vesterlund gave participants a choice. They could perform a series of addition problems and get paid based on their performance on each problem. Alternatively, they could complete the problems, and then enter a winner-takes-all tournament, where the one who had performed the best would get all the money. For a given performance, the average amount that could be earned in either option was the same. Men were twice as likely to choose the tournament compared to women, even though there was no difference in actual performance. Where does this difference arise from? Predictably, it is confidence that drives the difference—men with lower performance were nonetheless more likely to enter the tournament, and women with high performance were less likely to do so. If you change the competition[31] and allow competitors to bluff about their performance and deter others from joining the competition, it was again men who were more likely to bluff, deterring women from entering competitions they could have won. Other studies have shown similar results: women are less likely to choose competitive environments, even when they perform as well as men. There is some evidence that this could explain why women miss out on career opportunities.[32] Across several studies, the gender difference in choosing competitive environments has sometimes been explained by differences in risk aversion or competitiveness. Yet, confidence remains a prominent factor in these studies.[33, 34] Overconfidence can thus reap the rewards that underconfidence fails to strive for.

In a 2014 article in the *Atlantic* magazine,[35] journalists Katty Kay and Claire Shipman call this difference between men and women a 'confidence gap'. Through interviews they conducted for their book

Womenomics,[36] they reveal the widespread real-life consequences of this gap. Women managers in the UK are less confident than their male counterparts. Male business school students are four times more likely to negotiate their salaries and ask for more money. Men are more likely to apply for a promotion even when they meet only 60 per cent of the criteria, women typically apply only when they meet 100 per cent of the criteria. Kay and Shipman implicate men's ability to be honestly overconfident—without faking it—as one reason for the confidence gap. The other side to the gap, they say, stems from women's perfectionism and risk aversion. Avoiding competitive environments prevents women from gaining valuable experience that could help them thrive better in those very same environments. It's a vicious cycle that's further perpetuated by the negative reactions women face when they actually do compete or assert their confidence. Incidentally, Kay herself realises that she attributes her professional profile to having an English accent in the US, echoing how people who feel like impostors can come up with the most creative reasons to explain away their success.

People have also looked at the implications gender differences in competition could have for leadership in groups. Depending on the stereotypes of the task involved, confidence and self-beliefs can be detrimental to performance in competitive environments. Groups choosing leaders based on claims of past performance are more likely to choose men than women.[37] This is driven by the overconfidence of the men and their biased estimates of past performance, rather than underconfidence on the part of women. Male overconfidence increases if leadership comes with financial incentives. In light of results such as these, it is easy to view overconfidence as a male trait, and perhaps underconfidence as being more female.

Things are not so simple, though. Take, for example, a study[38] comparing the tendency of men and women to choose competitive environments among the Masai in Tanzania and the Khasi in India. This study used a similar idea to that used by Niederle and Vesterlund we discussed above. People participating could get rewarded for every successful performance on a task. Or they could choose to compete with another person and get rewarded three times as much for each success if they did better than their competitor. The task was a simple one—they had to toss a tennis ball into a bucket from three metres away, with a score based on how many times they succeeded out of ten attempts. The decision to compete or not was made before the people attempted to toss the ball into the bucket. In the more patriarchal Masai society, men were twice as likely to compete as women. In contrast, in the matrilineal Khasi society in Meghalaya, it was women who were more likely to compete than men. Another study[39] used the same task and pay-offs in the Nandi society in Kenya. Since a woman's property in this society is inherited only by men, women without sons take on the role of a female husband to a younger woman. The sons of this younger woman then go on to inherit the property of the husband. When the economics professor Ignacio Palacios-Huerte ran a competition study similar to those we've been talking about, he found that female husbands were just as overconfident as the men and were markedly different to the wives. The roles we play in society, it would appear, cast longer shadows than we give them credit for. The social and cultural environment clearly influences how competitive men and women are, and could also have an influence on who ends up being overconfident and underconfident.

Some researchers have sought to explain the differences in confidence between men and women based on the social role played by confidence. The suggestion is that women (at least in some societies) perceive a greater social cost to being overconfident—and prefer to make lower self-estimates rather than risk future effects on their social image.[40] This seems to occur even when there isn't an explicitly strategic advantage to being underconfident, suggesting it could well be an internalised attitude. Of course, this could be also true for any underconfident person.

If this is true and we do use confidence strategically in social settings, there should be tell-tale signs showing that underconfidence occurs differently in social settings compared to private settings. Studies that set out to look for the social role of underconfidence have found some evidence for it. Take the worse-than-average effect. Does believing that they are worse than average help people by giving them suitable social outcomes or motivating them towards better future performance?[41] Some studies suggest this is true. Believing you are worse than your peers or receiving a negative evaluation often leads immediately to poor performance. However, it could motivate people to seek out helpful advice and do better in the long term. It could be argued that it motivates people to put in more effort.[42] For instance, students who start off at university believing they had made fewer friends than average go on to make more close friends over three months.[43] That's true even after we take into account the actual number of friends they have to begin with.

The impostor phenomenon also shows a social pattern. People who score highly on the impostor scale make different self-predictions if they think their predictions are going to be publicly discussed compared to when the predictions are anonymous.[44] Their predictions are lower when public and are more accurate if made anonymously. Impostors thus might not always have a strongly held private belief in their low performance. It is only when they present themselves to others that they differ from non-impostors in how they rate themselves. The evidence points towards their professed underconfidence serving a social function.

Yet, what advantage could something like the impostor phenomenon have at all? Let's start by thinking about the possible advantages of underconfidence. In our paper,[45] Shakti Lamba and I suggest a possibility linked to social signalling. We discuss how underconfidence could serve as a way of lowering people's expectations and convincing others we aren't threatening. This in turn could lead to them underestimating us and giving us an advantage—rather in the same way that underdogs pull off upsets in sporting events. Or it could just be a simple strategy to avoid conflict or status competition by signalling the lack of threat. This would also fit in well with the idea of confidence as a signal of status. Another take on the idea is that signalling underconfidence helps us get support and encouragement from others. That's certainly something that could be helpful even outside of competitive environments.

Evolutionary biologist Robert Trivers also suggests that underconfidence serves as a social signal.[46] However, he argues that it helps convince others that you are not competent and, therefore, gets you out of being assigned roles you don't want. It's a kind of an acceptable way of signalling laziness.

Another kind of social explanation for underconfidence flows directly from the theoretical model for the evolution of overconfidence we discussed earlier. The idea there was that signalling greater confidence in your abilities would help you win more competitions on average. But this is only true if the costs were largely outweighed by the potential benefits. So, for example, if you had a chance of everlasting fame as a superstar, and you were rich enough so that funding your own movie was small change, you might be overconfident about your chances of pulling it off. This would be true regardless of how great all the other actors around you appeared to be. But what happens if the benefits of the contest were small and the costs were large? Imagine you had to really struggle and spend all your savings to get a walk-on role in a TV sitcom. In this case, the model would predict that you'd actually be underconfident about your success.

Looking at the costs of overconfidence gives us further ideas of how underconfidence could help. For instance, underconfident people are judged to be more likeable than overconfident people. Not only do participants choose to reward underconfidence, people sometimes even bet that underconfident people would do better than overconfident ones in the long term.[47] Participants in that study thought that underconfident people would be more likely to try to better themselves, while overconfident people would strive less. This prediction seems to contradict the studies showing that overconfidence convinces others of people's abilities. One difference in this study was that it was clear who had been underconfident and who had been overconfident. In previous studies, all people had to go by was the self-predictions of performance. This suggests that, as performance is compared to prediction, we re-evaluate our estimates about the future performance of others. That fits with the results showing that people's trust in overconfident people goes down over time.

Studies ranging from academic performance in college, alcohol consumption and resilience after trauma also suggest that overconfidence boosts self-esteem and engagement only for a short period of time.[48] Over longer periods of time, it can lead to lowered motivation and social gains. This is true of social interactions as well—overconfident people go on to be less well-liked over time. Starting off underconfident in contrast seems to lead to better long-term adjustment and motivation. I'm reminded of an excellent article in *First Post* by the writer and teacher Vijeta Kumar written in remembrance of Rohith Vemula. She observes from her first-hand experience how caste privilege can interfere with a student's learning if they assume that they've already learnt all there is to learn.[49]

The bustling cities of overconfidence might bring their thrills to you, but the quiet woods of underconfidence have their own charms, it would appear. Stereotypes, innate preferences and the environments we find ourselves in all have a role to play in determining how underconfident we are. Ultimately, however, it is the societies we live in and our strategies for navigating them that give us the advantages we seek as underdogs. It is also our societies that bear the costs and successes of both our underconfidence and our overconfidence. What we need then is to step out of the lab and see how several of our ideas play out in the world we live in.

As we move back to talking about overconfidence, we can begin to ask how it works in several fields, from finance to politics. Defining and measuring overconfidence in the real world is hard. To do so, we will still have to rely on some controlled studies with implications for the larger world, but we can also make use of data from ongoing events, as others have done. In my attempt to test these results against our worst-case scenario, I have tried to be led by these studies. Some parts of the discussion are certainly speculative, and perhaps I might appear too cautious in others. Where I do seem too speculative, think of it as a way of having the conversation, to jog you into thinking about how best to capture real-world overconfidence. Ultimately, without getting closer to the real world, we cannot confirm the validity of our ideas or determine how generalisable our understanding of the psychology of confidence really is.

NINE

Very Smart People with a Lot of Money

2008—THE YEAR THAT NEVER ENDED. THE POLITICAL AND FINANCIAL aftershocks of that year's economic crisis are still reshaping our world.[1] People could no longer pay their mortgages, unemployment rose, the economic growth of countries was derailed. The World Bank estimated that the crisis would trap 89 million people in extreme poverty.[2] Even fertility levels have declined more rapidly since the crisis.[3] The counterfactual impulse cannot help but ask where we might be today if not for the endless shadow of that year. Was there a way it could have been prevented? It is easy to think of the financial crisis as something inevitable, an unpredictable black swan event that none of the banks and companies saw coming or had a warning about. That would not be true.

In 2006, the Indian economist Raghuram Rajan published a paper arguing that financial development had made the world riskier.[4] He laid down the arguments warning us that we could expect further 'turmoil' in major economic countries. His arguments did not go down well. In fact, recalling the response in 2019,[5] Rajan described some economists coming up to him to say that his diagnosis did not pose a problem because the private sector was full of 'very smart people' who would not take the risks he mentioned. Rajan's viewpoint was heavily criticised, his warnings ignored. Two years later, the economic crisis bore out his paper.

The financial community does seem to have been complacent about the possibility of a meltdown, but were they overconfident? You could argue that there were few people making the case for caution, as Rajan had. Perhaps it just seemed more sensible to go with the majority opinion at the time: that this was a golden era of moderation, that there wouldn't be the sort of booms and busts that had been the pattern for centuries. After all, given the strong financial incentives to get things right, companies could be expected to act rationally rather than with overconfidence. Even so, is it possible that when we survey the landscape of businesses, with its clusters of CEOs, stock markets and entrepreneurs, that we might find persistent pockets of overconfidence? And could they explain financial crashes such as the one in 2008?

To begin this survey, we first need measures of overconfidence suited for the financial world. The idea of overconfidence in economics, finance and business is not new. In 1986, the US economist Richard Roll coined the term 'The Hubris Hypothesis' to describe the phenomenon of executives acquiring firms in the false belief that they were more competent than they really were.[6] Typically, such acquisitions are undertaken in the belief that they would add value to the acquiring company. So, one way of measuring overconfidence or 'hubris' would be to see if the value of the 'bidding firm' decreased in the time period between the announcement of the takeover and the completion. Roll found that the evidence for hubris wasn't conclusive across the board, but at least some findings were consistent with the idea.

Roll's paper was very influential, but other measures of CEO overconfidence have proven more widespread. Those measures came from the work of the economists Ulrike Malmendier and Geoffrey Tate. To understand them, let's begin by noting that the compensation packages of CEOs often include stocks and options. Options are guaranteed prices for shares in the company that a CEO can choose to exercise, i.e., decide when to avail of their guaranteed price. This is her choice to make, but it is constrained, as the options are typically subject to an expiration date. If the stock prices increase, CEOs stand to make gains when they exercise their options. But if the stock prices fall, CEOs have no obligation to purchase the shares and thus do not face any losses, although of course they also do not make any gains. Now, if a CEO expects the stock prices to keep rising, she might correspondingly delay exercising her options so that she can make the most gains. On the other hand, if a CEO was a bit more risk-averse, he would wait until the stock reached a certain high level and exercise his options at that point. In a paper in 2005,[7] Malmendier and Tate came up with a benchmark at which we should expect CEOs to exercise their options. CEOs delaying exercising their options past the benchmark would thus be classified as overconfident. As a separate measure, they also classified as overconfident any CEOs who waited even further until the expiration date of their options. These CEOs are effectively optimistic that the share prices will keep rising until the very last minute, and they can benefit from the price rise. The strength of these measures lies in the fact that they are, at least in principle, independent of any other behaviour of the company or the CEO. We can therefore ask how these measures of overconfidence predict other factors, such as the investment behaviours of the CEO.

In a later paper,[8] Malmendier and Tate come up with yet another measure of overconfidence, this time based on the portrayal of the CEOs in the press. In articles published in six leading papers and magazines—including the *New York Times*, the *Financial Times* and the *Wall Street Journal*—they looked for the occurrence of two sets of words used to describe a given CEO. The first set included words like 'confident' or 'optimistic', the second included words like 'cautious' or 'reliable'. CEOs that were more likely to be described in the press by the first set of words compared to the second were classified as confident. While the measure might seem a bit subjective, this indicator of CEO confidence correlated well with the previous measure that relied on CEO decision-making around exercising options.

These measures have come to define how overconfidence is measured in finance. A large number of studies use some version of these measures. Some studies look at the difference between the option price and the market price as a measure, and others analyse the language used by CEOs, instead of the language used to describe them. But the broad ideas remain: focusing on the portfolio choices of the CEOs and the language used to either describe them or used by them. Some of the other measures we have discussed previously in the book—including better-than-average effects, personality questionnaires and confidence intervals that indicate levels of precision—have also been used to get at financial overconfidence.

In combination, these measures and Malmendier and Tate's measures give us the tools with which we can get to grips with overconfidence in the real financial world. They have been used to reveal overconfidence in stock markets across the world, from the US to Pakistan,[9] Indonesia[10] and Tunisia.[11]

Let's begin by looking at the degree of overconfidence revealed by these measures. Remember that the measure of overconfidence is based on how these CEOs plan for their own personal profits. That's a high incentive to get things correct, and these are smart people who've earned their prestigious roles. So by all accounts, we should expect almost all of them to make the right call. Yet, a large proportion of them still make the same error. In one of Malmendier and Tate's studies, 58 out of 113 CEOs meet their criterion for overconfidence—51 per cent of all the CEOs they studied. In another study with a similar measure,[12] 40 per cent of all CEOs were overconfident.[13] That proportion is certainly not negligible.

If CEOs were only overconfident about their own personal gains, that wouldn't harm anyone except themselves. It would only matter if these overconfident CEOs do worse than other CEOs at managing companies. A good starting point to look at this is Roll's original question of acquisitions. Are overconfident CEOs more likely to acquire other companies? Malmendier and Tate provide a resoundingly positive answer.[14] Their measures of overconfidence predict which CEOs will show a higher degree of acquisitiveness when they have plenty of internal resources. The acquisitions depend on overconfident CEOs believing that their company is undervalued as well as overestimating how much the acquisition will benefit the company. In fact, acquisitions made by overconfident CEOs who have the resources lead to a decrease, rather than an increase, in the values of company shares post mergers. Markets typically react negatively to announcements of these mergers. As Malmendier and Tate point out, US firms had over 12,000 mergers in the two decades preceding 2008 and spent over US$ 3.4 trillion on them. However, the shareholders of the companies that were acquiring others between 1980 and 2001 had losses of more than US$ 220 billion when the mergers were announced. That's a damning indictment of the pursuit of acquisition as an act of hubris, one that harms CEO and shareholder alike.

This isn't a phenomenon peculiar to the US. Data from firms around the world show similar results. One study, looking at 500 global firms, found that CEOs were overconfident around the world, and their overconfidence predicted the number of offers they would make to acquire other companies.[15] These CEOs think the market value of their companies is undervalued and prefer to use cash for acquisitions rather than equity.

There are some differences between CEOs. Firstly, CEOs in countries (or cultures) where people are typically considered more individualistic show greater overconfidence. So for example, 100 per cent of CEOs in Australia were found to be overconfident, and 88.5 per cent of CEOs in Germany, but only 29.9 per cent of CEOs in Japan were found to be overconfident. In addition, CEOs in certain industries seem to be more likely to be overconfident. About 78 per cent of CEOs in service industries were seen to be overconfident, and about 65.5 per cent in technical industries. Trade and Manufacturing are not all that far behind, with about 55 per cent and 62 per cent.

Other studies have also made the point that the premiums paid to CEOs are rarely justified.[16] CEOs who are paid higher premiums typically have more power in their companies, and this adds to the costs of acquisitions. The returns from these acquisitions subsequently don't match up to the premiums paid to CEOs. The suggestion is that the successes of obtaining power and garnering praise from the media lead to CEOs thinking they are better than they are and making poor decisions.

Let's pause to think about options for a second. Options powerfully tie the CEO's own profits to the company's performance. The better a company does, the higher the value of its shares and the greater the profit the CEO stands to make, giving them a strong incentive to help the company profit. However, it is because they stand to gain so much that they could be led to overoptimism—the incentives provide fertile ground for the seeds of motivated cognition. So, a CEO who is poor at assessing himself ends up being even more committed to his inaccuracies, believing he will earn more for both the company and for himself. As David Dunning and his co-authors put it in their review on flawed self-assessment,[17] providing such incentives to someone who is clueless only ends up making the person 'clueless and committed'.

Acquisitions are thus influenced by overconfidence. But few of us are in a position where we need to worry about acquisitions. A bigger area for many people is investments. In January 2021, the stock prices of GameStop, a video game company, soared. This was largely due to a coordinated effort by a community on Reddit, leading to huge losses for hedge fund managers who had shorted the company, i.e., bet that its value would decrease.[18] For those who invested, however, there was a bonanza to be made, with prices surging by 1500 per cent.[19] However, being overly certain of this trend and not selling at the right time could prove costly—the volatility in the share price led at some points to the price dropping by 40 per cent in twenty-five minutes.[20] A sharper example is in the craze for investing in cryptocurrencies. There, too, the prices of cryptocurrencies soared, with the actor Matt Damon even appearing in an ad for one of them declaring 'Fortune favours the brave'.[21] It was certainly odd to see that advert as a trailer before movies in my local cinema. Then, the value of several cryptocurrencies came crashing down in 2022, including the value of what is possibly the most famous one, Bitcoin.[22] The crypto company FTX, which was valued at US$ 32 billion, imploded and went bankrupt, and the founder was charged with fraud. Matt Damon has gone on to be ridiculed, and the YouTube version of his ad has bravely been made private,[23, 24] an example of how misplaced confidence can be punished. It's certainly worth thinking twice before following the latest investing trend.

So what is the relationship between overconfidence and investments? Some studies make the simplistic prediction that overconfidence would lead to greater trading activity. There is some evidence for this.[25] One way this could happen is through an assessment of insider information. Being excessively confident—overprecise—about any insider information they have could lead investors to make greater share purchases than they should. However, such information would be transitory, and what Malmendier and Tate's measures capture is more persistent risky behaviour, potentially something companies and markets should be more wary of. Malmendier and Tate do not simply predict that overconfidence increases investment. They make a more precise hypothesis—overconfident CEOs or investors are likely to show excessive trading, but mostly when the companies have internal cash flow. Their work confirms this hypothesis.[26]

So far, the story's clear. But what if we used the psychological measures of overconfidence we've discussed throughout the book: overestimation, overplacement and overprecision? One way of figuring this out is to move away from actual stock markets to experimental scenarios. Artificial trading experiments give researchers a greater ability to explore questions and measures of overconfidence. These experiments allow us to ask which of the different forms of overconfidence drives increases and failures in stock trading. Researchers who asked this question first tested people's financial knowledge and compared their declared confidence levels with the average number of questions they got right.[27] They also asked them how well they thought they had performed compared to the average person. These are effectively the measures of overprecision and overplacement that are often used in psychology. People who had high overconfidence on both measures made excessive levels of investment. However, people with moderate levels of overconfidence made more accurate investments. Perhaps it is only those with higher overconfidence that choose too high a level of investment. And perhaps too much underconfidence also leads to inaccurate levels of investment.

Other researchers asked the same question, but in a real-world setting,[28] studying investors working at a bank. They measured all three psychological measurements of overconfidence—overestimation (false belief in your abilities), overplacement (false belief in your abilities relative to others) and overprecision (excessive certainty in your beliefs). The investors were given a survey on their expectations for the future performance of their portfolios—in terms of actual earnings, performance relative to the market and projected confidence intervals. Comparing these expectations and the actual performance provided the three measures of overconfidence. The comparisons revealed that overconfidence was widespread among the investors, regardless of which measure was used. However, it was only when investors thought they were better than others (overplacement) that they had higher trading activity. The other two measures of overconfidence, overestimation and overprecision, were associated with risk-taking, but not with increased trading activity. Different forms of overconfidence seem to have different influences on investing behaviours.

One recurrent theme in studies of overconfidence has been that men are often more overconfident than women. Researchers in finance have also been curious about this question. One of the earlier studies looking for signs of overconfidence in investment actually uses this difference as a proxy for demonstrating the existence of overconfidence.[29] By following households and their investments across six years, the study shows that men do indeed trade more than women—45 per cent more, in fact. If this leads to greater earnings, then of course this wouldn't be overconfidence. But the reverse is true. The returns of both men and women are reduced when they trade more, but men's earnings reduce about a percentage point more. So, while men are more overconfident compared to women, it isn't by a large amount. This difference is a bit greater when you compare single men and single women. In this case, men trade 67 per cent more, but their returns reduce by more than 1.44 percentage points per year compared to those of single women. As the authors point out, this is driven primarily by the fact that men are more likely to trade despite having less ability—they tend to invest in smaller stocks that have a higher level of risk. It could be that women trade when they are more confident of their investments.

The investment app Stash ran its own study,[30, 31] and found the interesting result that, on days when the stock market is most volatile, male investors on the app were more likely to panic and sell shares, while women investors were more likely to be level-headed. This seems to paint a picture of male investors as more emotional, with panic selling being the flipside of exuberant purchasing. But these differences between men and women aren't always present. Take research that measured overprecision and overestimation in a simulated trading session,[32] with real financial incentives to be accurate. Here, men and women didn't differ in how much they traded or in how overconfident they were.

If overconfidence leads CEOs and investors to overestimate future earnings, it certainly poses a significant danger. But there could be further knock-on effects, apart from the errors in investments and acquisitions we've discussed. Overestimating earnings could lead to greater borrowing and delays in acknowledging losses. It could even lead to misstatements about earnings, which might begin unintentionally, but then spill over to intentional misstatements. In fact, there is evidence that overconfidence is linked to the likelihood of committing fraud.[33] In general, overconfidence could contribute to financial problems and increases in a company's debt because managers have underestimated the probability of losses. Risk-taking by CEOs could also be exacerbated by government guarantees of bailouts,[34] leading to taxpayers having to bear a greater burden.

It isn't just CEOs whose overconfidence matters. Daniel Kahneman, in his book *Thinking Fast and Slow*,[35] makes the point that traders in general believe they are making informed guesses about risks that are worth taking, but actually do no better than blind guesses. Overconfidence has been implicated in retirement planning, negotiations between buyers and sellers, and credit card applications. Others have argued that, when overconfidence increases trading volume, this in turn leads to greater volatility in the stock market as a whole.[36] Small wonder then that a popular Wall Street saying advises you not to confuse brains with a bull market.

Overcoming these various negative effects requires that we first understand how financial overconfidence originates. Early on, Roll suggested that overconfidence is simply a product of the fact that, over their careers, CEOs rarely have to execute mergers. As a result, they have no way of calibrating themselves against past failures. This points towards a more general idea that the feedback about financial decisions can often be poor or ambiguous. If so, we already know that this would provide the right environment for overconfidence to develop. One of the clearest ways in which this plays out is through the self-serving or self-attribution bias.

Self-serving bias, you might recall, describes the tendency of people to attribute successes to their own efforts, while simultaneously explaining away failures as a result of external uncontrollable factors. Famous examples abound. Finance professors Imad Moosa and Vikash Ramiah give us a good cross-section of them in their review of self-serving biases.[37] Even in the face of financial collapse in 2008, the CEO of Lehman Brothers found others to blame, claiming that 'only Lehman was denied that expanded access' to bailout funds.[38] In September 2007, he had proudly declared in an email that 'the BRos [i.e. Lehman Brothers] always wins'.[39] The CFO of Citigroup chose to cite 'unforeseen events'. The CFO of Goldman explained away the heavy losses saying that the events were effectively something that you only expect to happen once in a billion years. Perhaps predictably, none of these statements resembles the introspection you might think a failure of this scale would generate.

How about the flipside? Does success lead to overconfident self-belief, and how could we look for this in CEOs? Let's return to the documentary *Bad Boy Billionaires of India* and Vijay Mallya. In the documentary, we see Vijay Mallya enjoying the fruits of his successful business as the CEO of United Breweries. The company famously produces Kingfisher Beer, the brand that for decades dominated the market for beer in India. He celebrates his success with lavish parties, earning the nickname the King of Good Times. Yet, rather than focusing on his successful business, Mallya seeks out ever newer industries to invest in, including, fatally, the airlines industry. We've discussed how people are most overconfident when they are inexperienced in a field. Mallya proves to be no exception. Despite mounting losses from his airline company, he refuses to cut his losses and eventually ends up facing huge debts and is accused of bank fraud. It might be worth pointing out that, despite his failing business, he still managed to convince banks to keep giving him loans. Perhaps this is the result of his overconfidence successfully convincing lenders. Or perhaps it is his reputation as a successful businessman leading to a cascade of availability biases on which he coasted. Either way, his overconfidence led to both himself and others ignoring failures long after they were readily apparent.

How could we look more rigorously for signs of overconfidence building up over a career? To begin with, investigate behaviour over the course of a career. If self-serving bias was what led to overconfidence, we would see overconfidence building up over time.[40] Initial successes would be followed by risky behaviour that only increases with time. This pattern is what researchers have found.[41, 42] Acquisition deals are more destructive if they are 'higher-order' deals, i.e., deals that are made after several other deals. If early acquisitions are successful, CEOs tend to acquire more and purchase more stock. These transactions, however, lead to losses rather than greater wealth, demonstrating the inherent overconfidence of the CEOs. Investors also seem to follow this pattern. For example, investors in China who had the good luck to be assigned shares in an initial public offering, subsequently went on to trade more and make more losses.[43] Success leads to greater investment, and increases in both overprecision and overestimation of future returns. We see the same pattern in both controlled experiments and real-world settings. Models of behaviour also make the same predictions.[44]

In fact, when running our businesses, we even remember things differently, thanks to self-serving biases. Take the example of store managers who were recruited by researchers to participate in a tournament-style competition.[45] The best performers had few errors in how they remembered their performance. Those who performed the worst had the worst recall of their performance, and what they did recall was dominated by positive memories. These memories weren't impossibly self-serving though—they were anchored in the reality of past performance, but enhanced the positives and downplayed the negatives. Yet, when it came to making predictions about future performance, it was exactly those who had poor memories of their past performance that made the most overconfident predictions. Investors in real markets also have inflated memories of their most important trades, and investors who had greater biases in their memory were also more overconfident and traded more frequently.[46] Once more, positive events influence what we learn about ourselves in a way that negative events never do. Interestingly, investors who looked up, rather than recalled, previous important trades were less likely to be overconfident.

It almost appears as if the poor performers needed motivated beliefs to keep them looking forward towards a positive future. Or to impress others about their future potential. This social aspect could be a crucial factor. Individuals are less likely to be overconfident with clear performance measures and incentives, but as we've seen, the presence of observers seems to enhance overconfidence. One suggestion is that settings that are highly selective and competitive are precisely where you expect to see the highest overconfidence. For example, CEOs have survived several rounds of selection and promotion. This is precisely what could lead to them overestimating their abilities. What makes this worse is that they are now in a position with the greatest decision-making power, with fewer checks and balances. In other words, it's more difficult for any overconfident decisions to be corrected.

And yet, there must be ways to prevent overconfidence from leading firms to disaster. Some suggestions have included cuts on bonuses in companies or sectors that want to deter overconfidence—for example, in banks that are bailed out by taxpayers. Another suggestion is to reduce CEO access to money for investment. Yet another possibility is to modify the composition of the board of directors. Ensuring that the members can have an outsider perspective on the company, from people who have no personal investment, could help work against overconfidence. Hiring the correct CEOs is obviously the most useful thing a company can do. Some studies have argued that the companies that do the very best have CEOs who are more humble and hardworking.[47]

Another possibility worth considering is the idea that women CEOs might do better than male CEOs. We've seen that women can often be less overconfident than men, both in studies of real companies as well as in experimental studies. Could having more women in management positions reduce risk-taking and overconfident decisions in companies? Women CEOs do differ from male CEOs—they make fewer acquisitions and take on less long-term debt.[48] The acquisitions made by firms with male CEOs go on to have a return about 2 per cent less than those of female-led firms. Male CEOs are more optimistic about the future earnings of the company and are less likely to be worried about long-term debt, even taking on more debt than would be rationally advisable. Women CEOs, on the other hand, are more likely to take on short-term debt, at least in one study of women CEOs in Europe.[49] This provides them greater immediate flexibility to either capitalise on current growth opportunities or swiftly resolve any difficulties the company faces.

Interestingly, this pattern appears to be enhanced in countries that score higher on indices of masculinity and gender inequality. In the study of women CEOs in Europe, for example, countries with a higher masculinity index included Austria, Ireland, Greece and Italy. Sweden, Norway and Denmark had the lowest scores of the index. It is almost as if, in countries with greater gender equality, women CEOs end up behaving more like the male CEOs, with a corresponding decrease in their cautious approach to debt structuring. That suggests that, in cultures where there are perhaps fewer negative consequences when women show confidence, they too make full use of the advantages of overconfidence.

The composition of company boards can make a difference too. Male CEOs are less likely to be overconfident if the board of directors at the company includes women.[50] Regulations in India require at least one woman on the board of any public company, and 96 per cent of companies surveyed comply with this regulation.[51] Other countries also have similar regulations, which is promising for efforts to curb CEO overconfidence. The effect of having women on boards is even reflected in personal decisions made by male (but not female) CEOs about when to exploit their stock options. They are less likely to hold onto options that they can make a profit from, i.e., they are less likely to overestimate future profits. As we know, decision-making about options has been a key measure of CEO overconfidence. Yet even this individual decision, independent of the firm's structure or composition, is affected by the presence of women directors on company boards, especially in industries where CEOs are prone to overconfident decision-making.[52] One explanation that has been offered for this is that having women directors on the board gives the CEO impetus to consider a wider range of alternatives and arguments during decision-making. Since having women directors on boards does not influence the overconfidence of female CEOs, there is potentially something about the gender dynamics of boards that is also at play here.

It also looks like firms with a greater number of women on their boards are less likely to chase after acquisition bids.[53] They are less likely to have aggressive investment policies and seem to improve the performance of their firms, at least in industries where CEOs tend to have higher overconfidence. Additionally, firms with female directors even did better during the financial crisis of 2008. Yet women are still underrepresented on boards. In 2021, the percentage of women directors in the financial service sector worldwide was 21.2 per cent.[54] As of 2020, in India, women are in leadership positions in only 11 per cent of firms and hold 17 per cent of positions on company boards.[55] In general, many firms that have women directors usually have only one on their board. This is increasing over time, yet there is much more progress to be made. If nothing else, the possibility for increased performance and decreased overconfidence should spur companies to work harder towards increased representation.

Thus far, the focus has been on the losses that stem from overconfidence and how companies could potentially avoid them. But what explains the prevalence of overconfidence in the first place? If narcissistic overconfident CEOs don't do as well as humble, hardworking ones, then why are there so many of them? What are the advantages of overconfidence to companies, or at least to the CEOs themselves? If these were to mirror the advantages we discussed earlier, we could hazard a few guesses. We should expect overconfidence to personally benefit people by increasing their status within the company. So, we should see them getting more promotions and reaching higher positions of power. We should also expect overconfidence to help in areas where motivation and perseverance are a benefit, perhaps when entrepreneurs are starting up or if the company thrives on innovation.

The first of these ideas seems to bear up. Overconfident managers are easily found, and they also seem more likely to become CEOs. Oddly enough, this isn't entirely a bad thing. In fact, managers with moderate levels of optimism and overconfidence seem to benefit companies. It is only excessive overconfidence that leads to losses.[56] Amongst the top 200 firms on the Bombay Stock Exchange, companies with overconfident CEOs even perform better in terms of the value of their assets.[57] Overconfident CEOs invest more in innovation and gain more patents.[58] They thrive in industries that require innovation, although this doesn't always lead to an overall increase in value for the company. These results seem to chime well with the motivational advantages to overconfidence.

Another key to understanding these advantages is making a distinction between confidence and attitudes to risk. An overconfident manager can be risk-averse. The difference between such a manager and a rational one is the perception of risk. So, an overconfident manager will generally end up taking a more risky course of action, not because they want to take on more risk but because they perceive the action to be less risky than a rational person might. This could benefit companies, especially if they are in industries that require risk-taking.[59]

Research models of how promotion works within companies also make the case that this could lead to overconfident managers getting promoted.[60] Their level of risk-taking would better match what suits the company or the shareholders. Also, models of overconfidence argue that overconfident people might perceive their potential earnings to be greater and therefore work harder, which would of course benefit the company.[61] Looked at through this lens, the fact that overconfidence leads to increased status could be a net gain for everybody. Of course, this only holds good if overconfidence can be reined in, failing which it leads to the well-documented losses we've discussed.

Other models show that overconfidence could also be an asset when trading stocks.[62] Being more willing to take a risk means that overconfident traders could benefit from being the first to capitalise on any information. One assumption here is that overconfident traders would learn from any mistakes, and therefore, eventually not trade based on unreliable sources of information. Given the evidence for self-serving biases, this might not always be the case.

Companies can also exploit overconfident managers for their own benefit. In industries that require high risk-taking, companies might typically have to negotiate higher performance-based incentives, such as bonuses, stocks and options, to hire a CEO. An overconfident CEO would be more likely to believe in their ability to boost the company's performance (and its share value), and are likely to be more happy to settle for lower performance-based compensation. If you believe the company won't perform well, you're probably going to ask for a larger percentage of the profits. But if you are overconfident and believe the company (under you) will do exceedingly well, then even a smaller percentage of the profits would give you a lot of money. Models of compensation correspondingly suggest that overconfident workers might earn less than others if companies adjust their offers to take their overconfidence into account.[63, 64] In general, a little bit of overconfidence could benefit both the CEO or employee looking to gain a promotion and the company looking to negotiate lower bonuses and take greater risks for less compensation.

Risk-taking might be particularly important for companies that are moving to a new product or starting up. Here, overconfidence ought to help increase motivation and innovation, and there is some evidence for this. Overconfident managers seem to be beneficial for innovation in competitive industries.[65] They are quicker to exploit opportunities for growth and invest more in research and development. What is crucial, however, is the relationship between how overconfident and how risk-averse the manager is. While a risk-averse overconfident manager could help with the right level of growth, a more risk-prone overconfident manager could well undo the foundations of a company before it gets off the ground.

This is of course a problem that entrepreneurs have to grapple with. The majority of new ventures are bound for failure. Within the first five years of being founded, about 60 per cent of all new businesses started in the US fail.[66] Within the first ten years, it's almost 80 per cent. Yet, one survey found that entrepreneurs in the US believed the chances of a firm like theirs succeeding was 60 per cent,[67] and 81 per cent of them believed their own chance of success was greater than 70 per cent. A good 33 per cent even said they had zero chance of failure. It is no surprise then that more people start a new company each day. The allure of the reward must loom large in their minds. Imagine becoming the next Amazon or Facebook! When the potential for profits is that high, it seems likely that the environment is conducive to overconfidence.

There is some evidence that people are inaccurate about their chances of success. For example, people seem to be poor judges of what markets to join, at least in an artificial skills-based market.[68] Participants in one study who were randomly assigned to a market performed well and made profits in 71 per cent of the rounds. Other participants who chose to enter a particular skills-market—i.e., self-selecting participants—only managed to make a profit in 6 per cent of the rounds. However, there is substantial variation on measures of overconfidence across the world.[69] Of people surveyed in Hungary and Argentina, 55 per cent believed they have the skills to succeed, compared to 11 per cent in Japan. Clearly, cultural perceptions of success or failure have a role to play.

It doesn't boil down to an ignorance of the facts. People acknowledge and are well aware of the high likelihood of failure, but simultaneously believe that this somehow doesn't apply to them. In this, they are similar to the examples we discussed before. PhD students in pursuit of academic careers and low-ranking members of a drug gang hoping to become the big boss someday share the same traits as starry-eyed entrepreneurs.

There's a pattern to entrepreneurial overconfidence. In other studies,[70, 71] people could choose to join a game involving difficult questions or easy ones. Predictably, most people joined the easy games. As a result, competition was high and most people made losses. The implication is that entrepreneurs will too often believe they can succeed if they enter industries perceived to be easy, but in doing so, they typically underestimate their competitors. Researchers argue that people focus too much on their own abilities and less on the competition—the availability bias is hard at work here. In fact, providing entrepreneurs with information about their competition moderates their overconfidence.

An Argentinian study[72] found strong better-than-average effects amongst the entrepreneurs they studied, with 80 per cent of them believing they were better than the median participant in the study. Assessments of their past performance were centred around the average, but there was a greater belief in above-average future performance, fitting the pattern of an optimism bias. This belief about future performance was, however, removed if the entrepreneurs were given information about the actual average performance of start-ups. As with most projects, a small reality check goes a long way. The 2008 financial crash was a mighty reality check, and has likely had an effect on the financial decisions of millennials.[73] They are less inclined to become entrepreneurs or invest in stocks compared to other generations.

More patterns emerge if you measure real-world overconfidence. A French study of thousands of entrepreneurs compared growth forecasts of entrepreneurs with their actual performance years later.[74] Entrepreneurs starting new ventures or ideas, rather than a more standard one, were more likely to be overconfident by this measure. Similar results were found from a study that used population surveys from eighteen different countries.[75] This fits some of the ideas we've talked about before. Overconfidence is more likely to be found when there is more ambiguity and less knowledge. This is more likely to be the case with a novel idea compared to a tried and tested one.

It seems likely that people who found small businesses could be more optimistic compared to mid-level managers.[76] This is unsurprising, given that they probably have a greater feeling of control in their position and over their lives. Self-serving bias could also no doubt reconfirm the self-views of entrepreneurs after every success. At one level, this optimism could lead to more risk-taking, simply because of a lowered perception of risk. Overconfident entrepreneurs are predicted to invest more of their own money or informally borrowed money into their ventures.[77] They are slower to abandon failing projects, leading to greater losses, as predicted by the sunk-cost fallacy. On the other hand, optimism and even overconfidence might be precisely what entrepreneurs require. Overconfidence might be just the right thing to convince potential funders or customers that you are going to succeed. This could be especially important for anyone selling a novel idea. Their overconfidence might help them gain more initial funding from venture capitalists.

The fact that several Silicon Valley companies retain funding and a high profile, despite struggling to make profits even after years, suggests this dynamic could be at work. Twitter was founded in 2006, but only first made a profit in 2017.[78] The company behind the car-hailing app Lyft admitted in 2019 that it has a history of making losses, and that it cannot ensure future profitability.[79] Yet, its stock opened at a price that was 21 per cent above the asking price.[80] Its rival, Uber, founded in 2009, has had losses since its inception, cumulatively amounting to US$ 14 billion in 2019.[81, 82] The idea that loss-making ventures might benefit from investment, thanks to their overconfidence is perhaps still relatively understudied. What does seem clearer are the motivational advantages of overconfidence. It can boost the morale of the company and lead to entrepreneurs potentially working longer hours and striving harder to find customers and appropriate technology.[83] Overconfidence could be the engine that propels action. In the end, rather than avoiding overconfidence, entrepreneurs need to harness its power while steering clear of risky accidents. What's required is an optimal level of self-deception—something that could be true for all our lives.

From investors to entrepreneurs, we've seen that overconfidence is well established in the everyday running of businesses. We can now return to our initial question: did this lead to the financial crisis of 2008? At the heart of the 2008 crisis in the US was the issue of credit. An optimistic belief in the strength of the housing market led to buyers using too much credit. A recent study shows that people with credit card debt fail to pay it off even when they have the financial ability.[84] This seems driven not by people's impulsivity or innumeracy, but by their overconfidence in their financial knowledge. Perhaps something similar was at play during the housing crisis. In addition, poor regulation also allowed banks to lend money too easily. The economist Robert Schiller in his book *Irrational Exuberance*[85] points out that it isn't that home buyers had a strong conviction that home prices would never fall. In fact, only 19 per cent of those surveyed in 2004 believed there was little or no risk. Instead, he implicates an avoidance of the idea that prices could fall. This resembles the mechanisms of information avoidance or optimism we've discussed before—we only search where the light is. Schiller also describes the phenomenon of speculative bubbles that lead to financial crashes. The first two editions of his book, both warning of market overvaluations, came out in 2000 and 2004, each foreshadowing crashes that occurred soon after, first in 2000 and then in 2008.

Schiller provides several disparate reasons for historical crashes, but one consistent phenomenon is a sort of psychological contagion, where news of booming markets lead to further investment from ever greater numbers of people. He links this to the economist John Maynard Keynes's idea of 'animal spirits', an urge to act rather than remain inactive, which seems to perfectly fit the idea that overconfidence can give us a motivational advantage.

External factors, including new technologies, news coverage or perceived onsets of historical eras (think Y2K) seem to lead to the behaviour of multiple individuals aligning, something which potentially correlates all their errors and leads to overconfident bubbles. None of this is new or unique to the 2008 crash. One of the most famous examples of markets booming only to crash is the craze for tulips in the 1600s. The original Dutch word for this phenomenon translates to 'wind trade', aptly capturing the fuel behind an ever-expanding bubble. Similarly, the period leading to the economic crash of 1929 was also called the Cocksure Era. The economist Charles Dice argued around that time that the market should go on increasing indefinitely—only for the market to crash immediately after his book was published. We've already talked about the difficulties experienced by cryptocurrencies. Bubbles occur time and again, and enclosed in these bubbles, we remain unaware of our own biases. In the survey from 2004, only 1 per cent of people talked about a bubble when discussing home price increases. They were far more likely to think of the increases as a natural consequence of supply and demand.

In 2007–8, when overconfident homeowners could no longer afford mortgages, they defaulted on loans. Property prices fell and the banks collapsed. A lot of risky investments were tied to the property market and credit. Based on all that we now know about overconfidence amongst investors, CEOs and companies, the potential fault lines should be clearly visible. The first of these is its contribution to stock market volatility. We know that overconfidence can lead to excessive trading of shares, leading to greater volatility. This is true for the period around the 2008 crisis as well. If we look at stock market trading across the world, there were pronounced drops in share prices from around mid-2007. In stock markets around the world, including in Australia, India, Brazil and Kuwait, the volatility of the stock market was related to overconfident investors.[86] The only two markets where this was not seen were in Japan and Singapore. Overconfidence thus could cause swings in stock prices, potentially leading to a downward spiral when things go wrong.

What about the CEOs of banks during crises? If they were to underestimate financial risks, it is possible that banks could make poor loans, leading to greater defaults. This in turn means that when a financial crisis occurs, these banks are the ones that would be the most vulnerable and the most likely to collapse. There is evidence of exactly this.[87, 88] CEOs of banks can be classified as overconfident or not based on how they exercise their options, similar to the measure proposed by Malmendier and Tate. Researchers have then investigated how banks with CEOs thus identified as overconfident did compared to other banks over several years, including more than one financial crisis. One study found that the percentage of banks with overconfident CEOs increased—from about 47 per cent to 62 per cent—in the years just preceding financial crises.[89] This adds to the idea that overconfidence contributes to crises. During both the 1998

Russian crisis and the 2008 crisis, these banks were more vulnerable due to poorer lending standards and more debt. For example, they had an 11 per cent greater increase in real estate loans and about a 5 per cent increase in other loans compared to other banks. They had more loan defaults, greater decreases in stock performances and higher chances of CEO turnover. A clear indication of increased risk-taking.

What was most striking was that the banks that had overconfident CEOs before the 1998 crisis were still the ones likely to have overconfident CEOs in 2006. Banks that performed badly in 1998 were the ones likely to fail in 2008.[90] It's as if banks don't learn from their mistakes and correct their course. In fact, it appears likely that there is a persistent risk culture. This ties in with some ideas we discussed earlier. Banks that want to take greater risks can actually gain from hiring overconfident CEOs as they could potentially provide them less compensation. It makes sense therefore that banks with a high-risk culture consistently hire overconfident CEOs, and subsequently have riskier approaches to loans and debt.

Viewed this way, while the overconfident CEOs are making risky decisions, they aren't actually driving the culture of the bank. Rather, it is banks with riskier cultures that prefer overconfident CEOs. There is evidence suggesting that this could be driven by institutional investors who own a large block of the shares in a bank.[91] Banks with overconfident CEOs are more likely to have this kind of institutional ownership than other banks.

In non-crisis years, measures of overconfidence based on options and those based on the language used by CEOs could have different implications.[92] Those found to be overconfident by the second, language-based measure had above-average compensation. Potentially, finding the right words could be helping CEOs convince companies to pay them more, providing what appears to be a neat example of how self-deception helps deceive others. However, after they have faced crises, CEO overconfidence appears to decline by both measures. This is especially true for the CEOs using overconfident language—their percentage went down from about 40 per cent to 13 per cent by this measure. If nothing else, crises teach them to use more cautious language. No doubt the high turnover of CEOs during crisis years contributes to a reconsideration of their self-assessments.

In the end, CEOs can still gain from their overconfidence, either through future hires by banks with a risky culture, or through higher compensation. Institutional shareholders also seem to benefit from CEO overconfidence in non-crisis years due to the right level of risk and innovation. During crisis years, overconfident banks do make losses, but even these might not always be disastrous. Some findings show that the difference between market losses of overconfident and non-overconfident banks could be only 3 percentage points.[93] This might even be offset by the gains they make during non-crisis years.

Thus, individually, people and firms could stand to gain from overconfidence. But there could be a knock-on effect on the market as a whole. The large-scale effects felt across the world was a result of multiple overconfidence biases exacerbating each other. Consumers overestimated their ability to pay back loans. Banks underestimated the probability of defaults. Hedge funds put too much of their trust in statistical models that believed the real estate market would go on increasing. This combination of optimistic beliefs eventually led to losses for huge numbers of people around the world. There is thus a skewed balance between who reaps the gains of overconfidence and who suffers the losses that can result. This is only thrown into starker relief when we consider other sorts of disasters, from wars to pandemics, where the losses often involve human lives.

TEN

Wars of Error

IN THE MAHABHARATA, YUDHISHTHIRA FAVOURS A REASONABLE approach to preventing war. Faced with impending conflict, he offers the Kauravas a way out, and sends word through Krishna that an offer of five villages would be enough to settle matters. In the Iliad, another classical war epic, we find an alternative possible solution. Before the Greek and Trojan armies meet each other, the Trojan prince Paris challenges Menelaus, the king of the Greeks, to a duel that would settle the war. Rather than whole legions of men fighting each other, the two of them could face-off and avoid the enormous costs of war. In its own way, this could be viewed as a rational means to avoid wholesale bloodshed. These approaches make sense. Nations bleed when they go to war. Their citizens die, or return wounded. There are often huge economic costs, and it can take years to recover. Rather than launching military campaigns, countries in conflict could instead rationally assess their strengths and weaknesses, decide who might win a war and settle their conflicts accordingly.

Why isn't this pacifist's dream the norm? Even *The Art of War*,[1] the classic and popular military text believed to be written by the Chinese general Sun Tzu from the fifth century BCE, has arguments in favour of avoiding wars. Here's one: 'Supreme excellence consists in breaking the enemy's resistance without fighting.' Perhaps even more telling: 'If you know your enemies and know yourself, you need not fear the result of a hundred battles.' Using self-knowledge and achieving your goals without actually fighting has been good advice for centuries.

Assumptions of rationality did underlie the major military strategy in the Cold War, forming the basis of deterrence theory and the related idea of mutually assured destruction. At its simplest, the idea is that countries needed credible threats, like stockpiled nuclear weapons capable of destroying each other, to prevent attacks by opponents. Deterrence theory and Thomas Schelling, the economist who laid the foundations for it, have been credited with maintaining relative stability during the Cold War period.[2, 3]

Given our discussions so far, though, we might naturally be sceptical about the assumptions of rationality underlying this theory. In both the Mahabharata and the Iliad, the outcome is predictably not the peaceable one. Duryodhana, the leader of the Kauravas, refuses to give the Pandavas a single inch of land, takes them to battle and loses in eighteen days. Paris and Menelaus fight it out, Paris is wounded but is sneaked away by the goddess Aphrodite. The Trojans break the agreed-upon truce and go on to lose the war. Wars that could have been avoided burst out in both cases, and in both cases, the ones who choose the military option lose, revealing their overconfidence. It's also interesting that the Pandavas, who go on to eventually win the war, were willing to sue for peace. The costs of war must surely have loomed heavily in their minds.

The assumption of rationality during wars has been challenged in both political discourse and popular culture. If you've seen Kubrick's comic masterpiece *Dr Strangelove*, you've encountered the argument that a few unpredictable agents could start an almost accidental nuclear war. In the documentary *The Fog of War*, even Robert McNamara, who had been US defence secretary from 1961 to 1968, stresses that we cannot assume that rationality will ensure peace. Rogue actors and despots who might welcome destruction would not, for instance, fit the narrative of deterrence theory. Critics of the theory have pointed out that such people might launch an attack regardless of the promise of destruction, indeed, even embrace it.

Then there is overconfidence, a specific form of irrationality that could colour perception of the conflict and work against deterrence. It might even be an advantage in wars—deceiving yourself might motivate you during battle or deceive an opponent.[4] We might predict that, when communication and information is less reliable between two countries, their perceptions might end up being biased towards overconfidence. Overconfident individuals might launch attacks in the blithe hope of winning outright before their opponents have a chance to respond. These scenarios tear away at the rational foundations of deterrence.

Perhaps this is why the classical epics point to the the role that irrational behaviour and overconfidence in particular can play in war. One of the foundational texts of Taoism—the Zhuangzi[5]—has a delightfully appropriate quote: 'Don't you know about the praying mantis that waved its arms angrily in front of an approaching carriage, unaware that it was incapable of stopping it? Such was the high opinion it had of its talents.'

What really is the role of overconfidence in wars, though? As with any attempt to apply psychological ideas in real-world situations, this question can be hard, even impossible, to answer. Yet, there might still be ways of approaching it. Let's return to two (of the three) forms of overconfidence: overestimation and overprecision.

Overestimation is the belief or claim that you have the ability to do something when you don't. Think of the general who thinks they can win a war that proves to be a disastrous military defeat. The strongest evidence for overestimation of this sort would be cases where the initial aggressor loses. Countries initiating wars surely do so with the intention of winning it. Models suggest that being overconfident might help you win more resources.[6] However, in experimental wargames, overconfident people are more likely to launch an attack, but are also more likely to fail.[7, 8] Several historical examples are testament to these misjudgements, generation after generation. Napoleon's decision to invade Russia in winter[9] eventually led to his troops being starved of food and heavily underprepared for surviving the cold. His overconfidence included an estimation of how long the war would last, because he was planning for a swift victory that would be achieved before the depths of winter. Napoleon had to withdraw, and the depletion of his forces left him underprepared for future conflicts. Eventually, this played into his downfall and capture. Looking at wars where the aggressor loses is a first step towards demonstrating overestimation.

There are, however, some difficulties with determining overestimation in this fashion. It would of course be convincing if the same general or leader launched multiple wars that failed. That would make a clear case: this leader persists in their biased beliefs even in the face of failure. But we don't often have the same person leading several wars. One way to address this gap could be to look at multiple military decisions within the same war. Or to look for particularly egregious errors or statements that could serve as tell-tale signs—rather than proof—of overconfidence. I'm imagining a leader making lofty claims like 'We will crush the enemy in a matter of minutes', or of the Roman Emperor Caligula declaring war on Neptune and launching an attack on the sea.[10]

However, it is a trivial argument to make that at least one of the two groups going to war must be overconfident, simply because they lost. This is unsatisfying and not even necessarily borne out. Luck or other factors could play a decisive role in determining the victor of a war, for instance. During the Battle of Longewala in the 1971 Indo-Pakistan war, Pakistani troops suffered a huge loss.[11] Yet, on paper, there were 2,000–3,000 Pakistani soldiers and thirty to forty tanks fighting 120 soldiers on the Indian side, albeit supported by some fighter aircraft. It doesn't seem entirely unreasonable for them to have fought expecting victory, even though they went on to lose. In other cases, even with an almost guaranteed loss, there could be several reasons for going to war that do not arise from overconfidence. One side could be fighting back, knowing that all the odds are stacked against it, because it is faced with an existential threat or fighting for its values or identity. This would apply to independence struggles, where people might prefer to go down fighting for an ideal. The 1857 war for independence in India was surely worth fighting, even if it resulted in a loss. To genuinely implicate overconfidence, we would have to look for decisions to go to war that don't fit into these categories.

The second form of overconfidence, overprecision, you will recall, is excessive certainty in your estimates. Such as a president who decides only a narrow range of outcomes or facts is probable, despite advice and evidence to the contrary. This kind of error could affect several aspects of war, starting with the decision and reasons to go to war and leading all the way up to how certain you are that you will win. In the case of overprecision, it's not just your belief that you will win that's under scrutiny, it's how certain you are about it.

Overprecision also has a role to play in countries' estimation of how long the war is going to last and how much loss of life it will entail. There are also positive illusions about the economic and social costs of going to war and, crucially, about the aftermath of war. The latter could affect both victor and vanquished, but it could also tie both of them together in unexpected ways. For example, the aftermath of war plays an important role when a country deposes the ruler of another nation, but has no plan for the governance of the country that loses. The supreme confidence at the moment they decide to go to war could prevent countries from having an honest and clear consideration of the consequences, playing into the human capacity for self-deception about our abilities to solve future problems and our illusions of control.

It is difficult to measure overprecision even in carefully controlled studies, but perhaps you could try to build up a case for it in the real world through circumstantial evidence. Evidence of the biases that lead to overconfidence would be the clue here. Confirmation biases, motivated cognition and sunk-cost thinking would all bias the information available during decision-making—reducing the likelihood of even thinking about negative outcomes. This would likely guarantee greater certainty in your estimates. Looking for evidence of these psychological biases could, therefore, be an important tool when looking for military overconfidence, perhaps even as decisions about wars are being made.

I also wonder whether we can take inspiration from Ulrike Malmendier and Geoffrey Tate's work on overconfident CEOs and apply one of their measures to politicians or generals. Their second measure for overconfidence had involved observing what words prominent business magazines used to describe CEOs. Others developed a similar measure based on the language the CEOs themselves used. These measures then predicted future overconfident behaviour. Perhaps a similar approach could be applied to politicians by looking at daily newspaper reports discussing them or by looking at the language they use in press conferences. Such a measure of political overconfidence would, of course, apply not just during wars but during other crises and normal governance too—topics we'll look at in the next two chapters.

In his book *Overconfidence and War*,[12] the political scientist Dominic Johnson applies insights from psychology and evolutionary biology to look at real-world examples of wars. The framework of Johnson's book is particularly useful in thinking of the various measures by which we can capture how our illusions play out during wars. Johnson makes a case for positive illusions governing Germany's decision to break its pact with the Soviet Union during the Second World War. That's an example where aggression initially led to success, but eventually led to failure. The German–Soviet Pact signed in August 1939 clearly marked out their areas of political interest and solidified their joint invasion of Poland. The pact also involved an agreement that neither country would ally itself with an enemy of the other. Two years later, however, Germany unilaterally broke the pact and invaded areas of Soviet-occupied Poland. Germany had no reason to add a war with the Soviets to its military campaign in the rest of Europe. Hitler, however, decided it would be a swift victory, calling it 'a child's game in a sandbox'. The actual attack that broke the pact—dubbed Operation Barbarossa—was a huge success for the Nazis, but it immediately created a powerful opponent. The USSR's entry into the Second World War eventually led to the defeat of the Nazis and the overthrow of Berlin.

Similarly, historian and author Barbara Tuchman briefly elaborates on Japan's decision to bomb Pearl Harbour in her book *The March of Folly*.[13] Despite advice against it, the belief was that this would demoralise the US and prevent them from entering the Second World War. Instead, of course, it rallied the country. Where previously the US had been non-interventionist, it now decisively entered the war and helped win it. Tuchman defines 'folly' as an action going against the interests of that country or organisation. This doesn't always mean overconfidence, but in this case that definition works well.

Another discussion of overconfidence in wars comes from the wars fought between India and Pakistan. In his book *Conflict Unending*,[14] Sumit Ganguly argues that, in the wars between the two countries in 1947-48, 1969 and 2000, nationalism and jingoism led to underestimation of the opponent's military capabilities by both sides. Ganguly also argues that the comparatively more democratic governments in India at the time led to less overconfidence about military competence compared to the relatively more authoritarian governments in Pakistan. That supports one of Johnson's primary arguments, namely, that overconfidence is exacerbated by governments that tend towards the authoritarian. A similar view is held by strategic studies expert Lawrence Freedman, who argues that Russia's failures in the ongoing war in Ukraine stem from Putin's authoritarianism.[15] He argues that Putin expected an easy victory because he only consulted with people who 'shared his prejudices' about the weaknesses of Ukraine's military.

Beyond decisions to launch offensive strikes, there are other aspects of overconfidence. Two often underestimated aspects about wars are their duration and the resultant loss of life. Tied into both of these is the sunk-cost fallacy, a characteristic of individual psychology that could play a role at a national level too. Once we invest in a course of action, we tend to persist with it even when it proves to be faulty and changing tack would be less costly. An often-cited example of this is the Concorde airline. Despite the fact that it proved to be economically unviable, British and French governments continued to invest in the airline because it became impossible to pull out. The analogy with war is clear. When the duration of war and the loss of life caused by it are underestimated, countries commit large amounts of resources to the conflict, assuming that it will only be for a short while. As the war continues beyond those initial expectations, it becomes difficult to pull out precisely because so much has been invested in the conflict already. Models of conflict show that overconfident leaders are not only more likely to start conflicts but also remain active for longer in a conflict.[16]

Johnson's book points out several examples from both the First and Second World Wars, where victory was often expected to be quick and with a relatively small number of troops. This optimism seemed to be widespread on both sides in the First World War. A British airmen's song back then perfectly encapsulated the optimism bias in lyric form: 'The Bells of Hell go ting-a-ling-a-ling / For you but not for me'. Both sides believed they would win and be able to gain large advantages from the war. This made for a dangerously strong enthusiasm for going to war, leading to a major disaster for all armies.

Perhaps the classic example of military overoptimism is US participation in the Vietnam War. Through several different governments, this war was consistently thought to be winnable with low involvement of troops. It ended up being extended over decades, and successive governments in the US made consistently optimistic choices over many years, bearing out the idea of overconfidence. The eventual result was a large number of casualties and a retreat on unfavourable terms. What makes this example particularly striking is that this was a war that had already been fought and lost by the French. It's for good reason that the first episode of Ken Burns and Lynn Novick's magisterial documentary on the Vietnam War is called 'Deja Vu'. The French president De Gaulle, who had seen France lose and pull out of Vietnam, was vocal in his pessimism about US involvement. He called Vietnam 'a hopeless place to fight',[17] and recommended withdrawal and negotiation as the only way to ensure peace. General Leclerc, once a commander in the war in Vietnam, also warned that it would take as many as 500,000 men to win the war, and even that might not be enough.[18] These warnings did little to change the US government's decision to steadily increase involvement in Vietnam. Perhaps they initially thought their army was stronger than the French army and the outcome would be different. Yet, the conviction about victory persisted despite the extended duration of, and the losses in, the war. The eventual number of soldiers deployed by the US in Vietnam ended up being greater than 500,000. Even that larger number of troops did not lead to victory.

Tuchman also partly blames the overconfidence of North Vietnam and the Viet Cong for the protracted duration of the Vietnam War, and for neglecting the possibility of a negotiated peaceful solution. She argues that the hope of a rapid and decisive victory in South Vietnam led to continuous military offensives despite multiple offers of peace talks. Tuchman uses the Tet Offensive as an example of folly on the part of the North Vietnamese. In January 1968, the North Vietnamese and the Viet Cong launched a major attack on several control centres in South Vietnam simultaneously. The idea was to achieve a blitz of victories and encourage an uprising in South Vietnam with the objective of winning over all of Vietnam without a negotiation with the US. As it turned out, the North Vietnamese troops and the Viet Cong suffered between thirty and forty thousand casualties and failed in their attempt to spark a rebellion in the South. It was only in 1973 that the Paris Peace Accords were signed and the

US withdrew its troops from Vietnam. Within two years, the North Vietnamese troops had conquered South Vietnam—but the war with the Americans had lasted nearly two decades.

Tuchman's book also lays out the evidence that the propaganda used to sell the war to the American public and the world ended up convincing the government itself to intensify its involvement in the war. Subsequently, the investment of money, troops and prestige in the war meant that the US could no longer disengage unless it won. The alternative would have been to back out of the war with a loss of prestige as well as thousands of lives and decades of spending. You've no doubt already clocked that this follows the pattern of a sunk-cost fallacy. There is an additional element of national prestige to this example of sunk costs, which undoubtedly raises the stakes.

Another aspect that propaganda feeds into is belief in the importance of going to war. In other words, it fuels excessive certainty—or overprecision—in the justification offered for going to war. In the case of the Vietnam War, this interacted with the fear of communism. The desire to prevent the spread of communism was a major factor through the Cold War period. In the context of Vietnam, this led to the espousal of 'domino theory'. It became a strongly held belief that if one country in Southeast Asia were to become communist, the ideology would rapidly spread to all the other countries and beyond to several countries in South Asia and East Asia. This fear fed the belief that going to war in Vietnam was necessary. However, the push to generate support for the war fed the fear of communism as well. What resulted was thus a feedback loop that Tuchman calls 'self-hypnosis'. The confidence with which the domino theory was held now appears misplaced. When Vietnam eventually did become communist, it did not spark a wave of communism across Asia. There is an alternative possibility, though—perhaps fighting the war, however disastrous and overconfident it was, fulfilled a signalling role to other countries, deterring them from becoming communist. In this view, it could then serve as another example of the role that overconfidence plays in social signalling, or as a sign of commitment.

Military goals also influenced the certainty with which the decision to go to war was made in another recent instance, the Iraq War. The justification for both the US and the UK in that case was famously the presence of weapons of mass destruction (WMD) in Iraq. In the UK, Iraq's possession of WMD was the justification the Blair government provided journalists with in a set of documents. These documents were shown to be plagiarised and based in part on older information.[19] The government's own experts questioned some of the claims about WMD in the report[20]—the dossier included these claims despite their objections. The fact that the primary reasons for going to war seemed to be based on hypotheticals by unverified external sources rather than facts eventually led to the dossier being dubbed 'the dodgy dossier'.

Despite being successful at toppling Saddam Hussein, the invasion of Iraq did not, in the end, find evidence of WMD, discrediting the entire reason for going to war. According to the book *The Silk Roads* by Peter Frankopan, the search for confirmatory evidence even led at one point to weather balloons being misidentified as the hypothetical weapons.[21] The push to go to war was thus based on faulty premises, repeatedly ignored objections and evidence to the contrary. In this, it seems to serve as a good example of how war can be initiated based on unjustified levels of confidence and certainty based on poor evidence.

The failure to actually find the weapons looms large in current assessments of the Iraq War. Even two-thirds of US army veterans now think that the war was not worth fighting.[22] A 2017 poll by YouGov found that 55 per cent of UK citizens think it was wrong to have gone to war in Iraq and only 18 per cent think it was the correct thing to have done.[23] When the decision to go to war was made in March 2003, however, a similar poll had 54 per cent approving of the war and 38 per cent disapproving.[24] Approval for the war remained consistently positive until September 2003.[25] This seems to reflect how decisions to go to war garner support when they are immediate. At the time, those supporting the war seem to have disregarded arguments against going to war, which were put forward by the press discussions of the 'dodgy dossier'. An interesting follow-up poll in 2015[26] asked people to recall whether they approved or disapproved of the war. In that poll, twelve years after the first one, 43 per cent of people remember disapproving and 37 per cent remember approving of the war, contradicting the results of the original poll. To my mind, this shows our own propensity to deceive ourselves and cast ourselves on the right side of current opinion. When all the pressure is for war and after war is actually initiated, we approve of it and are certain it is justified. But without that pressure, if the difficulties become obvious and the war is later perceived to have failed, we would rather think of ourselves as having always disapproved of it. In this way, our view of ourselves can more easily align with the subsequent evidence, potentially reducing cognitive dissonance. We don't then always learn from our misplaced confidence. In fact, it looks like we might well misremember our past decisions and preserve the illusion of our accuracy.

The huge political support for the Iraq War in both the US and the UK suggests an interesting idea. We have discussed the idea that overconfidence can help deceive people better. We now know that, by ignoring advice against the invasion, George Bush and Tony Blair were overconfident and, if we are generous, self-deceived about their evidence to go to war. Could this self-deception have actually helped them sell their case to the Senate and Parliament, resulting in strong support from politicians? This is what we would expect based on the social signalling theory of the evolution of overconfidence. The more confident the politician, the more convincing their case for war should be, regardless of the actual outcome of the war. It would make for an interesting study: are the wars that end up lasting far longer, or costing more lives and money than predicted, precisely the ones that have strong political support as evidenced by votes in the houses of government? Of course, the same might be true about wars that resulted in swift and decisive victories reflecting true confidence rather than overconfidence. This would demonstrate both the confidence bias and how overconfidence could hack into this bias.

The lack of evidence for WMD is not the only reason that the Iraq War is assessed so negatively. While the US and the UK might well have defeated Saddam Hussein, one of the major criticisms is how underprepared both countries were for dealing with the aftermath. This can be another measure of overconfidence during wars. The focus is on victory, so there is often little discussion on how to manage the situation after a leader is deposed.

The journalist and speechwriter James Fallows wrote incisively about this for *The Atlantic*[27] on the eve of the invasion of Iraq in 2002. Through interviews with several experts on foreign policy, the Middle East and the army, he laid out all the non-military areas that would be of prime importance after the initial invasion of Iraq. These included refugees and relief, police control, manpower and intelligence, forming a government and territorial integrity. The experts he interviewed also warned of the possibility of political instability due to a lack of leadership after Saddam Hussein was deposed, infrastructural responsibilities, post-conflict reconstruction efforts, 'a humanitarian crisis' and a 'bloody civil war'. It was obvious that the US would effectively have to govern Iraq for a long while, with at least an estimated 75,000 soldiers to maintain law and order. Fallows even highlights this in the title of his article, calling Iraq the 'Fifty-first American State'. This was evidently an endeavour that would demand a lot of the US, and advocates of the invasion of Iraq had to be highly optimistic or ignoring the consequences. Importantly, Fallows states that, amongst the people he interviewed, 'the strongest advocates of pre-emptive attack, within the government and in the press, had neither served in the military nor lived in Arab societies'. This seems to have suggestions of the Dunning-Kruger effect, where people with experience were more realistic in their predictions compared to non-experts. In the First World War, a related sentiment was more pithily encapsulated by the phrase 'lions led by donkeys', highlighting the bravery of soldiers and the incompetence of leaders.

Fallows's article and others like it from before the invasion have turned out to be prescient. The situation in Iraq turned out exactly as several experts had argued it would be, with a massive humanitarian crisis and widespread internal conflict. The US was eventually forced to increase its military presence in the country. In the end, its troops reached a peak of 170,300 in 2007, and had to remain in Iraq until December 2011. The withdrawal led to continued sectarian violence and political instability, including the rise of the Islamic State in the country. This, in turn, has led to further US involvement. On the fifteenth anniversary of the invasion, Iraqi-American author Sinaan Antoon wrote a poignant article about the aftermath of the war in the *New York Times*.[28] Despite growing up hating Saddam Hussein, he describes the legacy of the US invasion as leaving Iraq 'dysfunctional' as a 'corrupt semi-state'. He points out that an estimated million Iraqis have lost their lives and ends by saying, 'I never thought that Iraq could ever be worse than it was during Saddam's reign, but that is what America's war achieved and bequeathed to Iraqis.' The human costs of overconfidence and unshakeable certainty in our righteousness can be catastrophic.

The wars in Vietnam and Iraq point towards both the analyses of folly by Tuchman and positive illusions by Johnson. The examples and processes they described closely resemble the factors we discussed earlier when looking at how overconfidence is built up within individuals. It appears as if similar processes play out structurally on a national scale in wars. For instance, Johnson argues that positive illusions increase with decreasing verifiability. So, military personnel should have the least positive illusions, followed by local decision-makers, but politicians who are far from the field should have the most illusions. This closely resembles the optimism described by Fallows in his interviews during the build-up towards the Iraq War—people with military or foreign expertise were less optimistic than government officials far removed from the area. We've seen how lab-based tests of overconfidence repeatedly show a similar effect, where verifiability reduces overconfidence. Leaders with higher self-esteem will also tend to have greater optimism. Again, we've talked about how a subjective sense of power leads to greater overconfidence. In a later chapter, we'll discuss in further detail how this interacts with the very personality traits that might help you become a leader.

There are, however, some factors that are relevant both at the individual and the national scale. The first of these is the prevalence of informational biases. If you recall, this appears to be one of the foundational aspects of the psychology of overconfidence. Evolutionary biologist Robert Trivers and psychologist William Von Hippel implicate informational biases as the definitive mechanisms by which we deceive ourselves,[29] both about our own capabilities but also about the world around us. Experiments by these researchers show that we avoid information detrimental to our goals, focusing on information that will help us achieve them.

The analysis of war-time decision-making shows the same pattern—at least for political leaders. In her book, Tuchman only considers case studies as folly if the failed action was taken despite contemporaneous information available about its inadvisability. In fact, the action taken was typically in direct contradiction to recommendations for other less disastrous courses of action.

Tuchman repeatedly implicates what she calls 'wooden-headedness' in how governments respond to problems. They tackle problems beginning with preconceived notions and ignore any contrary opinions. For example, Tuchman demonstrates how the Lyndon Johnson administration persisted in an optimistic view of the Vietnam War, ignoring the preponderance of pessimistic intelligence reports and the estimates that further military troops would be required. This was despite no senior serving officers believing that the war could be won with the methods the US was then using. She further makes the point that, even if the US eventually did win the war, the government would still have hugely overestimated their capacity and underestimated how difficult the war would prove to be. In his book, Dominic Johnson also points out that, as information flowed from the battlefield to the president, it would have been skewed by the 'incremental optimism' of decision-makers at each level, until it might have been impossible for President Johnson to actually make a realistic assessment of the chances of victory or defeat.

A similar pattern can be seen in the build-up to the Iraq War, especially in terms of managing the aftermath of the invasion. James Fallows had a follow-up to his 2001 article in 2004 called 'Blind into Baghdad'.[30] In this article and a 2006 book[31] with the same title, he makes a clear case that the optimism about the post-war situation had led to many warnings being ignored and actively suppressed. An economic advisor, who made unfavourable estimates of the cost of the war from US$ 43 billion to US$ 93 billion, was forced to resign (the estimated cost of the Iraq War in 2013 was US$ 1.3 trillion). The optimism about post-war efforts was also based on the notion that the Iraqis would celebrate the removal of Saddam Hussein and look at the US troops as liberators. Even before the invasion, there were warnings that any such view would rapidly change into viewing the US as invaders. Nevertheless, the optimistic view persisted. Some former generals argue that this resulted in the army being understaffed to deal with the disruption that followed, despite warnings before the invasion that larger numbers of troops would be needed for exactly these reasons.

In *The Fog Of War*, McNamara says: 'We see what we want to believe.' Our goals are fundamental to how we process information.

But information biases can actually make us better at making arguments that convince others. For most politicians, the fundamental goal is arguably to get elected or re-elected. This surely influences their perceptions of an active war. Burns and Novicki's documentary series shows the extent to which elections dominated the thinking of successive presidents about the Vietnam War. For years, public support for the war was high, and no presidential candidate could hope to win an election standing on an anti-war plank. This could only have led to consistently optimistic declarations about the possibility of winning, even if this meant further commitment in terms of the number of troops sent in. Commitment to the war continued until public opinion became much more divided and escalating the war became an electoral liability. Only then did presidential candidates run on platforms of reducing involvement in the war—even if they still stopped short of declaring the war effort a failure.

We could argue that the declarations of optimism were purely electoral rhetoric and did not actually reflect deeply-held overconfidence. Both Tuchman and Johnson argue against this. Tuchman's analysis argues that the entire system appeared to fall prey to a form of 'self-hypnosis'. The greater the propaganda promoting the war and the commitment of troops, the more important it was for the US to actually win the war, and therefore, the more optimism was called for about the prospects of victory. This is the sunk-cost fallacy once again increasing the motivation for optimism. It also chimes perfectly with the description of self-deception put forward by Trivers and von Hippel. In his book, Johnson quotes Chester Cooper, a US diplomat, observing that the optimism reflected 'genuinely held beliefs' that the war would end soon, and that 'views to the contrary were not favourably received'.

It is important to highlight how information contrary to military (and political) goals is dealt with. Wars inevitably involve difficult choices, and the politicians of the time have to choose one path rather than the other. In hindsight, it might be easy to see which decisions were wrong, but how do we decide if those mistakes were due to overconfidence? I would suggest that a strong indicator for motivated cognition and an optimism bias is the suppression of contrary opinions. When advisors are sacked or experts excluded from decision-making simply for raising points that don't agree with the government's narrative, this fits the exact pattern by which our own brains filter feedback from the world. Such actions doubly reinforce overprecision. Firstly, they remove views that could provide a wider range of opinions which leaders can use to make their decisions. Secondly, they actively discourage others from disagreeing with important points in the future, easily leading to groupthink and a world of confirmation biases. This picture is strengthened when similar actions recur to reinforce errors in the same direction. This is the signature that can be observed through the examples of Vietnam, Iraq and beyond.

As discussed before, being buffered from the consequences of failure could exacerbate any biases towards overconfidence. Winning competitions by bluffing or cheating gives people as much confidence as a real victory, even if there has been no test of ability. This plays out during war as well. In military campaigns, this shows up when countries experience a string of victories. In some cases, such victories have led to overoptimism about future success and drastic moves that result in failure. When we discussed Germany's decision to break its truce with Russia and launch a military offensive earlier in this chapter, it was an example of overoptimism. In his book, Dominic Johnson shows how this was fuelled by previous victories, especially the victory over France, which led to Hitler ignoring contrary advice and proceeding with the assumption of an early victory. The same could also be said of Napoleon. History might be written by the winners, but it is the losers who learn its lessons.

When thinking of motivated cognition or information biases, it is important to distinguish between the individual leaders involved and the response of the countries. If a prime minister goes to war thinking of the next election, that's a perfectly rational selfish choice. They might potentially be overconfident about the benefits to the country, but they could be clear-eyed about the reasons for their choices.

Similarly, information could be skewed at every stage towards positive outcomes because the major is trying to please the colonel and the colonel's trying to please the general. Each person there is succeeding in their goals. Whether or not anyone is overconfident in this depends on how aware they are of their choices—something we'd be hard pressed to get at. But even when every person makes their choices knowingly, the net result is that everyone's errors align in the same direction, biasing how estimates are formed. What motivated cognition and information biases do is lead to systemic overconfidence. This, in turn, leads countries to disastrous defeats even as their leaders achieve the desired electoral outcomes. In many ways, this echoes exactly what our worst-case scenario suggested at the very beginning of the book.

As individuals, our overconfidence can be increased when combined with other biases and beliefs. We can trace similar patterns at the national stage during wars. Perhaps the most obvious of these is the role that racism might play in military overconfidence. Dominic Johnson and other commentators have made this point about the Russo-Japanese war of 1904–5. Despite suffering multiple defeats over the course of the war, Tsar Nicholas II was convinced Russia couldn't lose to Japan, partly because of assumptions of racial superiority. As a result, opportunities for armistices or treaties were ignored, and Russia suffered far greater losses than it needed to. Johnson's book also makes this point about overconfidence in the First World War, such as German attitudes towards the French, characterising them as weaker and inferior, and then going on to lose the war.

More recently, a belief in the superiority of Western civilisation could certainly have played a part in the outbreak of both the Vietnam and Iraq wars. Tuchman makes a subtler point about the domino theory that served to galvanise US involvement in Vietnam. She argues that this theory about the spread of communism throughout East Asia stemmed from a panic about the spectre of the 'Yellow Peril', and ignored the fact that each country in East Asia was unique. The idea that each of these countries would respond uniformly also stemmed from underlying Western biases that viewed them as the same based on ethnicity. She points out that, when these race-based biases were absent, the US supported Tito's communist regime in Yugoslavia without being similarly worried that all of Europe would turn communist. In addition, Kennedy insisted that the US could win in Vietnam where France failed, because the US was fighting for freedom, betraying a lack of self-awareness that their Vietnamese opponents would still view a war with the US as a 'White man's war'. It was also conveniently ignoring the fact that the US had earlier refused to help Ho Chi Minh when he had appealed to them for help against the French (as the Burns and Novicki documentary shows). Even later on, in the middle of the war in Vietnam, there was a strong sense that it would be impossible to lose to guerrillas in what Lyndon Johnson described as a 'fourth-rate country'.

If these examples are anything to go by, one prediction we might make is that wars are more likely to break out between countries of different races or ethnicities, especially if at least one of them perceives themselves as being superior. Furthermore, these wars would then last longer because the belief in superiority should create more positive illusions about ongoing military action and strengthen sunk-cost fallacies. In other words, if you're driven by a need to feel superior to your opponent, you are more likely to ignore information to the contrary and it will be more difficult for you to pull out of such a war without losing face. This might prove to be a difficult prediction to evaluate, though, as perceptions of superiority and what constitutes a different ethnicity have varied throughout history. Some potential evidence for this comes from studies of civil wars. Ethnic fractionalisation in a country doesn't by itself predict the duration of a civil war.[32] But wars that result from ruling governments socially excluding specific ethnic groups last longer.[33]

Could sexism also play a role in military overconfidence? A popular argument goes that the world would be more peaceful if we had women leaders. At first glance, if we put together two lines of research, this seems to be a possibility—the first showing that, on average, women are often less overconfident than men and, second, that overconfidence increases the likelihood of war. So having women in charge should reduce such a likelihood. Kittur Rani Chennamma and Rani Laxmibai might not look kindly on that assessment, but it definitely merits a direct and thorough research programme.

Certainly some examples—Indira Gandhi, Margaret Thatcher, Golda Meir—demonstrate that women leaders are no guarantee of peace and that they can lead effectively during wartime. So, might women leaders be more likely to go to war? And also more likely to win wars? All three of these leaders, however, were responding to external acts, rather than initiating wars. Perhaps this raises questions about whether female leaders are more likely to face aggressions because they are perceived to be weaker. Such a perception would have been proven wrong in these three cases. Gandhi and Thatcher decisively won the wars they were involved in, the 1971 war against Pakistan and the Falklands war, respectively. The third, Golda Meir, has been criticised for her handling of the early phase of the Yom Kippur war. Critics argue that she underestimated the likelihood of the war. On the basis of these three examples at least, women leaders can lead countries during wartime without overconfidence, at least in terms of achieving military gains.

There is also some evidence that, rather than the presence of a woman leader, higher levels of gender equality reduced the severity of violence used by a country during conflicts.[34] It would be interesting to see what patterns can be observed in a systematic study of women leaders, their likelihood of going to war and the success and duration of their military campaigns. In other words, how overconfident they are in comparison to male leaders. In the twentieth century, however, only twenty-four states had women leaders. Only four of these have led during military crises, so such patterns would be almost impossible to test systematically for modern times.

One paper has, however, addressed some of these questions for medieval Europe. In a paper, delightfully titled 'Queens',[35] Oeindrilla Dube from the University of Chicago and S.P. Harish at the College of William and Mary investigated Europe between the fifteenth and twentieth centuries.[36, 37] They looked at realms ruled over by women in this period, and asked if there was a greater or lesser likelihood of wars in these regions. They found that queens were actually more likely to go to war than kings. But it turns out that there's more to this finding. It matters whether the queens were married or not. If we look only at unmarried rulers, queens were more likely to be attacked than kings. Among married rulers, though, queens were more likely to attack others than kings. One interpretation of the first result is that the unmarried queens were perceived as weaker, and were therefore attacked more often. This seems to illustrate a potential role for sexism playing a part in medieval wars. Centuries later, when talking about Indira Gandhi during the 1971 Indo-Pakistan war, President Yahya Khan of Pakistan said, 'If that woman thinks she is going to cow me down, I refuse to take it.'[38] He also stated that his response would have been less violent if the Indian leader had been male. Sexist assumptions inform conflicts in modern times too.

One explanation for the results about married queens is that marriage was used to secure new alliances. This enabled queens to share the division of labour with their spouses, which placed them in stronger positions to attack others. Given the gender norms of the centuries studied, kings would have been less likely to similarly involve their spouses, thus leading to fewer military ventures and potentially fewer gains through war. It's worth noting that these results depend on the gender norms of the age. Gender norms might well play a role in what kind of women leaders get elected to power in modern times as well. A 2018 US survey shows that women politicians are perceived as weaker on defence and national security.[39] Perhaps women leaders might, therefore, end up being more ideologically conservative and hawkish about wars to compensate for these perceptions.[40]

A third important bias, which has historically played an important role in wars, is religiosity. Knowing that you have the gods on your side could well do wonders to boost your belief that you will win a war. It could also enhance your certainty that a war is just and deserves to be fought. The problem with religious wars is often that both sides might believe that God is on their side—sometimes even if it is the same God that both sides believe in. Overconfidence is likely to be widespread in such wars. As with wars between different ethnicities, wars between opponents with strong religious convictions and differences should also last longer. The Crusades, with their duration of about four centuries, constitute a classic example. The Thirty Years War in Europe, between Catholics and Protestants, and the later conflicts of the Anglo-French wars also involved participants divided on religious lines. Modern times aren't immune to religious conflicts and divides either. The Sri Lankan civil war, which lasted about twenty-five years, had opponents who differed both ethnically and religiously. The war in Iraq was explicitly linked to religious beliefs, with then US president George Bush stating that the invasions in Afghanistan and Iraq were 'a mission from God'.[41]

The lessons for Duryodhana from the Mahabharata and Paris from the Iliad, it would appear, are still relevant for the rest of us. Overconfidence leads to failed military campaigns, longer conflicts, ever increasing costs, growing loss of life and disastrous aftermaths. Biases and prejudice have their part to play as do the motivational goals of our leaders. The privileging of constant positive estimates and feedback over negative information traps us in a feedback loop of positive illusions, which are only bolstered by the sunk-cost fallacy. Countries and leaders work towards their goals rather than acknowledging facts, but the rush to war also places the rest of us at the centre of a conflict of our own. Dominic Johnson puts it best: 'The question remains where duty lies: to loyalty or to truth?'

ELEVEN

Pandemics Don't Bluff

WHAT USE IS OVERCONFIDENCE IN A HURRICANE? WEATHERMAN Michael Fish is famous in the UK for his error about the Great Storm of 1987.[1] Mocking the idea that a hurricane could hit the UK, he reassured viewers that they had nothing to fear. When the storm did hit, it killed eighteen people and resulted in damages costing UK£ 1 billion. During wars, as we have seen, overconfidence could possibly help a leader. With other kinds of disasters, though, overconfidence cannot pave the way to victory. Nuclear fallout does not care about bluster, rhetoric will not stop a pandemic. Yet, the same biases we have been talking about in the context of war also occur during other calamities.

The podcast *Cautionary Tales*, hosted by the economist Tim Hartford, is a veritable catalogue of such overconfident disasters. The episode called *That Turn to Pascagoula*[2] talks about Hurricane Katrina. In September 2004, New Orleans faced a major disaster as another hurricane, Hurricane Ivan, threatened to blow through the city. But it turned away at the last minute and the city was spared. You might think that this served as an early warning that should have left the city well prepared when Hurricane Katrina arrived in 2005. Yet, as Hartford argues, near misses can actually have the opposite effect—in this case, Ivan confirmed the idea that the storms always take the 'turn to Pascagoula', a city in the neighbouring state of Mississippi. For some, this reduced the fear of future storms. As we have seen before, initial success can leave you unprepared for future failures.

Overconfidence and unrealistic estimates have also been implicated in other disasters.[3] Take the 1986 Chernobyl nuclear accident.[4, 5] Warnings from the KGB in 1979 about the possibility of accidents at the nuclear plant were ignored. A smaller accident in 1982, which led to radiation release, was covered up. Even after the incident, the Soviet Union denied that it had occurred, and subsequently downplayed its scale. Citizens were not told to stay indoors, and a May Day parade was allowed to take place a week after the accident. This sequence of events makes a strong case for information avoidance, denial and self-deception building up to overconfidence that an accident wouldn't occur, and then, even after the accident occurred, that it wasn't serious.

Several other accidents serve as examples. The *Titanic* was famously hailed as being unsinkable, and had only twenty lifeboats (enough for 1,178 people). In fact, the number was cut down from thirty-two to reduce deck clutter. This meant that there weren't enough for everyone when disaster struck—there were 2,208 people on board—and the maximum capacity was actually 3,457 passengers and crew.[6] Self-deception and overcertainty have been implicated in plane crashes, where the certainty of pilots silenced the doubts of co-pilots.[7, 8] The loss of the *Columbia* and *Challenger* space shuttles have also been suggested to have been influenced by overconfidence.[9] The physicist Richard Feynman, who was part of the investigating commission into the *Challenger* disaster, concluded his findings by saying, 'For a successful technology, reality must take precedence over public relations, for nature cannot be fooled.' A telling remark that points towards how biases begin to operate once we are working towards a decided-upon goal. The goal could, for example, be to present a successful front to the public. But optimising for this could end up compromising other, more important goals, such as safety. These examples show how informational biases are particularly salient in disasters. Another reminder of our worst-case scenario.

The importance of overcoming our biases in favour of good policies is something that many of us saw play out on our screens in 2020. The COVID-19 pandemic overturned what we thought of as normal life, changing how we relate to each other, and exposing the strengths and weaknesses of governments. It also showed us the utter futility of boastful posturing in the face of a calamity. In this, it is the perfect example of the failures of overconfidence in the face of natural disasters. In what ways then could overconfidence have played a part in the pandemic?

A good starting point is the relative preparedness of different countries for a pandemic. Underfunded or poorly structured healthcare systems represent a form of overconfidence. A country that doesn't bother to fix its healthcare system when it can afford to do so is effectively betting against the possibility of a pandemic-style medical emergency. When one does arrive, these countries would thus be underprepared. Writing in the *Atlantic* magazine, Ed Yong makes a scathing critique of the US response to the COVID-19 pandemic.[10] He points out that, despite spending impressive amounts on healthcare, the system has no incentives in place to prepare for pandemics. The pressures on hospitals meant that they weren't prepared for an emergency that would last for months.

Even when plans for a pandemic are in place, things can go wrong if they lack funding or active implementation. The UK actually had an emergency plan specifically for pandemics. But after years of cuts to the health budget, the planned-for emergency protective equipment was no longer up-to-date or available in the necessary quantities in 2020.[11] Training for pandemics had also not been prioritised. In fact, in 2016, after the last rehearsal for a pandemic was run, the highlighted areas of concern included intensive care ventilators and protective equipment, items that were in short supply when the COVID-19 pandemic hit the UK.

A key element that we know reinforces overconfidence is lack of feedback. It's hard to be perfectly ready for a pandemic when you don't know what to expect. It is in these uncertain areas that cognitive biases can kick in. The availability bias ensures that we make use of what we are most familiar with to form our estimates. So, it was perhaps to be expected that the first point of comparison for many countries was a disease that they encountered more regularly. In many Western countries, this bias could have been what led to people thinking of the new virus as something like the flu. This, in turn, led to lowered risk assessments and a slower response. For a lot of countries in Asia, however, the recent experience of the SARS epidemic meant that they took rapid action against the new virus from the outset. They were quicker to respond and better prepared for the COVID-19 pandemic. Even China, which bore the brunt of the initial emergence of the virus, managed to contain it through aggressive measures and quarantining cities. Memories of SARS meant that these countries didn't stop at telling their citizens to wash their hands and not touch their faces.

COVID-19 was first identified in China in December 2019. By 30 January 2020, the World Health Organization had declared it a public health emergency of international concern. Yet, across Europe and the US, it took months before strict rules on flights and quarantine were in place. Within Europe, Italy was the first country to be hit badly. This could have provided other European countries another warning. Once again, countries differed in the speed with which they brought in stricter measures. One measure of how complacent countries were could involve measuring when their lockdown measures came into place. The speed with which countries imposed lockdowns turned out to be vital in reducing the number of deaths.[12] We can see this by looking at the number of deaths in 2020, and comparing that to the average for previous years. The percentage increase (or decrease) gives us a measure of excess deaths that can be attributed to the pandemic. For example, Austria imposed their lockdown on 16 March, when there was a single death attributed to COVID-19 in the country, and had a peak excess death toll of 14 per cent in the initial wave of the pandemic. The Netherlands, which waited until its excess death toll was 17 per cent before initiating a lockdown, reached a peak of 74 per cent excess deaths. This pattern appears true across the world. An analysis by the *Financial Times* shows that the countries that imposed lockdowns when only a few cases of COVID-19 had been reported were the ones that had the lowest levels of excess deaths.[13] Countries like Chile or Germany, which imposed their lockdowns with less than 300 cases per million people had less than 100 excess deaths per million people. Countries like the UK and Spain, that only locked down when the number of cases exceeded 3,000 per million, had a peak number of excess deaths that were close to 1,000 per million. Based on public statements in the UK at least, one element that could have contributed to the delay might well have been governments being underconfident that people would comply with the restrictions of lockdowns. Of course, interventions like lockdowns, including travel restrictions, isolations, social distancing and quarantines, have now been shown to be effective at reducing the spread of the disease.[14, 15] One study[16] of six key countries (including China and Italy) argues that, in just these countries, the interventions prevented around 450 million infections. It was the countries that delayed embracing these interventions that were hit the hardest.

One reason countries might have been reluctant to lock down was the perceived impact this might have on the economy. This debate raged early in the course of the pandemic. Sweden is a good example to look at in this context. Compared to other European countries and especially other Scandinavian countries, Sweden chose to pursue a unique response to the pandemic with far less stringent restrictions on movement and businesses. Scientists who criticised this policy have faced a strong backlash, not the best indicator of good policy.[17] As might be expected, this resulted in a high number of cases and deaths. The number of deaths in the first half of 2020 was the highest tally in Sweden for a comparable period of time in 150 years.[18] The number of deaths as a proportion of the population was six to twelve times higher than that in other Scandinavian countries. Excess deaths reached a peak that was 46 per cent more than other years.

So, did keeping the country more open keep the economy in good shape and reduce economic hardship? The data indicates otherwise.[19] The unemployment rate in Sweden increased from 7.1 to 9 per cent between March and May 2020, and the economy contracted by about 4.2 percentage points in 2020[20]. However, other Scandinavian countries had similar contraction in their economies, between 2.4 (Norway)[21] and 4 (Denmark)[22] percentage points. The unemployment rate in Denmark increased from 4.1 per cent to 5.6 per cent between March and May 2020. This seems to suggest that while a less restrictive lockdown led to greater spread of the disease, it did not help Sweden's economy fare considerably better than its neighbours'.

A recent analysis of the 1918 flu pandemic in the US[23] also shows that cities that locked down earlier and with more restrictions didn't do worse economically. In fact, they potentially grew faster after that pandemic. An article in the *Financial Times* during the first part of the current COVID-19 pandemic cites a study that shows related results.[24, 25] In general, countries with the highest levels of excess deaths per million, like the UK and Spain, also show the highest loss to their GDP in mid-2020. With some exceptions, countries like South Korea, Norway and Indonesia, with fewer deaths, also have a lower forecast GDP loss. If the interventions that prevent excess deaths also help the economy, delaying or diluting the interventions seems misguided.

Perhaps even more importantly, countries could have prepared for the pandemic by ensuring they rapidly developed testing systems and an adequate supply of ventilators, protective clothing and equipment. In fact, South Korea shows us that a rigorous testing and isolation policy could work to combat the spread of the pandemic even without an internal lockdown. Germany's success (within Europe) in testing and tracking the spread of the virus is also credited with giving it relatively better control over the pandemic.

In the UK, a damning report in the *Times*,[26] indicted the government for not taking these issues seriously enough, despite several of these points being brought up in advisory meetings. The first case of local transmission of the virus in the UK was on 29 February 2020. By then, the severity of the virus was known from China as well as the fact that drastic measures might be needed in response. By mid-March, the World Health Organization was urging countries to test. The UK had time to prepare on a variety of fronts—including testing, contact tracing and ensuring the supply of ventilators and protective equipment. Instead, on 12 March, the response actively moved away from testing and recommended self-isolation.[27] Ironically, the UK was one of the first countries to develop a test, but then proceeded to test much less than other countries. Comparisons with South Korea and Greece show that the lack of early intensive testing, isolation procedures and PPE added to the UK's failings.[28, 29, 30] Lack of proper testing was a problem for the US as well. The fifteenth case of COVID-19 in the US was reported on 14 February. Three weeks later, only about 10,000 tests had been carried out in a population of 328 million.[31] Without adequate testing, there was no way to effectively carry out contact tracing and local isolations. President Trump nonetheless insisted that testing was going smoothly. Meanwhile, in the UK, the government provided televised reassurances that the testing system was 'world-beating'. A reminder to all of us that repeatedly stating something and wanting fervently for it to be true does not make it so.

In contrast, other countries like Senegal, Bhutan, Vietnam and South Korea heeded the warnings. Senegal began preparing contingency plans when COVID was declared an international public health emergency in January.[32] It went on to increase testing capacity by using mobile labs and turning hospitals into quarantine facilities. As of September 2020, it had less than twenty deaths per million due to COVID-19. Bhutan put in place a response plan as early as 11 January and started screening passengers for possible symptoms from 15 January.[33] It went on to have strong quarantine and tracking policies, and as of February 2021 had a single death from COVID-19. Vietnam shares a border with China, and has a population larger than Germany. One might expect it to have a high casualty rate as the pandemic spread. Instead, it took the threat seriously early on. Its emergency plan came into action on 23 January, when the first case was reported in the country.[34] Travel restrictions, border checks, an extensive testing programme and contact tracing were rapidly initiated. Importantly, it also communicated well with the general public through public health advertisements and even SMS messages. The result: as of September 2020, the country had still to document a single death from COVID-19. South Korea also started on its plan early—on 2 February, when it registered its fifteenth confirmed case.[35] Tests were available within a week. In another couple of weeks, large gatherings were banned and public spaces were closed. An intensive testing campaign was mobilised, and about 10,000 people were tested each day.[36] Here too, deaths due to COVID-19 are low: around 7.1 per million people.

The onset of the pandemic was an uncertain time. Information could be conflicting and insufficient to make clear decisions. Several unknowns about the virus remain to this day. Is it fair then to indict governments as being overconfident for their failures? Scientists were also not free from error. In March 2020, the World Health Organization was quick and confident in its assessment that the disease was not airborne.[37, 38] It took them until December 2021 to acknowledge that error. As with wars, errors and incompetence can explain failures, but not all incompetence is overconfidence.

One approach is to use the overblown statements of politicians (or scientists) as an indicator. As with CEOs, perhaps developing an index of language used by leaders, or about them, could form a measure of overconfidence.

Observing how governments respond to developments and news that don't fit their plans or statements can be more revealing. The surest signs of overconfidence would be the same ones that fuel our individual overoptimism—repeated missteps in the same direction and a refusal to take on board bad news. If we take this as our starting point, we can trace the thread of overconfidence throughout the pattern of the pandemic. In fact, not only did governments ignore inconvenient facts, they actively took action against the bearers of bad news. Whether this was to prioritise economic interests or to save face, individuals in power might have had their reasons. Yet, even if they were not themselves self-deceived, the result is a failure to avert a disaster. So, at the very least we can say that, when the powerful penalise negative reports, it's an easy route to systemic overconfidence.

At the very beginning of this story is the Chinese response to the pandemic. The response was eventually rapid and stringent, but several people have pointed out that, in the earlier stages, the government played down the idea that the virus was being transmitted. In fact, doctors who tried to put out warnings were threatened. In what is now the most famous case, Dr Li Wenliang, who made several public and insistent warnings about the virus, was detained by the police and forced to stop.[39, 40] The police also warned other doctors in Wuhan who were discussing the virus to stop. Li would later go on to die from COVID-19, and his death sparked a swell of support and anger amongst Chinese citizens on social media.[41] He was hailed as a whistle-blower about the virus, and was eventually cleared posthumously of any criminal wrongdoing. Meanwhile, the refusal to listen to his warnings and the suppression of negative reports exacerbated the widescale spread of the virus.

Some commentators have argued that this was a symptom of the authoritarian style of the current Chinese government. Could there be a link between government style and pandemics? A graph in the *Economist*[42] suggests that there is. Over the past sixty years, epidemics have been less deadly in democracies, especially for countries with a greater GDP per person. Yet, as we can see in Vietnam, you don't need to be a democracy to take the threat of a pandemic seriously. In the current pandemic, it certainly seems like the suppression of inconvenient truths or politically contradictory voices has been a hallmark of countries around the world, democracies or otherwise. And the evidence for overconfidence in several countries is demonstrated right at the top.

In Brazil, President Bolsonaro was utterly incautious about the prospects of catching the disease.[43] He didn't wear masks and attended mass rallies, proudly shaking hands with multiple people. He stated that the virus is not a threat to healthy people and compared it to a flu or a cold.[44] Later, he urged the country to return to normal, calling social distancing 'mass confinement'. By every measure, Bolsonaro refused to take the threat of the pandemic seriously, endangering his own health as well as that of supporters at his rallies. It gets worse. He railed against lockdowns implemented by state governors. When the Brazilian health minister, Luiz Mandetta, disagreed with him about his opposition to health warnings, Bolsonaro went on to fire him.[45] That minister's successor also clashed with Bolsonaro over his stance on the pandemic and left within a month. He was then replaced with a successor who had no healthcare experience.[46] The health ministry removed data detailing the spread of the pandemic in the states.[47] It also stopped providing a count of confirmed COVID-19 cases in the country. The intolerance of dissenting views, the shredding of transparency and the wilful disregard for warnings makes for a perfect recipe for overconfidence in the face of an emergency. The result of Bolsonaro's irresponsible and foolhardy pandemic response: the death toll towards the end of March 2021 was 303,462 or 1,438 deaths per million people.

In the United Kingdom, Boris Johnson was 'shaking hands with everybody' during a hospital visit,[48, 49] saying that the virus would not stop him. His government's pattern of resisting lockdowns seems to reflect repeated behaviour biased in a particular direction. In particular, during the second wave, despite expert opinion, repeated calls by the opposition and clear warnings from the first wave, Johnson's government resisted putting in place a national lockdown for weeks. The second wave of the pandemic, when it came, hit the country far worse, aided no doubt by the presence of a new variant. Travel restrictions that could have contained some of the variants were only brought into place about a year into the pandemic, and were still laxer than in many countries in the world.

President Trump in the United States also responded similarly.[50] He didn't wear face masks in public, urged organisations to continue as normal and spent two months rejecting the views of experts, saying the virus would disappear 'like a miracle'. Later, he pushed unproven cures for the virus, including at one point suggesting that drinking bleach could help. Meanwhile, doctors and nurses who warned the media about shortages of masks or equipment lost their jobs.[51] When Dr Anthony Fauci, the director of the National Institute of Allergy and Infectious Disease, called for a more urgent and strict response, the government resisted his advice. Even soldiers were not immune to retaliation. Captain Brett Crozier, who argued for the safety of his sailors when more than a hundred of them tested positive for the virus, was relieved of the command of his aircraft carrier.[52] The United States never really suppressed the first wave of the pandemic, and in March 2021, had one of the highest death rates of any country, with around 1,659 deaths per million people.

India has a different story to tell. While the death rate (as in, deaths per million) was not as high as several Western countries, it had one of the highest number of deaths due to the pandemic. During the first wave, India did impose a lockdown admirably early, and strong restrictions on travel were put in place. In fact, the lockdown was one of the most severe in the world. It was criticised for the lack of a wider consultation with public health experts and for insufficient financial support for workers,[53, 54] but it was also credited with saving lives. As the course of the pandemic continued, after an initial rise in cases for months, the number of cases and deaths came down dramatically. Many explanations were proposed for this, including the suggestion that herd immunity had been achieved. Serosurveys, however, indicated that only about 20 per cent of the population had antibodies against the virus.[55] In fact, people in the age group forty to seventy actually had a high death rate even in the first wave, comparable to several other countries. The notion of herd immunity was a source of false optimism.[56, 57]

This perceived decline in cases might have led to a specific sort of systemically overconfident response. During the period of declining case numbers, warnings about new variants and the shortage of hospital beds and oxygen were ignored.[58, 59] The national scientific task force on COVID-19 held no meetings between 11 January and 15 April 2020. Temporary hospitals were dismantled and the treatment protocol for COVID was not updated after July 2020. Meanwhile, rules about social activities were relaxed. People were allowed access to pubs, cinemas, religious gatherings, election events and other large public gatherings. This aided the accelerated spike in cases in March 2021, resulting in the second wave of the pandemic. The second wave proved to be disastrous, with the death rate rocketing upwards, fuelled by new variants of the virus as well as a lack of hospital beds and oxygen. This is the 'turn to Pascagoula' phenomenon—escaping disastrous consequences leads to overconfidence about future possibilities.

Consider these overblown statements before the second wave. At the World Economic Forum in January 2021, Prime Minister Modi declared that India had saved humanity. His party passed a resolution praising him, saying that India had defeated Covid under his 'able, sensitive, committed and visionary leadership'.[60] In March 2021, the health minister, Harsh Vardhan, declared that India was in the 'endgame' of the pandemic,[61] and insisted even in late April 2021 that the death rate was one of the lowest in the world.

Unlike the first wave, where action was taken, in the second wave, there was a resistance not only to implementing restrictions but even to facing the facts. These are classic signs of informational biases that could lead to systemic overconfidence. Data from cremation grounds and mathematical models pointed to the fact that the official count severely underreported the number of deaths.[62, 63] The chief minister of Uttar Pradesh reportedly said that there was no scarcity of oxygen in the state, and asked administrators to take action against hospitals that complained about an oxygen shortage.[64] The Union government even went on to quash court orders favouring restrictions and lockdowns. In Uttarakhand, a chief minister who advocated hosting the Kumbh Mela in a limited capacity, following safety rules, was replaced.[65] All in all, the overconfidence of leaders cost the country dearly. In the first week of May 2021, there were over 3,000 deaths every day—and that is on the official record.

Newspaper articles have indicted several other countries, from Nicaragua to Belarus, that show patterns of denial. In Mexico, the government put out posters saying the virus was not serious. In Turkmenistan, there are reports of people being arrested for discussing the pandemic. In Tanzania, President John Magufuli declared that god had eliminated COVID and dismissed vaccines as a priority. The Brazil-based political scientist Oliver Steunkel coined a term that perfectly encapsulates the response of several of these world leaders—he called them the 'ostrich alliance'.[66] An apt metaphor for how the brain of an overconfident optimist deals with bad news.

One factor common to all these countries is that they are all led by men. Could male overconfidence have made all the difference? If overconfidence contributed to the pandemic death toll, we should expect better news in countries run by women leaders. How did these countries fare?[67] Much has been made of Germany's response at the onset of the pandemic. Angela Merkel, the chancellor of Germany, certainly took the virus seriously and launched an extensive testing programme. Compared to several other countries in western Europe, Germany initially did better, but the death toll in Germany is still high compared to countries in Asia. Tsai Ing-wen in Taiwan was amongst the first leaders to respond. She introduced measures to block the virus as early as January, pre-empting the need for a complete lockdown. Taiwan would go on to assist the US and Europe by exporting face masks to them. Jacinda Arden in New Zealand also brought in self-isolation for entrants to the country early, when there were only six cases in the country. Foreigners were banned from entry soon after. Prime Minister Katrin Jakobsdottir in Iceland provided free testing to all its citizens. The comprehensive tracking system meant that schools were not shut down and the country did not need to lock down. All of these countries have had far fewer deaths in the first wave of the pandemic than their neighbours, with the last three having less than fifty deaths per million citizens in total.

Are these cases evidence of a clear pattern? Would the pattern hold up in a more in-depth study? As it happens, we do have evidence from exactly such a study.[68, 69] Supriya Garikipati and Uma Kambhampati from the universities of Liverpool and Reading set out to look at measures of public health in countries during the first quarter of the pandemic, and whether they were different in countries led by women and men. They looked at data from 193 countries up to 19 May 2020. The number of deaths due to COVID-19 in male-led countries were almost double the number in female-led ones. However, of all these countries, only nineteen were led by women and 174 were led by men. Clearly, there was an imbalance here that made it difficult to compare them. To address this, Garikipati and Kambhampati matched each female-led country with a nearest neighbour. They used demographic and economic measures such as GDP and population—factors that would be important contributors to the spread of COVID-19—to match up these neighbours. Comparing these matched countries was revelatory. Female-led countries did better on several fronts. They locked down earlier and, most importantly, they had fewer deaths. For instance, New Zealand had about 1,500 deaths less than Ireland; both countries have populations less than five million. Bangladesh, led by Sheikh Hasina, had about 2,000 deaths less than Pakistan; both countries have a population greater than 150 million. Perhaps more strikingly, Germany had 30,000 less deaths than the UK. Even if the major countries that have been in the news—the US, Germany and New Zealand—were excluded from the analysis, the results still held.

Interestingly, since the World Bank, a major source of the data, doesn't cover either Taiwan or Hong Kong—both led by women—these were not included in the study. Including them would only strengthen the results, as both performed well through the pandemic. At least two other studies focusing on a lower number of countries also found similar results.[70] Women-led countries had fewer deaths and a more rapid 'flattening of the curve'. Only one major study found that differences in testing or the rate of spread of the disease was not statistically different between countries led by women or men.[71] Even here, the trend was still in the same direction.

How do we make sense of this? Does this confirm our initial hypothesis that women, being less overconfident, make more sensible leaders? Perhaps. Another way of looking at this is that women leaders were more risk averse when lives were in danger, but could be seen as more willing to take risks with the economy by imposing strict lockdowns. In addition, perhaps it isn't the leaders alone who had strong responses to the pandemic. Countries that are willing to elect female leaders might already have an ethos that lends itself well to taking pandemics seriously.

It's also worth thinking of other suggestions from psychological studies of overconfidence and what hypotheses they could suggest. One possibility is that there are differences in national cultures of overconfidence. We discussed how studies that compared countries across the world found less overconfidence in people from East Asian countries, at least on specific skill-related tasks. It is tempting to see the successful response to the pandemic in Vietnam, Taiwan, Singapore and South Korea as vindication of the idea that the cultures in these countries do reflect a better, less overconfident attitude to governance. We don't know this for certain, of course. What we'd need is a more detailed study building in a variety of factors to confirm this hypothesis.

An opinion piece in the science journal *Nature*[72] made a case for the study of 'hubris' as a factor influencing national responses to the pandemic. In particular, the article argued that studying how strong a country's exceptionalist view of itself was would prove fruitful to our understanding of the spread of the virus. A research article in the journal *Lancet Planetary Health*[73] also provides evidence that countries with more 'permissive' cultures had greater death rates during the pandemic compared to those with 'tighter' cultures. The degree to which citizens identify with their country also predicted support for the public health policies and greater physical distancing during the pandemic.[74] The role of national cultures in the pandemic response is an aspect that could certainly be studied more.

Garikipati, one of the authors of the study comparing men and women leaders, makes an important point. She acknowledges that their study covers only an early period of the pandemic,[75] and the final word would need to wait until after we reach the end of the pandemic. This caveat is an important one. The effect on the economies of countries would be something we might only see several years after we control the pandemic and learn how to fight it. All of this no doubt relies on both the culture of countries and our everyday individual actions. Do we follow the government's rules? Do we perceive risks as less or more than they really are? Perhaps far more than individual action, the results depend on how our leaders approach crises and what kind of leaders we elect—the clearheaded premiers or the visionary blowhards. These leaders and us, the people who elect them to power, are what we turn to next.

TWELVE

Politicians and Partisans

THE PHOTO WAS TAKEN AT ST LOUIS UNION STATION, MISSOURI. A passenger on his way to Washington, D.C. has just stepped off the train onto the platform. It's a portrait in black-and-white. The passenger is slightly off-centre, suited and bespectacled. He is holding up a newspaper—the *Chicago Daily Tribune*—and his face is lit up with a wide-open grin. The date on the paper is 3 November 1948. The headline is one of the most notorious in print history: 'Dewey Defeats Truman'. The man holding the newspaper is the newly re-elected president of the United States: President Harry Truman, only too happy to oblige journalists with this iconic photo of him triumphing over pre-emptive reports of his defeat.

But that infamous headline wasn't the only one making the wrong call. Throughout the election, every poll indicated that it was 'inevitable' that Thomas Edmund Dewey would win the election by 333 seats to Truman's eighty-two, that he would sweep twenty-seven, maybe even thirty, of the fifty US states.[1,2] There was trouble brewing in Truman's Democratic Party.[3] His moderate approach to civil rights had caused his support to be split, with liberals in the party calling for far more sweeping changes and more conservative Democrats remaining unappeased, wanting to add amendments to his platform. Things got heated enough that the conservative Democrats walked out of the convention, protesting Truman's stance on civil rights. The party fragmented even further. A third party was formed in early 1948—the Progressive Party—splitting the Democratic vote. The Southern Democrats who opposed Truman formed a party of their own, the States Rights Democratic Party. They came to be called the Dixiecrats. The Democratic Party was, in other words, in utter disarray. It was easy to think its internal differences would be fatal to Truman's electoral chances.

Dewey's lead in the polls seemed impossible to overcome. Truman's campaign was strapped for cash and produced lacklustre campaign film reels. Even Truman's wife doubted her husband's chances. When the *Chicago Tribune*'s correspondent Arthur Hennig made his prediction, it was no wonder he thought the Republican nominee Thomas Dewey was unbeatable. In fact, several other famous columnists had their columns about Dewey's victory penned and ready for publication the next day.[4] *Life* magazine had photos with speculations about the Dewey presidency in its edition before the election. The *Manchester Guardian* published an article on election day that read 'Harry Truman: A study of a failure'. It wasn't just one paper that got it wrong. Almost the entire establishment, from the journalists to the pollsters to Thomas Dewey himself, was guilty of the same error. That error was, of course, overconfidence.

The 1948 US election and the *Chicago Tribune* might have gone down in history as the ultimate example of electoral overconfidence, but it is only the most cited one. In fact, in time it might be superseded by another, more recent one. Scenes from Michael Moore's 2018 documentary *Fahrenheit 11/9* tell the tale best. The opening segment lays down the scene before the 2016 US election. Over the course of the campaign, we see scenes of politicians, voters and journalists all supremely confident about the election of Hillary Clinton as the first woman president of the US. In one clip from a news channel, the very mention of President Trump ends up with everybody—guests and host alike—unable to suppress their laughter. It's a riveting clip in hindsight, because we know just how cruel history is going to be to everyone in it. Yet, few people did better in their predictions of the election results. The betting odds massively favoured a Clinton victory, and both Democrats and Republicans were confident of her win. To complete the echo of Dewey and Truman, a regional daily in Germany even prepared an edition on the morning of 9 November 2016 with the headline: 'Good Morning, Mrs. President!' (although, to be fair, they had prepared a headline for the alternative result too)[5]. Once again, our collective belief in a preordained political future was proven wrong. We don't even need to forget the past to be doomed to repeat it.

Other examples abound. In the 2004 Indian elections, the ruling National Democratic Alliance, led by the Bharatiya Janata Party, topped all the pollsters' predictions for victory. The BJP had just won four state elections. Buoyed by this success, they called elections six months early. The ultimate sign of their utter conviction was their slogan: 'India Shining'. In this, they were not only overconfident about being re-elected, they were overconfident about their performance in government and the state of the country.[6] Today, the slogan is perhaps best remembered for the mismatch in the image it projected with what people appeared to see around them. That mismatch would lead to the electorate punishing the ruling party and handing victory to the opposition: the United Progressive Alliance led by the Indian National Congress. The situation was perhaps reversed in the 2019 Indian elections, with several journalists predicting a reduced majority for the BJP. The party instead went on to win a massive outright majority, something that hadn't been seen for decades.

We could also cite one last example from more recent times—the Brexit referendum. As with the previous examples, all conventional wisdom and polling predicted a victory for the Remain campaign. Britain, everybody was sure, would vote to stay in the EU. Yet, as the results came in, the pollsters were left facing another unpredicted upset. It's striking that at least some Leave voters insisted afterwards that they only voted because they were sure they would never win but wanted to register a protest. The perception of a Remain victory was so strong that even some of those opposing it believed it.[7]

It's clear to see how strong a role overconfidence could play in elections. But can we use overconfidence to look at both elections and voters more systematically? Surely this should be possible, given the key role some theories give to overconfidence in social interactions. For example, we might naively predict that being overconfident is a good thing for a candidate's popularity. This is not what we see happening, though, certainly not in the US elections of 1948 or 2016. A closer look at the role of overconfidence could offer an explanation. In experiments where students were overconfident about their grades, classmates were correspondingly convinced of their higher intelligence. What if this idea were applied to someone running for elections?

The idea is that, if you were running for office in your country and were supremely overconfident about your victory, your very confidence would convince others of the same. Your supporters then would have less incentive to come out and vote for you, since you are going to win anyway. The reduced turnout could easily work against you if the race turned out to be closer than thought. There are also the classic ways in which overconfidence builds and reinforces itself. Confirmation biases and motivated cognition would flourish, and you might ignore evidence in the latest polls showing your lead slipping away. So, while the other candidates worked hard on their campaigns, your own might be a bit too complacent.

Here again, the Dewey-Truman race is a fascinating case study. As the anointed victor who only had to deal with the slight detail of elections, Thomas Dewey avoided anything controversial. His speeches were full of visions of unity and optimism, rather than issues that might have really mattered to voters. This left them in the end with what they might well have thought of as glorious nothings. Truman, on the other hand, toured extensively with passionate, evocative speeches, casting himself as the candidate who would go down fighting. Being an underdog strikes a chord with people, and large crowds gathered to hear him. 'Give 'em hell Harry,' they yelled. Truman's growing popularity should have been a warning sign to Dewey and his advisors, especially compared to Dewey's own dwindling crowds. Yet, in the end, they decided against a stronger fighting stance and chose to sit the election out, again potentially allowing the self-deception of innate biases to triumph over the ground data.

Similarly, in Clinton's 2016 campaign, critics have cited her team's decision not to focus more on so-called battleground states, like Wisconsin and Michigan, as a fundamental reason behind the electoral defeat.[8, 9] The campaign ignored several voices advocating precisely this, pointing towards overoptimism about victory in these states. Clinton, however, points out that she didn't ignore these states, and that decisions about campaigns were made when all the polling indicated that there wasn't much danger of her losing these states.[10] There's a case to be made then that, once again, it was systemic overconfidence that drove both the expectations and the efforts.

It's easy to single out these cases, but overconfidence could be widespread in campaigns across the board. Take the case of the staffers of US state campaigns, or those on Obama's 2012 presidential campaign.[11] These elections had high stakes, and the staffers would presumably have benefited from accuracy rather than optimism. Nonetheless, when predicting outcomes, they were three times more likely to predict better outcomes than those actually obtained. It is tempting to view this optimism as serving a more motivational function than a social-signalling function.

During the same campaigns, across the political spectrum, the general public were even more over-optimistic about their preferred candidates' vote share than the political staff—but only if they were affiliated to a particular party. Independent voters made predictions that were closer to being equally split between overconfidence and underconfidence. The difference between the general public and campaigners is particularly interesting because it suggests that when accurate predictions are more important to your job, as with political operatives, your predictions remain biased in favour of the preferred candidate, but you do get more accurate. Conversely, if you have fewer real stakes in the game (like the general public), you're freer to be inaccurate, which makes sense. It also suggests that overoptimism is stronger when you're invested in a candidate and affiliated to their 'group', another signature of overconfidence and the optimism bias.

Of all the campaigns, incumbent campaigns—the ones that were campaigning for re-election of a sitting candidate—were the most accurate in their predictions, and were occasionally even pessimistic about the size of their victory compared to the final result. In contrast, all campaigns that went on to lose, over-perceived how close the campaigns were, and expected an equal vote share as the winning party. Again, this seems to fit a motivational account of overconfidence; you need that extra shot of optimism when you are fighting a tough campaign. That optimism could also help convince operatives and voters that there still is a chance of victory. This could, in turn, help convince voters that races are closer than they really are, and get them out to vote.

If that's so, what type of campaign confidence actually motivates voters in close races? Todd Rogers and Don Moore looked at this in a range of ways, using archival records, field experiments and surveys.[12] Across these approaches, the results clearly demonstrate that people are more likely to vote, volunteer for and donate to campaigns when races are perceived to be close. This is even more true in the case of losing races. Campaigns do appear to use this to their advantage. Emails from campaigns that talk about how close the races are tend to emphasise that they are losing. It is the belief that they might lose, rather than overconfidence about winning, that helps motivate voters. In other words, underdogs have the motivational advantage, or as the title of the paper puts it, this is the 'motivating power of underconfidence'. In this light, both Clinton's campaign and the Remain campaign in the Brexit referendum had a problem from the very beginning.

Alright—so overconfidence in victory seems to benefit campaigns perceived to be losing. Let's shift focus to achievements now. The social function of overconfidence predicts that people who were self-deceived about their capabilities would be able to convince others about them. We should, therefore, expect politicians who oversell themselves and are full of bluster to be successful and have a faithful following. Their success could well be divorced from their actual achievements. In controlled experiments, overconfidence does lead to greater status, after all.[13] Several other results corroborate this pattern, especially among narcissists. Narcissists emerge as leaders in groups of unacquainted people, and are also rated as leaders by expert observers.[14] Narcissistic leaders do not, however, perform better at assigned tasks than other participants. Men seem to end up in leadership positions because they are more overconfident about their performance.[15] Perhaps this can explain why parties in India field men as their candidates rather than women. Men are, after all, more likely than women to be narcissists.[16] In the 2019 Lok Sabha elections, women did better than men, with an electoral success rate of 10.9 per cent compared to 6.4 per cent for men.[17] Yet, only about 10 per cent of the candidates were women. Of course, this could be because women had particularly high influence in the constituencies they were selected from rather than women being naturally better at elections. The true pattern can perhaps only emerge when the number of women and men selected are more comparable.

In the workplace, we've seen how overconfident people tend to be in leadership roles despite risky decision-making and poor performance. Overconfidence can mask stress during presentations to panels, and candidates are rated as having leadership potential based on their confidence rather than their competence. This was also true in the 2016 US primaries.[18] When candidates were perceived as being both confident and competent, voting intention for them was high. Yet, confidence influenced voting intention even for candidates who had low perceived competence. This fits the pattern of overconfidence leading to greater status and greater persuasion even in real-world settings.

There is no dearth of potential examples of this playing out in recent politics. When Donald Trump took office as the president, one of his major campaign promises was to repeal Obama's flagship Affordable Health Care Act. The bold promise was that it would be replaced by a new bill with 'insurance for everybody'.[19] Barely months into the presidency, the plan floundered and Trump was left declaring that 'nobody knew health care could be so complicated'.[20] Several others, including his opponent Hillary Clinton, certainly did, but evidently many voters preferred confidence, real or otherwise, over an honest assessment of complications. A similar bias towards believing bold statements might explain Donald Trump's reputation for being a good businessman despite multiple bankruptcies. Some of Trump's other major promises also proved unachievable, including the building of a wall between Mexico and the US (funded by the Mexicans). Yet, even as late as July 2019, the percentage of people approving of his performance was comparable to the percentage approving the performance of Obama or Reagan at a similar point in their presidencies.[21]

British politics is not far behind. Most British people now think that Brexit has gone badly.[22] We can also look at specific claims made during the campaign about the Brexit process and the state of the country just after the Brexit vote. For instance, claims of immediate economic instability after a leave referendum vote have not played out. Britain's economy was still growing, and unemployment continued to decrease immediately after the vote, although the value of the pound sterling declined. Similarly, claims that a leave vote would immediately lead to Scotland voting to leave the union have also not so far been borne out. In fact, from the Brexit vote to mid-2022, there appeared, for the most part, to be less support for Scottish independence.[23] These claims thus seem to be overly pessimistic and underconfident—the Leave side has often characterised the predictions of the Remain side as 'Project Fear'. Of course, how predictions of financial and political crises post Brexit stand up will depend on the still-unfolding future. Since the split from the EU came into effect, there are already stories of increased paperwork, large pile-ups of cars at the border in Kent and supply chain problems, leading some to suggest that Project Fear is now Project Here.[24]

Claims by the Leave campaign have not proved to be accurate either. In particular, claims about the ease of the Brexit process are now easily mocked. Billboards around Britain reminded us of Liam Fox's statement: 'The free trade agreement that we will have to do with the European Union should be one of the easiest in human history.' It stands in stark contrast to the difficulty of passing any sort of agreement through parliament. Other promises of a Brexit dividend for the NHS, or the swift signing of several trade deals before the country even left the EU have also not been fulfilled. You could, therefore, make a case that the Leave campaign was pretty overconfident about the immediate success of the Leave vote. Meanwhile, dissenting or moderating voices from judges to negotiators have been attacked, reinforcing a purely optimistic view of the future. Again it is this overconfidence (or optimism), rather than the pessimism of the Remain campaign, that seems to have won out. Another feather in the cap for the social advantages of being overconfident.

Perhaps the social influence of overconfidence could also explain the persistence of some politicians who fail upwards. Where you might expect failures at their jobs to lead to future difficulties, they go on to greater success. Boris Johnson, for example, seems to have had a bafflingly extended political career. As a journalist, he was fired twice, once for making up a quote and another time for a false assurance to the Conservative vice-chair.[25, 26] His term as Mayor of London was generally judged to be competent, but also involved expensive mistakes, including plans for a massive Garden Bridge that had spiralling costs and eventually fell through.[27] Now, there's a prime example of the planning fallacy not just extending a project but eating it up from the inside out. His term as foreign secretary did not cover him with glory either. Despite all these missteps, he went on to succeed Theresa May as the leader of the conservative party and the prime minister of the country. It's tempting to argue this was helped by his capacity for bold statements and optimistic promises.

Politics appears to be particularly susceptible to the charms of overconfidence. We've discussed how a bias towards overestimation and overplacement appear when the task or trait in question is less poorly defined or multiple measures of success are possible. This could surely apply to politics. There's also good reason to expect leaders to display overprecision, privileging excessive certainty over accuracy if that's what voters reward.[28] Measuring performance can be tricky. Good performance can be claimed on the basis of specific economic metrics, general well-being, cultural factors. It's easy to latch on to the one measure on which you are succeeding and trumpet that one. Most issues at stake for countries are complex, so it's easy to selectively focus on particular successes, while finding appropriate reasons for failures—that's the self-serving bias again. This would be true both for politicians and the people who vote for them. In addition, purely using electoral success as a measure complicates things. Electoral success is strongly dependent on social influence. So, overconfidence (which wins you social influence) will simply lead to further success. This means it wouldn't be perceived as overconfidence at all—it would simply be seen as an accurate confidence in success, regardless of actual performance.

It wouldn't be unreasonable at this point to ask if this isn't how things really should be. Perhaps the narcissists, charismatic charmers and bombastic leaders are what a country needs? They could even end up being the best dealmakers or figureheads that we could get. Is there really a reason to be wary of their overconfidence? Of course there is. The performance of overconfident leaders isn't better than that of people in laboratory studies.[29] They fail to spot deficiencies in plans and have overly positive expectations. In fact, lower levels of confidence were important to form effective plans. There is, however, one advantage to being overconfident. Overconfident people are the best at preparing inspiring and appealing vision statements—no wonder they win votes.

Fascinatingly, the overconfidence of politicians spills over even into politicians' estimates of their own chances at re-election. Let's look at actual members of parliament from Belgium, Canada and Israel.[30] As part of a study, these politicians were asked to estimate their likelihood of getting re-elected. They also had to provide responses to a question that measured risk-taking behaviour (overconfidence, we know by now, comes with risky behaviour). Politicians who were overconfident about being re-elected were twice as likely to choose the risky option. Could it be that the politicians who made risky choices had relatively safe seats? That doesn't hold up. An objective measure of how 'safe' the politician's seats were did not predict risky behaviour. It really was excessive confidence in getting re-elected that correlated with the politicians' risky behaviour.

These results pose a major challenge to the efficacy of electoral checks on politics. We might naively believe that the fear of losing an upcoming election might cause politicians to be more cautious. But that logic would not work if politicians are overconfident about their electoral success. Furthermore, corrections to overconfidence work with frequent and accurate feedback—as with the underconfidence-with-practice phenomenon we discussed earlier. Most politicians face only a few rounds of elections, each perhaps four or five years apart, and the results can usually be justified with ambiguous and unreliable reasons. With corrections like that, we can see how it might be difficult to change the risky behaviour of politicians, especially if being overconfident actually gives you electoral gains.

Overconfidence also biases how both politicians and the general public process information. We've seen that tasks or motivations help build up overconfidence because of the way they influence the search for information. It turns out that prior beliefs and attitudes can also influence how politicians make decisions. Take the case of a study[31] where Danish politicians were offered a choice between two organisations that supplied public services, either schools or road maintenance. One of the organisations was from the private sector and the other from the public sector. For every choice, the evidence unambiguously showed which of the two performed best. This should have been the one that the politicians chose. However, the results clearly showed a bias due to prior attitudes. Politicians who were pro-public sector were more likely to choose the public sector organisation and the reverse was true for politicians who were against it. When further information was provided that again supported one option over the other, the expectation was that the politicians would now make the right decision. However, the new information only helped increase correct choices when they were in accordance with the politician's prior attitudes. When prior attitudes conflicted with the right decision, the politicians were not more likely to make the right decision. The politicians were making decisions in spite of the evidence—a hallmark of overprecision as I've defined it in this book.

The limited effect of evidence on overconfident decision-making is exacerbated by another factor: power. People who are primed to feel powerful are more sure of their answers than people who are primed to feel less powerful, but their answers are more likely to be inaccurate.[32] People with more powerful roles at work make overconfident bets on their trivia knowledge, for instance, losing more money than people with less powerful roles. This was also true when participants in a study were randomly assigned the role of supervisor or production worker. In general, a feeling of power leads to increased optimism and downgrading perceptions of risk. These effects are similar to what we see in narcissistic behaviour. People who score high on the Narcissistic Personality Inventory are also overconfident in study tasks. In fact, when these participants are primed to feel powerful as well, this has an additive effect on the level of overconfidence.[33]

When combined with power, overconfidence leads to a greater discounting of advice.[34, 35] Once an initial decision is made, people tend to give greater importance to their own judgement and less to any subsequent advice and evidence. 'Good advice that you just didn't take,' sang Alanis Morisette. Isn't it ironic? No—it's overconfident. In the experiments investigating this, people were first assessed as powerful or not, based on their response on a scale. People assessed as powerful had increased confidence in their judgements and, as a result, were then rated by their co-workers as less likely to take into account other people's advice or reconsider their own opinion in the light of such advice. A similar pattern was seen even when people were simply primed to feel more powerful by being asked to recall a time when they felt powerful. People who feel powerful also appear to discount advice from both experienced and novice advisors. People who feel less powerful, by contrast, listen to experienced advisors, while correctly discounting advice from less experienced ones. This could be driven by the fact that powerful decision-makers view other experts with a competitive mindset.

Ignoring advice is also relevant to another characteristic of overconfident people—they persevere on a course of action they have decided on even when all the evidence suggests that it isn't a good one. In other words, an 'escalation of commitment'. We're all guilty of it. When things go wrong, your instinctual response is to justify the actions that led to it, even if you should really be correcting yourself. Perseverance is no bad thing for a leader to have, and the confidence to work through difficult times is definitely one of the character traits that we look for when we vote. However, when it is led by overconfidence, it could lead to obvious missteps and harmful policies. One study that compiled data from a large number of other studies found an important relationship between overconfidence and escalation of commitment.[36] This 'meta-study' concluded that overconfidence only leads to escalation of commitment in particular contexts—when the primary promises or decisions were made publicly. When these were made privately, on the other hand, people were more willing to take heed of evidence. This is obviously worrying in the context of politicians, who speak and act under intense public scrutiny. The very scrutiny that we expect to hold them to account would be what causes them to double down on their failing policies.

This could lead to a perfect storm of risky decision-makers. Narcissists are more likely to be overconfident. They are also more likely to seek power. Being self-deceived about their capabilities would help them convince others to actually appoint them to positions of power. Finally, the experience of power would lead to them feeling even more overconfident and taking more risks. This is particularly relevant at a time when authoritarian regimes or leaders with a tendency to centralise power are on the rise in several countries around the world. The belief in their confident rhetoric could lead to repeated electoral victories when the true measure of their abilities should be their success at governance. Leaders who centralise authority tend to limit their circle of advisors, and are far less likely to tolerate dissenting voices or advice. This often could lead to groupthink and sudden and dramatic policy moves, which might be ill-advised and harmful to countries.

Demonetisation—changing the notes or currency of a country—as the Indian government did in 2016, could be one such example. In countries such as Zimbabwe, Myanmar and the USSR, demonetisation led to slowed economic growth and national unrest.[37] The governments in question all had a high degree of centralised authority. In India as well, the decision was made rapidly in the face of advice against it, including by Raghuram Rajan, then governor of the Reserve Bank of India.[38] Several commentators have implicated that move in a fall in India's economic growth.[39, 40]

We could cite several other historical examples. Muhammad bin Tughlaq, the fourteenth-century ruler of Delhi, is now legendary for his combination of authoritarianism and rash decisions, including experiments with changing currency.[41] More recently, between 1999 and 2008, AIDS denialism in South Africa influenced President Thabo Mbeki's decision to not implement treatment programmes with antiretrovirals. That decision is estimated to have cost more than 330,000 lives.[42] Hitler expressed beliefs in an intuitive prediction of weather, and planned to recruit people with a sixth sense for it.[43] On his invasion of Russia, as the first snowfall began, German troops had not been issued winter clothing. Stalin's support for the unscientific theories of the agronomist Trofim Lysenko had dire consequences for crop failure in the USSR, and led to the persecution of other scientists.[44, 45] Mao's Great Leap Forward in China has been linked to an economic crash and millions of deaths as a result of famine.[46] Conversely, the economist Amartya Sen argues, famines do not occur in democracies because people are able to hold politicians to account.[47] That said, it was the democratically elected Sri Lankan government's rapid ban on chemical fertilisers in 2021 that has been implicated in drastic food shortages in the country.[48, 49]

There are counter-examples, where centralisation of authority in governments has led to successful countries—Singapore and present-day China are often cited as examples. One argument suggests that these two countries were never democracies, and it is the change from democracy towards centralised control that makes the difference in other countries such as Venezuela, Turkey and Hungary.[50] Support for the idea that authoritarian and non-inclusive governance is generally not beneficial can be found in the influential book *Why Nations Fail* by Turkish-American economist Daron Acemoglu and

British political scientist James Robinson.[51] In the book, they use case studies to argue that countries with more inclusive political and economic institutions are the ones that succeed. This pattern stays true on several measures, from economic prosperity to reduced infant mortality.[52]

Authoritarian overconfidence could even lead to the collapse of the authoritarian government itself. In 1975, India's prime minister Indira Gandhi responded to protests across the country by declaring a state of emergency and arrogating several powers to her own office. Over the course of the emergency, she established her authority by arresting opposition politicians and censoring the press. Having complete power perhaps led to her believing that she would win a majority if she called elections and legitimised her style of governance. Instead, the elections, called in 1977, led to a massive loss for her party, and she herself lost her seat. As the Russian-American journalist Masha Gessen puts it: 'Dictators fall when they're overconfident; they stay in power when they're paranoid.'[53] Combining these ideas appears to make it clear that, without vigilance and several checks and balances, most organisations and countries might end up with leaders who are narcissistic and overconfident—ready to take risks at home and abroad. Our worst-case scenario from the introduction is perhaps most dangerously at play in the world of politics.

All of this is troubling, but it might not make us question ourselves. It's easy to blame the politicians. In fact, it probably confirms what we've suspected all along. Certainly, in recent times, mistrust of politicians is high, and we wouldn't be surprised if they all turned out to be overconfident narcissists. But what about us, the voters? Are we certain our own political choices and decisions are any less overconfident? Of course we are certain. As certain as any overconfident person would be. To paraphrase a Kabir doha, you might search the world for faults, but take a look at yourself and you'll find there's nobody worse than you. To discover the truth about ourselves, let's turn to studies of voters and their attitudes, looking out particularly for overprecision. Think of those unending political arguments with friends and family members, where they insist they know the truth about immigration or taxes, even as you pull up the reports that prove them wrong.

The trouble is your friends and family aren't alone in their misperceptions. Most of us are often wrong on political issues. A survey from 2018 by the market research company Ipsos Mori provides us with data from thirty-seven countries that demonstrates this.[54] For example, people from some countries with high firearm usage, such as Colombia and the US, tend to underestimate the percentage of violent deaths due to firearms. People of all nationalities underestimate the level of sexual harassment in their countries, with people from Denmark, Netherlands and France having the least accurate estimates. Citizens of all countries overestimate the percentage of unemployed people in the workforce, and almost all of them greatly overestimate the number of immigrants in the country. People from some countries, Colombia, Peru and Brazil among them, believe that over 30 per cent of their country's population was born out of the country. The actual figure is less than 1 per cent! Similarly, people from all countries, except Turkey, overestimate the percentage of the population that is Muslim. It would be one thing if people were merely mistaken on these issues, with individual errors pointing in different directions. What is striking about this catalogue of errors is that they often point in the same direction across individuals and countries. Even without measures of confidence, there is a clear possibility of overprecision here. Politically salient topics, it would appear, are rife with misperceptions. How do they combine with overconfidence?

To begin with, both models of behaviour and actual empirical data shows that overconfidence in voters leads to them being more ideologically extreme.[55] More ideologically extreme voters, driven by overconfidence, are also more likely to vote. Overconfidence predicts voter turnout better than income, education or race. The move towards extreme views is driven by the fact that overconfident people are more likely to show what's called 'correlational neglect'. We're constantly getting information about politics, now more so than ever, and we're trying to figure out what's true and what's not. As we hear a fact over and over and from different sources, we're more likely to believe it. What we neglect is how these sources of information might be correlated. So, while we think we're getting information from different independent sources, they might all be influenced by the same limited number of sources, including information that we have passed on ourselves. That WhatsApp forward you sent out has done the rounds and come back to outrage you all over again. Here's a real example: two-thirds of all anti-vaccination content on Twitter and Facebook come from just twelve people.[56] As a result, we end up believing certain political news to be facts purely because we encounter them more often.

We're all guilty of this, but overconfident people are guilty of this to a greater degree. Even as they neglect these correlations, overconfident people tend to seek out more confirmatory sources and reinforce their beliefs. They are also less likely to use any difference in opinion to change their own beliefs, ending up being more ideologically extreme and consequently more likely to vote. Interestingly, in this study, overconfidence was correlated with age. I wonder if that could partly be why older people are more likely to vote than younger people.

It isn't only ideology that is affected by overconfidence. The other major influence it has is on partisanship. Data from the Pew Research Centre[57] shows that, in the US, over the two decades between 1994 and 2014, people with consistent Republican or Democratic ideology increased from 10 per cent to 20 per cent. In terms of ideology, 92 per cent of all Republicans were to the right of the median Democrat and 94 per cent of all Democrats were to the left of the median Republican in 2014. Clearly, identifying with a particular political party is causing people to drift apart. We also tend to see parties in terms of their stereotypes, overestimating various traits of party members.[58] For example, people think 32 per cent of Democrats are LGBT and 38 per cent of Republicans earn above US$ 250,000 a year. In reality, 6 per cent of Democrats are LGBT and only 2 per cent of Republicans earn above that figure. These misperceptions then fuel our images of the other and lead to further emotional or moral distancing from rival parties.

A big question is how much being a member of a party influences our perceptions. One strand of work argues that being partisan creates a perceptual screen.[59,60] We end up only seeing the things that support our political point of view. Partisans are more optimistic about their party's success in elections. This can provide greater motivation to campaign and vote in close races, but it could also of course delude people into false security and suppress the vote. People who identify with a particular party are also less likely to see their party as being corrupt and more likely to blame others for failures.[61, 62] They are more likely than people identifying with another party to evaluate their own party as doing well—and this gap in perception has been increasing in the US over the last fifty years. The perception gap is particularly high amongst those with the highest political awareness, and almost absent for those with the lowest political awareness.

In India, one year before Narendra Modi was re-elected in 2019, 59 per cent of BJP voters said job opportunities had got worse and 62 per cent said that the prices of goods and services had got worse since he came to power in 2014.[63] In comparison, 80 per cent and 70 per cent of Congress voters said jobs and prices respectively had gotten worse. Partisans are also more likely to remember false information that supports their political positions.[64]

In comparison, independents who don't identify with any political party are far more accurate in their predictions and factual estimates. In the US, retrospective evaluations have become increasingly polarised over the last century, driven by the attitudes of the political elite.[65] Strikingly, some studies argue that it is politically better-informed people who are more likely to show these partisan effects. They are of course very knowledgeable about information that supports their point of view, but when faced with conflicting information, they are more likely to ignore or discount it. They are also more likely to seek out counterarguments and confirmatory information, thereby reinforcing their original beliefs.

In an influential study, Charles Taber and Milton Lodge, two political scientists from Stony Brook University, New York, found evidence that people's political views come from biased information processing, or 'motivated scepticism'.[66] They argue that partisan goals are driven by emotional processes, and that all reasoning is motivated in this fashion, although it might be constrained to varying extents by accuracy. They measured people's attitudes towards affirmative action and gun control, two politically salient questions in the US. Participants could read arguments on these two topics by clicking on pieces of information that were hidden until clicked upon. People's ratings of these arguments strongly reflected their prior attitudes. The amount of time people spent reading arguments and their responses also revealed a confirmation bias for supportive information. Conversely, when they disagreed with a political stance, there was a disconfirmation bias.

Perhaps the most striking result was that knowledge of politics didn't make things better—in fact, it strengthened the partisan bias. What's worse, those who were more biased in their search for information and those more knowledgeable ended up being more polarised after the task than they were before.

This process of biased information search is, of course, one of the mechanisms underlying overconfidence. It is no wonder then that we end up being overly certain about things our minds are made up about. In real-life arguments, there might of course be other factors to consider, such as underlying stances. For instance, people might be more prone to considering the other's viewpoint if they share the same moral objective, let's say, equal opportunities for all citizens. It would be different if there are deeper differences, such as if some people believe people of certain religions or races are inferior. Given fundamental moral differences like this, people might well rate all arguments of their opponents as poor and vice versa, regardless of knowledge level or political affiliation.

Several subsequent studies have confirmed our biased information-seeking for political information. These confirmation biases have even been demonstrated[67] in how people viewed a real-life event—the 2012 US presidential election where Barack Obama beat Mitt Romney. Before the election, when participants were faced with expert predictions that the candidate they opposed would win the election, they found arguments to dispute the expert opinion. However, after the election, they showed a different bias. They were more likely to find arguments that supported the reality, thus working towards accuracy goals rather than ideologically motivated ones. This seems like a strategic deployment of motivated reasoning. It suits us to be overconfident when it could convince and motivate us and others towards a specific goal, like the election of a preferred candidate. When this goal is no longer possible, we would be expected to no longer deceive ourselves and move towards greater accuracy.

Taber and Lodge acknowledge the value of being sceptical about new information or arguments. If you've arrived at your opinion after careful consideration, you shouldn't be immediately swayed by the first contradictory position you encounter. As they put it: 'To the extent one's attitude reflects considerable prior thought, it may well be more trustworthy than new information.' But they go on to caution against being too resistant to changing our minds: 'skepticism becomes bias when it becomes unreasonably resistant to change and especially when it leads one to avoid information'.

So, even when faced with the same information, people with different attitudes appear to confirm their prior attitudes and become further politically polarised.[68] This is definitely not conducive to democratic societies if we need to use facts to decide policy.

But there's a deeper issue to worry about. Could the 'perceptual screen' raised by political attitudes be distorting perceptions of actual facts? Identities are often strongly tied to political parties or groups. This, in turn, leads to overoptimism. However, facts could act as a check in these situations. You believe your group had the rally with the biggest supporters, say, or the presidential inauguration with the largest crowd. This could be easily contradicted by, say, photographic evidence. When facing such clear evidence, there's a conflict between our motivational and accuracy goals, which could generate cognitive dissonance. We attempt to reduce this as much as we can, including sometimes sacrificing accuracy to preserve our core beliefs. This means that we could misperceive factual evidence, but only if we think our ideological beliefs are part of our core identity.

Evidence for this comes from looking at how the maths skills of people are affected by political identification.[69] People in a US study who performed well at maths were given problems that contained political content—data about cities in which handguns were banned or not. When given these problems, performance at maths no longer predicted how correct people were. Predictably, now political identity mattered more. If the solution proved that banning guns reduces crime, liberals were good at solving it. If it proved the opposite, conservatives were good at solving the problem. The polarisation in performance was not explained by the level of maths skills the people had. People with higher maths skills were actually more polarised in their answers. These results have been explained by what has been called 'identity-protective cognition'.[70] Our mistakes serve as social signals to the groups we are committed to. In fact, people start making errors in problems they are perfectly capable of solving if they are 'contaminated' by culturally or politically unwelcome ideas.

Other researchers made a fascinating discovery[71] when they looked at how being dogmatic about one's political views was related to a low-level task of visual perception. In this case, the task was far removed from politics. Participants were faced with two patches of flickering dots, and had to judge which one had more dots and then rate their confidence in their answer. You would expect people to be more confident about accurate decisions compared to inaccurate ones. Yet, as predicted, politically dogmatic people were more likely to be confident even about their inaccurate choices in this visual task. The most dogmatic individuals thus were unlikely to change their minds, and this was driven by the simple act of choosing. Once they chose an option, they believed that option had a greater probability of being true. Further evidence was less likely to be included in any decision they made.

One argument against generalising these results is that they might not reflect the real world. We might expect people to be less dogmatic about something with serious consequences,, like the COVID-19 pandemic, for example, where concerns about safety should prevail over political affiliations. However, in the US at least, behaviour during the pandemic still fell along partisan lines, and led to differential infection rates. Compared to Democrats, Republicans saw the virus as less of a threat, were less likely to wear masks, more likely to go out and more sceptical about social distancing.[72] Local policy interventions appear to be ineffective at changing the partisan difference in mask-wearing. The lack of physical distancing was linked to increases in COVID-19 cases and to more deaths in counties that voted for Trump. Some of this might be due to cues gained from President Trump. Initially, he resisted mask-wearing, but his use of a mask in July led to greater engagement on mask-related topics on social media. The divide on mask-wearing certainly seems to be influenced by political cues.

These results raise an alarming question: once we become political, can we no longer trust our faculties of judgement or even our own senses? If this were so, it would be deeply concerning for the ability to reach out across political divides or to convince people of facts and find common solutions to problems. Some findings argue that this fear isn't entirely justified. Despite the partisan divide, 60–75 per cent of US citizens practised social distancing during the pandemic, according to a survey in June 2020, and the partisan gap appeared to be narrowing.[73]

Another behaviour that changed in response to the pandemic was how people sought out information. Researchers at the University of Michigan Office for Social Media Responsibility developed a tool called the 'Iffy Quotient', which measures the proportion of news from unreliable sites shared on Facebook and Twitter. During the early months of the pandemic in the US, this quotient showed that people moved away from more unreliable sites to more mainstream sites.[74, 75] So, perhaps we aren't stuck in our habits. Given that information search is an important route by which we can deceive ourselves, it is comforting to know we can seek out accuracy when faced with serious concerns.

The pandemic provided people with a very strong incentive to be accurate. There are other, less extreme ways of achieving the same, such as the tried-and-tested route of paying people. A study gave people small payments for answering factual questions correctly or saying that they didn't know.[76] When these incentivised options were available, the differences between supposed partisans dramatically decreased. People are also more likely to report a politically unfavourable study as convincing if they were provided monetary incentives to be accurate.[77] If partisans responded the same way with and without payments, this would have shown us that they genuinely believed in their reported misperceptions, i.e., the 'partisan screen' had distorted their view of facts. However, the fact that the answers were less partisan when payments were made shows that people do know the facts. Researchers argue that, in several of these studies, people respond in the way they are 'meant to' in order to make their party appear better. Even where a bias towards favourable facts persists, the number of people with this bias isn't large and the bias is reduced when there are incentives. In addition, when the task to be performed is made easier, the bias is almost entirely removed.

These results suggest that there are two different aspects to motivated cognition. The first could be called 'motivated learning', where our goals change how we learn or remember facts. This would include the information-search biases we've discussed. The second component of motivated cognition would be 'motivated responding'. As in the study with incentives, this involves people knowing what they don't know, but responding so as to make their group look good. Without financial incentives, we might be misinterpreting motivated responding and overestimating the amount of motivated learning. When we respond to a question—whether in a psychological study or otherwise—it's easy for us to say the 'right' thing that doesn't necessarily reflect our beliefs and subsequent behaviour. This seems reminiscent of the 'shy Tory' effect in the United Kingdom, where most surveys of voting intention regularly underestimate the number of voters for the Conservative (or Tory) party, simply because voters appear reluctant to admit that they vote for the Conservatives.

Mistrust in politicians runs high in several countries. In the UK, for example, they are the second most distrusted professionals—after advertising executives.[78] If the cycle of narcissism, self-deception and overconfidence is what is helping propel them to power, the scepticism would be eminently justified. We should be holding their pronouncements to account and scrupulously judging their performance in government. Yet, we almost certainly fail to hold our own views up to similar scrutiny. As countries, we are grossly misinformed on several vital issues. Those of us who support any political party appear to be guilty of large failures of understanding. At the very least, we are guilty of misinterpreting facts when we should be admitting we don't know.

One argument against the persistence of poorly performing overconfident politicians is that, at least in a democratic system, failures due to risk-taking will be punished. This doesn't always seem to be the case. Facts and political understanding can be biased once we identify with a political party. So, we tend to interpret facts to best defend 'our' party, and might well not immediately punish politicians electorally, especially when the results of a political action are unclear or spun to appear so. In addition, there is also an escalation of commitment. Once we make a choice, we motivate ourselves to defend it. The more dogmatic amongst us do this even for visual decisions! Motivated cognition makes us overconfident about our facts, and our identification with political stances causes that overconfidence to spread outwards favourably to include *our* parties and *our* politicians. Leaders, who come to power leading the 'true people' against elites—and are often called populist—go on to stay in power longer than non-populists.[79] The cycle that begins with the election of overconfident politicians is completed by overconfident and partisan voters.

This scenario is almost certainly overstated. To take just one example, poor performance in preventing death tolls in the pandemic affected the popularity of world leaders.[80] When Bolsonaro began his presidency, his government had an approval rating of 45 per cent. After months when COVID-19 spread through the country and led to one of the highest death tolls in the world, the ratings fell to 35 per cent. In May 2020, Narendra Modi had an approval rating of close to 80 per cent—perhaps reflecting India's low death rate, rather than the high absolute number of deaths. After the second wave in May 2021, his approval rating climbed down to 63 per cent, as India was hit with a grim death toll and the death rate skyrocketed. Trump's disapproval rating was at its highest during his mismanagement of the pandemic response. He trailed Joe Biden, his opponent in the 2020 presidential election, by fourteen points at one stage and then went on to lose the election. Approval of Boris Johnson's handling of the crisis fell by twenty points, and his party lost a large lead to be almost equal in the ratings with Labour, the opposition party.

In 2021, after the second wave, and as vaccination efforts started growing, these polls changed—maybe we are quick to forget negative consequences. More data is needed to test these ideas, especially from countries outside of the US and Europe.

The cycle of overconfidence isn't true of every election. What this picture does guide us towards are the possible weaknesses of electoral politics, especially the assumption that performance in government and performance in elections are correlated. To shift the focus from rhetoric to performance, what we need then are ways to sift true confidence from overconfidence. This should be a focus for journalists, and for politicians themselves.

But there is a related question about our own lives: how do we understand each other better in our daily conversations? How can we discuss facts without ideological bias and allow them to change our minds? Do we even want that? That's what we turn to next.

THIRTEEN

Overcoming Overconfidence

OVERCONFIDENCE CATALYSES A HOST OF CALAMITIES: ECONOMIC crises, wars, pandemics and inept leaders. Ideally, our societies would have developed to restrict the effects of overconfidence. However, what we see is that, while these disasters might destroy societies, the people whose overconfidence catalyses them prosper. The politician who overclaims and underdelivers gains all the benefits of power, the aggressive Wall Street professional gains a reputation for being successful. We are surrounded by examples of successful but incompetent people—testament to the fact that being overconfident could actually be beneficial. It could help with motivation, better mental health or to deceive others about our abilities. In the face of this evidence, surely everyone should end up wanting to be overconfident?

The clash between the advantages to the individual and the possibility of major societal crises is, however, a problem. It's clear that we can't just rely on our better natures. Staving off the harmful effects of overconfidence will require collective work. In this, the costs of overconfidence to the individual can help. One, a large degree of overconfidence might lead a person to take on tasks they are bound to fail at. Two, overconfident individuals are themselves susceptible to being fooled by other people's overconfidence. Finally, appearing narcissistic has social costs—you could lose the trust of others, for example. For some of us, these costs are sufficient to act as deterrents.

Most of us probably also want to overcome at least one particular kind of overconfidence—other people's overconfidence. Consider the wisdom of our urban planners and the projections of city contractors.

Wouldn't it be a relief if we could just rely on their proposed budgets and timelines? It's easy to see why the planning fallacy persists: everybody wants projects to happen quickly, with as low a budget as possible. Any person who bids to be in charge of a project inevitably faces pressures to shrink the costs and durations. It's easy then for the gears of motivated cognition and self-deception to begin to turn. What better way is there of convincing others of your ability to deliver what they want than to believe in it yourself? The onus is on the people handing out the projects to anticipate this optimism and work against its seductive charms. These concerns are, of course, well recognised by organisations as well as governments, and a range of policies are often in place to ensure that the pitfalls of overconfidence are avoided as best as possible.[1]

The UK government, for example, explicitly acknowledges the prevalence of overconfidence in the planning process in its guidelines for project assessment.[2] The guidelines recommend making adjustments to the costs and the duration of projects based on actual data. Other organisations similarly add buffer times to projects—a simple and effective solution. What we need to remain prepared for is overconfidence in any aspect of a project that we are seeking to optimise or convince others about. Engineering projects, for example, add safety factors while designing systems. Imagine you're designing a lift. You would make your calculations to build it strong enough to bear a given load. Adding a safety factor would mean that you make the lift stronger than your calculations recommend by some fixed standard factor. Implementing safety factors as part of the automatic design process thus provides a buffer against any overconfidence that might be involved in your estimation of material strength. The automation of similar processes and constant quality control is a simple way of combating human error, motivated or otherwise. It is certainly preferable to only conducting whole process reviews after large-scale disasters occur. What we need are safety factors for our societies and companies as well.

These societal safety factors would involve systemic approaches—checks and balances to avoid organisational or systemic over-confidence. For instance, people with narcissistic tendencies are known to make risky decisions, but paradoxically, they are also more likely to occupy leadership positions. Distributing power beyond the leader alone could work against risky decision-making by leaders. This could involve giving more power to board members, worker and employee representatives in corporations, and arranging for independent assessments of finances and accounts. Many democratic systems in the world also attempt to build in these checks by having multiple houses of parliament and strong independent judiciaries. The hope is that these different entities would help fight tendencies towards authoritarian overconfidence in presidents and prime ministers. The test is how these checks fare when the leaders have strong support from the public who might view any pushback as undemocratic or obstructionist. This is especially true when a country is in the middle of, or gearing up for, a war.

On a smaller scale, in our everyday work meetings, it's helpful to encourage people to write down independent summaries of their ideas or estimations before discussion. This allows for diversity of opinion and dissent, which discussion led by one person's point of view might disallow. In *Kill Bill*, the character O-Ren Ishii played by Lucy Liu has a classic monologue at a work meeting. 'As your leader,' she says, 'I encourage you from time to time … to question my logic. If you're unconvinced that a particular plan of action I've decided is the wisest, tell me so.' We should all be more O-Ren, cultivating opposition and multiple viewpoints. It would probably help if, unlike her, we haven't just beheaded one of the people at the meeting with a katana. Diversity of opinion also helps decorrelate error.[3] We all make errors during planning. But we don't make the same errors, and so, combining truly independent assessments effectively allows different errors to cancel each other out. By contrast, if we all align ourselves to agree with our CEOs or with O-Ren, our errors could easily point in the same direction, allowing us as a group to open the door to overconfidence. There, too, an average of independent evaluations without an initial estimate can counter the bias and lead to better accuracy. It's best to keep our katanas sheathed.

It's interesting to speculate how much this correlation of error leads to forms of large-scale consensus—could this be why the majority of people believed that Iraq was guaranteed to have weapons of mass destruction? Could it be why so many people thought that Hillary Clinton was definitely going to win? That's a case made by the psephologist Nate Silver.[4] He argues that the lack of diversity and independence of opinion among political journalists and their centralisation in limited parts of the country all contributed to the idea that Trump could not win. Could it be possible that errors such as this are only going to get worse when social media can rapidly spread information or opinion, and it suddenly seems like everyone is saying the same thing? The authority of a leader, media messages or the current zeitgeist can all act as powerful magnets, aligning our individual errors to point in the same direction. That is when we move towards failed wars, poor governance or booms and busts in financial markets.

Not only do we need multiple independent voices, it also matters who is responsible for quality checks and decision-making. We've touched upon this before. People are overconfident about promotions, but their peers' estimates are more accurate. We underestimate the likelihood of negative events happening to us, but are accurate about other people. Political predictions are most accurate when made by independents rather than people partisan to a particular political party. The pattern suggests that an outsider's perspective steers individuals and groups towards accuracy. Sometimes this could be as simple as discarding a belief in the exceptionalism of your project and simply being guided by the data from other projects similar to yours. These projects have an advantage in terms of realism—they have already happened, while your project still belongs in the realms of possibility. Paying attention to the details of these other projects, whether in terms of their costs, duration or other factors, could give you guidelines that your own project would benefit from. Training with these past cases has been shown to reduce overconfidence. Geologists at Royal Dutch Shell, for example, were less overconfident while assessing drilling sites after this kind of training.[5] In other cases, it might even be worth handing over the control of decision-making to others who don't stand to gain from your project. For instance, taking away access to investment money from CEOs appears to reduce overconfident acquisition of other companies.[6]

We could potentially go one step further and pay attention to the criticisms of our rivals and competitors, who of course have the most to gain by pointing out the faults in our proposals. Cybersecurity and intelligence, for example, use the idea of a 'red team' where one group plays the role of an adversary and tests the detection and response capabilities of a system.[7] An apt quote from Shakespeare's *Twelfth Night* compares friends to enemies: friends 'praise me and make an ass of me, now my foes tell me plainly I am an ass. So that by my foes, sir, I profit in the knowledge of myself, and by my friends, I am abused.' A Kabir doha similarly tells you to keep your critics close, they will keep you clean without soap or water. The behavioural economist Daniel Kahneman prescribes what he calls 'adversarial collaboration' as a way to reduce confirmation bias.[8] This involves designing experiments or projects with people we disagree with. Figuring out ways to effectively overcome our faults and address the criticisms is hard. Yet, in many ways, the hardest part of all is sacrificing our own overoptimism. When success depends on ignoring negative information, the inner momentum we build is often sufficient to drown out all other voices. Overconfidence can be both our ladder to success and the weight that drags us back into the depths of failure.

The ultimate outsider perspective could come from a mainstay of contemporary life, the faceless statistical algorithm. Across a range of fields from high school performance to clinical evaluations, algorithms end up being more accurate than expert judgement.[9] This isn't all due to human overconfidence. Other cognitive biases no doubt have their own part to play. The more interesting question is when algorithms are more effective and when humans are. Kahneman points out that a key factor is the predictability of the environment. Simpler, predictable or 'high-validity' environments (as he calls them) gives humans the advantage. But when there are multiple variables involved and the complex environment is significantly unpredictable, human judgements, including those of experts, aren't as reliable as an algorithm would be. What are examples of these 'low-validity' environments? The stock market and politics are decidedly complex worlds to navigate, and long-term forecasts of these aren't likely to yield a high degree of accuracy. Specialised algorithms arguably stand a better chance there. Even interviews where several aspects of the candidates need to be considered could end up being derailed by our trust in our own intuitions.

While algorithms might seem to be a promising way to overcome our biases, they are not a panacea against overconfidence and all forms of prejudice. Algorithms could themselves have their own biases, arising from a range of sources.[10, 11, 12] These include the data they are trained on, aspects of the world that the software developer failed to consider or the developer's own prejudices and biases. Results from new papers analysing 'objective' algorithms have demonstrated exactly these kinds of biases. It's certainly worth testing algorithms for their own cognitive biases—including for any forms of overconfidence—before embracing them. Now there's a whole new field of research!

So far, so good. Almost everybody wants organisations—from councils to corporations—to prevent losses due to overconfidence. How about our interpersonal interactions? If only we could overcome other people's overconfidence there too. Remember your friend's unshakeable confidence in his views or your boss's obstinate pursuit of a foolhardy course of action? How can you reach through their certitude to show them how wrong they are? And how right you are? Luckily, there is some research on this as well. Choose from four different approaches: feedback, details, training and framing.

STRATEGY ONE: FEEDBACK

Feedback has been a running thread in how we've talked about overconfidence. Lack of clear feedback is an essential component to maintaining overconfidence in a variety of situations, from the Dunning-Kruger Effect to authoritarian governments. If we reverse the logic, providing feedback should help us reduce overconfidence. There are different ways in which this works.[13] At the most basic level, feedback comes to us all, over time. As we get older, we are less optimistic about medical conditions. Experience of accidents and disasters decreases our optimism, at least for a while after we experience them. We're especially likely to take on board feedback when it's personalised: in one study, people who took a questionnaire on health risks changed their assessment of the risks of having a stroke or cancer after feedback about their actual risks.[14] This did not, however, affect their perception of the risk of, say, heart attacks or motor vehicle crashes. Also, feedback about other people impacts how convincing their overconfidence and self-assessments appear to be, and this also changes over time. In the study with my collaborator Shakti Lamba,[15] people were initially deceived by other people's overconfidence, but this effect faded over six weeks. Interestingly, this change only occurred when people compared and ranked their peers, but not when they made absolute judgements on peer ability. This suggests another way we could try to counter other people's overconfidence: perhaps rankings and comparative judgements would work better than trying to assess how good someone is without a reference benchmark.

Feedback also improves performance on tasks. This is seen in the underconfidence-with-practice effect we've discussed earlier, something seen in adults but not young children. It matters what the tasks are. Feedback leads to people being better able to distinguish correct and incorrect judgements on difficult tasks than on easy tasks.[16] Specific feedback on how someone is wrong is more likely to help than just knowledge of the outcome. Knowing you've passed or failed a test is far less useful than telling you exactly why your essay was awful. In fact, this idea of feedback does resemble a school setting, where there's time for detailed and continuous evaluation and updating of expectations.

How is this going to help you when you're arguing with your know-it-all uncle? Let's look at the one topic where you might feel most strongly about this—politics. With headlines about fake news and media accountability rapidly becoming the soundtrack of our lives, political fact-checking has naturally been a focus of recent research. How does fact-checking influence our political opinions? One study in the US tested the impact of fact-checking statements made by President Trump in the run-up to the 2016 US election.[17] They found that fact-checking reduced belief in inaccurate statements that had been corrected, but did not change people's feelings about Trump or how they planned to vote. That leads one to wonder how important the truth is to us once we have formed our political views.

A challenge to this idea comes from all the way across the globe. Researchers in Australia pointed out that the US study presented participants with an equal number of false and true statements.[18] So, while the inaccuracies were pointed out, there was a balance maintained by affirming factual statements made by Trump. This balance might of course not reflect reality. Different politicians might be more or less prone to inaccuracies, and our views on them might change based on how factual they were. The Australian researchers set out to test this by including statements from multiple politicians, and presenting participants with a varying ratio of inaccurate to accurate statements previously made by each politician. Their results threw up a golden ratio—the ratio of inaccuracies to factual statements at which support for a politician falls. That ratio is 4:1. We need four times the number of inaccuracies compared to factual statements to lose faith in our chosen leaders. Interestingly, this particular study also found no support for motivated cognition. The participants were not influenced by how much they already agreed or disagreed with the politician. Fact-checking changed their minds about statements regardless of who made the statements. This golden ratio, however, might not work in the US. At least one other study[19] that contrasted statements by Trump and Bernie Sanders found a very reduced effect of fact-checking on political support, even with high ratios of inaccurate to accurate statements. Perhaps there's something to dig into there about differences between countries or even voting systems.

STRATEGY TWO: CONSIDER THE DETAILS

This isn't so far from feedback. In some ways, what stopping to consider the details does is force you to look for information about whatever judgement you are making. For example, when study participants have to list arguments to justify their choices first, levels of overconfidence go down.[20] We are also more likely to reconsider our own positions if we're asked to think of reasons that go against them. Even the politically partisan amongst us aren't immune to this. Being asked to give precise numbers—for instance, what percentage of the other party earns above a certain limit or is of a particular religion or ethnicity—describing a party they don't like reduces the likelihood of someone holding inaccurate representations of the composition of the party based on stereotypes.[21] It goes further than that; it even makes them a little more likely to feel warmly towards the other. Early on, when discussing the better-than-average effect, we discussed how even adding a little bit of real detail, like being able to see the back of someone's head, reduced our tendency to believe we were better than them. Thinking of details and considering real people seems to break down our confidence in stereotypes and forces us to see each other more clearly.

STRATEGY THREE: TRAINING

Training, whether over shorter or extended periods of time, helps reduce overconfidence, and this is our third strategy.[22] Training works for us just as much as for others. Admittedly, it would encompass several different approaches, so perhaps it isn't a strategy in itself but something that brings other strategies together. For example, providing feedback or getting people to consider details could be built into a training programme. This is often how actual university courses work in an attempt to get students to improve performances and self-assessments. And it works even for non-academic topics. For example, junior high school students[23] were given information about the actual rates of consumption of alcohol, marijuana and tobacco and true levels of acceptability. Over the course of a year, this led to reduced consumption of all three. Students who drink and smoke typically overestimate how prevalent and acceptable drinking and smoking are, and the training effectively overcame that bias.

Other forms of training are also possible. When we considered the Dunning-Kruger effect, you'll recall the studies finding that overconfidence is high if our actual skill levels are low. One of the solutions to that problem is to just increase the skill level. As we get better, the effect reduces, and we become more accurate in our estimates.[24] There's also evidence that people who do better on tests of cognitive reflection are less susceptible to believing fake news, even if it supports their partisan points of view.[25, 26] Training or supporting people to think more analytically could, therefore, reduce the overconfidence that is born out of partisanship. There is plenty of evidence suggesting that cognitive reflection, natural or induced, makes people more discerning and less likely to believe fake news.[27] Another approach with beneficial effects involves guiding people's attention.[28] Directing people towards the harder aspects of a task reduced overconfidence, and had the added benefit of increasing learning outcomes, which could then have additional effects on reducing overconfidence. In addition, encouraging people to believe that intelligence can change also leads to both better performance and reduced overconfidence, a double benefit again.

It's worth designing the training appropriately of course. Young drivers who underwent training programmes grew to be even more optimistic than they were.[29] It was only when the training specifically directed drivers to past risky behaviour or negative experiences that overoptimism reduced. It seems like personalised and individual training and feedback are important if we want to successfully increase accuracy and reduce overconfidence.

STRATEGY FOUR: FRAMING

Context is everything. Both the manner in which feedback is provided and the nature of the training programme impact overconfidence. Which is why it's worth considering a whole bunch of strategies, which we'll group together under strategy four. At its simplest, framing entails how we have conversations with others. It matters why people are overconfident or why they choose the views they have. If it's a manifestation of a desire to take control of the situation, for example, feedback might not change that.[30] There might also be barriers to how responsive people are going to be to feedback. If we want people to listen, the way we have conversations needs to take that into account and address it. One suggestion for reducing overconfidence amongst physicians is to ask them to consider other people's contributions to their success and highlighting effort rather than skills.[31] In the context of combating doubt about vaccinations, we had discussed a study that showed conversations that provide information while empowering people to make their own choices were more likely to lead to changes in behaviour.[32]

Tasks or projects can be framed so that they reduce the likelihood of biases. One interesting phenomenon is our difficulty making probabilistic judgements compared to judgements based on frequency. For example, asking the question 'How likely is it that the bus arrives on time in the next five days?' is more difficult to tackle compared to 'How many times in the next five days will the bus arrive late?' Bus schedulers might well answer the first question with a lower, more inaccurate estimate. However, when asked to measure frequencies rather than probabilities, overconfidence was reduced.[33] Reducing ambiguity is another way of doing this. The better defined our measures of performance or criteria for success, the less likely it is that people can interpret them to suit their self-views. For example, when students graded themselves in a study, their grades correlated better with the eventual grades if the assignments had well-defined solutions.[34] Clearer, better defined evaluation criteria are a simple way to tackle several forms of overconfidence, and it's certainly a simple method we could use.

Framing could also tackle motivated cognition. For instance, making the facts easier to grasp is a simple way to counter motivated cognition.[35] When facts become obvious, even those who have strong reasons to dislike the facts can no longer deny them. Our capacity for motivated reasoning is typically bound by reality—if it's clear where that reality lies, there's only so far we can deviate from it. Other factors can influence motivated reasoning too. Since reasoning can be influenced by motivations towards both goals and accuracy, what if we increased our motivations towards accuracy, by, for example, including encouragement or monetary incentives? Bonus caps or taxes might reduce how much CEOs overvalue their bonuses and reduce their risk-taking behaviour.[36] Incentives could even make us more receptive to facts that might not fit our partisan worldviews. Making people accountable for the accuracy or inaccuracy of their views also changes their reasoning.[37] They rely less on first impressions and use less biased search strategies for facts.[38]

Even very simple corrections can have a role to play in tackling misinformation. Two political scientists, Sumitra Badrinathan and Simon Chauchard, conducted a study of social media users in India after the 2019 elections, and looked at how interventions could work against misinformation.[39] They provided the participants screenshots of rumours as well as corrections to those rumours made by different sources. The rumours were purportedly made by media outlets or politicians and were on a range of topics, including the effectiveness of cow urine to boost immunity, the link between vaccines and autism, and a claim that UNESCO declared Modi the best prime minister in 2016. The corrections were made by a random person, an expert or a specialised fact-checking service. Belief in the rumours was high, but corrections had a significant—though sometimes small—effect in reducing this belief. What was most striking is that corrections by the random person were just as effective as those by experts or fact-checkers. Perhaps even more interestingly, there was no evidence for motivated reasoning. Corrections were effective regardless of which political party people supported, whether the rumour was attributed to a politician or media outlet supporting that party, or whether the content was for or against that party. This seems to suggest that simply hearing contradictory opinions can lead to reduced confidence in rumours.

Ideally, a study should not just present participants with constructed examples, but track actual behaviour related to misinformation on social media platforms. A recent comprehensive study by the psychologists Gordon Pennycook and David Rand and their co-authors set out to do just that.[40] It investigated how people in the US share misinformation online. People were clear that sharing accurate information was very important to them. They were also able to strongly distinguish true from false headlines, regardless of whether it fit their political views. Yet, when a similar group of people were asked which headline they would consider sharing, they based their decision far more on how it fit their political views than on its accuracy. What explains this disconnect? The authors hypothesise that this is because, when sharing information, your attention is focused on signalling to a group or pleasing your followers or friends, rather than on accuracy. So, if you directed people to instead think of accuracy, they would share less content that was false. The researchers tested this by first asking participants to rate the accuracy of a headline and then asking them about their sharing intentions. Doing this decreased the likelihood of people sharing false information. It did not affect their attitudes towards sharing true information.

One question to ask is which headlines people are likely to share when they aren't directed to think of accuracy. They might share favourable headlines even when people generally rate them inaccurate. This would be evidence of a partisan bias. Alternatively, these could be false headlines that people nonetheless think are accurate—indicating the headlines aren't clearly inaccurate and that people are confused about them. Finally, there could be often-shared headlines that people stop sharing when thinking about accuracy. This final category, the authors describe as shared due to an inattention towards accuracy. The majority of the headlines (58 per cent) fell into the third category. In fact only 15.8 per cent of headlines fit the partisan sharing category. This suggests that, even when the headlines shared are clearly inaccurate, people aren't necessarily sharing them due to a specific political stance. They are simply not thinking about accuracy. This chimes with Pennycook and Rand's earlier work on how thinking analytically or having better cognitive skills increases accuracy and reduces overconfidence.

A final test of this idea came in a study involving an active intervention focusing on Twitter users who shared a high number of articles from sources that regularly had misleading headlines. These users were sent a message asking them to rate the accuracy of a single non-political headline. Simply receiving this message changed their sharing behaviour. The content they shared moved from misleading partisan news sources to mainstream news sources compared to similar users who didn't encounter the intervention.

Taking all the results of this study together, we can see an excellent demonstration of how even a simple nudge towards attending to accuracy can change partisan behaviour online. In fact, it even shows that our public profiles don't necessarily reflect deeply held beliefs. Perhaps we aren't so overconfident after all. We just like to show others we are.

We need all the strategies we can get because the path to accuracy does not run smooth. For, despite all the information about the possible pitfalls we might fall into, we're still prone to believing ourselves uniquely immune to bias. For example, 75 per cent of US citizens overestimate their ability to distinguish fake and accurate headlines.[41] In fact, overconfident individuals are even more likely to fail at distinguishing true and false claims and to visit untrustworthy websites. There appears to be a kind of Dunning-Kruger effect at play: those who are least likely to spot fake news are the ones who most overestimate their ability to do so.

The 'bias blind spot', as some researchers have called it,[42] prevents easy corrections. You might have read a whole book about overconfidence, but you'll walk away shocked at how biased everybody else is, especially compared to you. Yes, we do receive feedback throughout our lives that should tell us where our inaccuracies lie. But that feedback is not as reliable as it should be. It is often infrequent, not delivered in time or given so lightly or vaguely that it's easily ignored. For some of us, living in our bubbles, where we only hear encouragement and praise, sometimes from childhood, negative feedback might well be a stranger. Sometimes, however, feedback from a particular performance measure does get through, and we are forced to accept our own biases. Even in these cases, we often end up distrusting the study or performance measure that delivered this judgement upon us. If you don't like the sentence, blame the judge.

It's no wonder that misinformation persists—even in cases where it is followed by a retraction. This is something we're rapidly getting familiar with. Once fake news is out there, corrections do not make much of a difference. This is especially true for more general facts rather than for specific details.[43] So, for instance, you might accept that you were wrong about one particular company breaking the law, but you'd be less likely to change your mind about corporations in general indulging in illegality. This is enhanced if misinformation chimes with an opinion you already held. People who have strong beliefs in the free market are less likely to change their views about climate change in response to further information.[44] Even here, though, when people are warned of the possibility of misinformation and provided with a general refutation before they actually hear it, the misinformation seems not to have a strong effect. This approach has been called 'inoculation' or 'pre-bunking'. This sort of inoculation seems to be a useful tool to help people become more discerning and less likely to fall for misinformation out there in the real world.[45]

Our prior attitudes don't always change our view of the facts themselves, but lead us to interpret them differently. In addition, prior attitudes also make it easier for us to accept corrections or retractions of misinformation that are in agreement with these attitudes. Now there's a silver lining! And then there's the identity-protective cognition we've discussed before.[46] We all understand the feeling of being under threat when some group identity we care about strongly—religion or a political affiliation—seems under attack by a fact-checker. It isn't surprising that we might bias the interpretation of the facts in a bid to retain our rosy picture of our identities.

One of the most worrying ways in which we tend to defend our views was demonstrated in an influential study by the political scientists Brendan Nyhan and Jason Reifler.[47] They set out to see whether corrections to misleading claims change people's misperceptions. They define misperception as a belief that is contrary to evidence and expert opinion. This would seem to be linked to the form of overconfidence we've been referring to as overprecision. Nyhan and Reifler gave the participants a realistic exposure to facts in the form of mock news articles. Studies often simply present facts that the participants are told are definitely true, which is not how we might encounter facts in real life. Nyhan and Ryfler's approach of using news articles moved closer to reality. They ran four studies where participants encountered false information in these news articles. Subsequently, one group was given corrective information, while another control group was not. Comparing the beliefs of the two groups could then reveal the effect of the corrections.

The news articles used in these studies covered different topics: whether Iraq had WMD, the effects of tax cuts and policies governing stem cell research. The results showed that people often don't change their minds if the corrections are against their political ideologies. This is in line with much of what we've discussed so far—motivated reasoning would ensure that we are defensive in the face of contrary information. What makes the findings of these studies even more worrying is what they call the 'backfire effect'. In several instances, not only did the corrections fail to work, they went on to intensify people's beliefs in the original misperception. Facts that contradict your views thus seem to backfire. The explanation for this appears to be that, when we receive unwelcome information, we defend against it by bringing to mind information that might support our positions. This, in turn, makes us more certain of the opinions we held before.

The backfire effect has been a hugely influential finding and was widely covered by the media. It created a storm of interest scientifically too, garnering a massive number of citations. The finding has troubling implications for our ability to convince each other using shared facts. Are we then doomed to further and further disagreements, each of us living in our own misperceived reality? Another study,[48] for example, found that when self-identifying Democrats and Republicans were paid to follow bots with opposing views on Twitter, their views became more polarised, largely because Republicans became more conservative.

In India, a study[49] by political scientist Sumitra Badrinathan, focused on Bihar during the 2019 elections. The study tried to counter misinformation by providing people with the tools and training to spot fake news. The results there once again found a sort of backfire effect. Supporters of the BJP who had received the training were *less* able to spot fake news if it supported their views. People who didn't support the BJP, on the other hand, got better at spotting misinformation after the training.

The bleak picture suggested by the backfire effect is not necessarily always true, but we would do well to take its lessons into account. Perhaps where facts fail, emotions or framing can help. We've talked of this before, but it bears repeating. Facts are more likely to convince people when you also affirm their self-worth and autonomy. If it is defensiveness that causes the backfire effect, it can be defused by ensuring people don't feel threatened. In some situations, information could be presented in a way that is not only non-threatening but even affirms certain aspects of identity.

Yet, even this has proved unsuccessful in some cases. You could frame the case for preventing climate change as beneficial to the economy and national security—two issues that Republicans in the US care about. This framing, however, fails to convince them to support government action against climate change, and could even lead to a backfire effect.[50, 51]

There is still some reason for hope. The backfire effect itself may not always manifest. Another pair of political scientists, Ethan Wood and Thomas Porter, embarked on a large-scale study testing the prevalence of the effect.[52] They enlisted more than 10,000 participants and assessed fifty-two issues that could have demonstrated a backfire effect. These included the original issues used in the first study—weapons of mass destruction, tax cuts and stem cells. In all fifty-two cases, including these, the study found not a single instance of the backfire effect. In fact, participants accepted factual corrections even when they were contrary to their political beliefs, although the effect was greater if the corrections were in line with their beliefs. Wood and Porter argue that these results make sense. People are generally averse to putting in thought or cognitive effort. It is easier to simply accept facts, rather than construct counterarguments.

Another way of thinking of the backfire effect is that focusing on facts is a distraction. When it comes to political partisanship, the issues are often seen as moral divides, rather than facts.[53] Respecting an opposing moral position seems like a hard ask. When asked, a majority of people say that they could respect opposing opinions if based on facts. Yet, when tested, people actually respected subjective personal opinions more than facts. Across comments on YouTube videos, TV interviews and field studies, personal stories, particularly where the opposing person had suffered some harm, were what helped bridge the moral divides about gun control and abortion in the US. The most effective stories were about personal experience compared to those about a friend or someone they had read about. Hearing or reading about these experiences led to people respecting their opponents more because they perceived them as more rational. After all, what could be more rational than trying to avoid a situation that might cause you harm? Experiences—as the authors put it—seem truer than facts.

One of the important differences Wood and Porter note between their study and previous studies showing the backfire effect is that the participants in other studies have often been university students. They point out that this population might be particularly prone to constructing arguments and counterarguments—they might, in fact, be encouraged constantly to put in the cognitive effort that others might not be ready to. In the general population, however, perhaps it isn't worth people's effort to actually find reasons to challenge corrections when they are presented as facts. This is reminiscent of a recurring theme—at least when it comes to politics—the more informed about an issue a person is, the more likely it is that they will be partisan and overconfident about their facts and interpretations. Some of the examples of the backfire effect, however, do not come from university students. Sumitra Badrinathan's study of people in Bihar is a case in point. So we can still find the effect outside of universities.

If university settings seem to help instil a culture of argumentation and defensiveness against correction, that might in itself be a problem we need to struggle with. There are other ways in which it might help, though. One particularly helpful trait that such a setting might help instil is curiosity. Scientific curiosity has been shown to help reduce polarisation.[54] People with a higher degree of science curiosity are, for instance, more likely to read news from sources contrary to their political beliefs. In a broader sense, curiosity is certainly one way of encouraging people to test their well-defended beliefs and correct themselves. Wondering why other people think the way they do, or where our failures stem from, forms the beginning of the route towards increased self-awareness.

Research into why misinformation persists and how to combat it is a rapidly developing field. Already there are several new approaches that might make the discussion above outdated. Some fascinating new results show that interactive argumentation with a chatbot helps fight misconceptions, because it provides people good arguments against their misperceptions as a discussion rather than simply providing facts.[55] It can even help people gain more positive attitudes towards COVID-19 vaccines.[56]

With or without all these technological advances, however, the take-home message seems to be that there might be hope after all for most people, if not always for the professionally partisan. If facts can change our minds and veer us towards accuracy, we may be able to counter overconfidence when we want to do so.

The bulk of this chapter has focused on how we might want to limit or change other people's overconfidence. Each one of the strategies could well be applied to the elephant lurking in the background of the whole discussion—ourselves. Ignoring this elephant is a strategy that might be worth preserving, whether to motivate ourselves, make social gains or perhaps even maintain our mental health. What then of our roles in keeping our societies, communities and nations functioning? One theory holds that the greater the perceived ratio of gain to risk, the higher our tendencies to overconfidence will run.[57] In that case, when making calculations of risk and gain, we could build in the risks and gains to societies and people more generally. To temper our overconfidence when we can calculate large risks to people is surely a goal worth striving for. How this can be achieved is well worth more study—perhaps our goodwill is, in the end, not the most reliable tool we have. A better call to arms is for each of us to temper the other's overconfidence when society needs it most. This at least we might be adept at.

FOURTEEN

Facing the Mirror

AS I WAS WRITING THIS BOOK, I BEGAN TO SEE OVERCONFIDENCE everywhere. There were narcissistic world leaders and unprepared institutions. There were boastful CEOs and celebrities in denial. Then there were inflexible colleagues and stubborn relatives. Most of all, perhaps, I found an echo of so much of the book in myself. The timeline for writing the book was thrown into disarray thanks to my planning fallacy. I frequently found myself out of depth and made up by further frantic reading. There were several points at which I was convinced I was an impostor, and wondered why I had taken on this project in the first place. I'm sure experts will spot the Dunning-Kruger effect in my ideas about wars or pandemics, and my own partisan biases have inevitably crept into the discussion on politics. Of course, the very fact that I see overconfidence everywhere is itself perhaps a sign of my confirmation biases.

Two years after my overconfident failure to obtain the fellowship I talked about in the introduction, I applied again. This time I prepared better, and took on board the comments made by reviewers. I talked to previous recipients of the award, and made important changes to my proposal. When I interviewed for the fellowship on a rainy day in Manchester, I did not think it went well. The questions were hard. I had prepared for many of them, but I could have given more convincing answers to others. I didn't hold much hope for success afterwards. I drowned my sorrows in travel, visiting friends and relatives in India. It was on a train journey between Bengaluru and Hyderabad that, having rescued it from my spam folder, I read the email saying I had got the fellowship. As I set up my lab now, I'm dealing with the difficulties of germinating all my planned experiments in the harsh light of reality. Having to deal with the hundred small things that can and do go wrong is a regular reminder of the many forms of overconfidence I still have to unlearn.

If I have seen all these signs within myself, no doubt you can see them in the book as well. All I can say in my defence is that I have tried to be led by the experts. I might have been free with my speculations and glib parallels with world events, but the bulk of the book comes from all the research I have read. And what is it that I have learnt? Let's revisit our worst-case scenario from the introduction and see how it holds up.

To begin with, we are not Chaplin's sheep. We are a different breed, more wary, more cynical. We are still ready to trust a confident voice when we don't know better or when it tells us what we want to hear. This works well for us, that is, until we run into overconfidence. Overconfidence isn't a rare possibility that we might only occasionally encounter—it is present in different forms all around us—in everyday estimates of performance, in health behaviours, education, finance and in leaders around the world. Different forms of overconfidence could also have different costs. I wonder if we need to make a stronger distinction between overconfidence born of avoiding information that might require action (denialism) and an overconfidence that fuels action even in the face of failure. Avoiding health check-ups because you believe in your natural immunity is foolhardy. On the other hand, adopting positive health behaviours in defiance of an awful diagnosis could have positive consequences, even if only in opening up new opportunities for your life. In fact, the different kinds of overconfidence could well be in conflict with each other. What's the use of winning an argument (through overprecision) if it leads to poor health and death (thanks to overestimation)?

Most often, overconfidence is born from ambiguity. The gap between what is known and what is not is filled with what we would like to be true and what we can get away with. Fuzzy notions of average performance helps us believe we are better than average. Where we lack the skills or feedback to evaluate ourselves, we assume the best. Tasks with less clear feedback or more subjective outcomes are easily co-opted to fit our goals. Successes obtained through luck, bluffing or cheating are taken as evidence of our capabilities. For many, it is only repeated and undeniable encounters with failure that finally drive home our limitations. For many others amongst us, criticism is rarer and less clear, and we could go through our lives fooling ourselves about our true abilities. Who is allowed to get away with overconfidence—and benefit from it—is a problem we all need to grapple with.

Yet, for all of overconfidence's diversions away from accuracy, it remains bound to reality. We might avoid information, question statistics and ignore evidence in service of our goals, building up our conviction in our abilities and opinions. But when push comes to shove, our actions don't always match the distorted beliefs we profess. When the stakes are higher—as in a pandemic—we are more likely to seek accuracy rather than twist the facts. The same happens when accuracy itself becomes a goal. If we're paid to be correct, or even just reminded to be accurate rather than merely confident, overconfidence fades. The success of interventions guiding us towards accuracy once again highlights that our statements might not reflect genuine self-deceived beliefs about the world or other people. Even when responses are anonymous, they might simply serve as signals to others or to researchers, displaying our allegiances to causes and communities. Confidence is not a signal of knowledge but a sign of our commitment. Looking for overconfidence in terms of error would be missing the point—we might well be overestimating true overconfidence. The more we rely on measurements of actions and performance rather than claims and stated beliefs, the better our understanding of real-world overconfidence will be.

The benefits of overconfidence preserve its apparent ubiquity. It helps keep us motivated, preserves our mental health, fools peers into thinking we are better than we are, and it even gets us greater status and chosen as CEOs and leaders. Overconfident, even absurd beliefs could help us form community or gain material advantages. The next time you hear someone unwaveringly committed to what you think is an unbelievable idea, look at what they stand to gain from it and what social costs they might be scared of. If you think people are voting against their interests, perhaps it is you who misunderstands what their interests really are.

Overconfidence also has costs of course—and these are what might limit how far into our delusions we drift. As individuals, at some point, we are less well liked, and in the longer term, we lose people's trust. We don't gain or pay attention to feedback that could help us do better. These are all the advantages of being underconfident. So, depending on what each of us values more—status or sociability—we might each go down the path of overconfidence or underconfidence.

The costs of overconfidence are, of course, not for individuals alone. When each of our small deviations from reality combine and reinforce each other, larger-scale overconfidence can spread. Our errors prop each other up and our societies reach false consensus—everyone reassuring everyone else about the booming stock market or the inevitability of an election's results. We are more likely to be overconfident in social contexts, and equally less likely to change our minds after committing to something publicly. Even more worrying is the possibility that it is the most overconfident ones who might well go on to gain positions of authority and power. Ultimately, that remains the most dangerous portent of overconfidence. Sure, our trust in others and their overconfidence is not limitless, but this need not prevent the pattern of overconfident leaders, who reap all the benefits it can give them. It is society that pays the costs rather than the individuals themselves. They could have some loss of reputation, but this rarely affects their earnings, their family life or even their future careers. In their own circle of friends, perhaps they don't even lose their reputations. In contrast, lives could be lost in wars or pandemics, and livelihoods might be ruined by disastrous economic choices. Why would this have persisted? Why haven't we evolved or learnt to be more wary?

We are wary in our individual interactions—why doesn't that work at the level of societies? I think the answer to that lies in our modern societies. In small-scale societies, we would repeatedly encounter others whom we interacted with, and rapidly figure out who was trustworthy enough to continue interacting with. Reputation loss could be catastrophic, and overconfident folks would lose any status they had garnered. In our massive modern societies, it is harder to gauge someone's trustworthiness, especially when there may not be opportunity for repeated interactions. Even when a much-scrutinised politician pushes a disastrous policy, we might not know their intent or why the policy failed. There's just enough uncertainty there for us to make excuses for them. We are happy to make these excuses and be fooled by overconfidence if these leaders are on 'our side', if they are pushing for the same goals as us. And then sometimes, even if we don't make excuses, by the time we do realise someone is incompetent and all hot air, it might well be too late. One thing that a whole range of recent events has—or should have—taught us is that a single outlier can do tremendous damage, even changing the fabric of our societies. More often than not, by the time we have realised the scale of the disaster on our hands, the beneficiaries of overconfidence have moved on, leaving their successors with the uninspiring task of cleaning up the mess. Whether this theory, that overconfidence persists due to the scale of society, holds up or not needs to be confirmed. Most urgently though, we need to ensure the benefits that overconfident people gain is not at the expense of everyone else.

I can only hope that this book—my own exercise in overconfidence—has not been at the expense of you, the reader. Let me return to the gambit at the beginning of this book. If there was enough in this book that you found worthwhile, perhaps I haven't been overconfident after all. And if I have, then that's what kept me motivated enough to finish the book. The least I can hope for is that the book earns the benefits of my overconfidence and is all the more convincing for it.

Notes

1. AN ENTOMOLOGIST ON MARS

1. Trivers, R. (2000). 'The elements of a scientific theory of self-deception'. Annals of the New York Academy of Sciences, 907(1), 114–131.
2. Trivers, R. (2011). *Deceit and self-deception: Fooling yourself the better to fool others*. Penguin UK, London.
3. Lamba, S. & Nityananda, V. (2014). 'Self-deceived individuals are better at deceiving others'. *PloS One,* 9(8), e104562.

2. TRUST IN ME

1. Price, P.C. & Stone, E.R. (2004). 'Intuitive Evaluation of Likelihood Judgment Producers: Evidence for a Confidence Heuristic'. *Journal of Behavioral Decision Making*, *17*(1), 39–57.
2. Yates, J.F., Price, P.C., Lee, J.W. & Ramirez, J. (1996). 'Good probabilistic forecasters: The "consumer's" perspective'. *International Journal of Forecasting*, *12*(1), 41–56.
3. Karmarkar, U.R. & Tormala, Z.L. (2010). 'Believe Me, I Have No Idea What I'm Talking About: The Effects of Source Certainty on Consumer Involvement and Persuasion'. *Journal of Consumer Research*, *36*(6), 1033–1049.
4. Zarnoth, P. & Sniezek, J.A. (1997). 'The Social Influence of Confidence in Group Decision Making'. *Journal of Experimental Social Psychology*, *33*(4), 345–366.
5. Barrick, M.R., Shaffer, J.A. & DeGrassi, S.W. (2009). 'What You See May Not Be What You Get: Relationships Among Self-Presentation Tactics and Ratings of Interview and Job Performance'. *Journal of Applied Psychology*, *94*(6), 1394–1411.
6. Barrick, M.R., Shaffer, J.A. & DeGrassi, S.W. (2009). 'What You See May Not Be What You Get: Relationships Among Self-Presentation Tactics and Ratings of Interview and Job Performance'. *Journal of Applied Psychology*, *94*(6), 1394–1411.

7. Ellis, R.A. & Taylor, M.S. (1983). 'Role of self-esteem within the job search process'. *Journal of Applied Psychology*, *68*(4), 632–640.
8. Murphy, S.C., von Hippel, W., Dubbs, S.L., Angilletta, M.J., Wilson, R.S., Trivers, R. & Barlow, F.K. (2015). 'The Role of Overconfidence in Romantic Desirability and Competition'. *Personality and Social Psychology Bulletin*, *41*(8), 1036–1052.
9. von Hippel, W., Ronay, R., Baker, E., Kjelsaas, K. & Murphy, S.C. (2016). 'Quick Thinkers Are Smooth Talkers: Mental Speed Facilitates Charisma'. *Psychological Science*, *27*(1), 119–122.
10. Zarnoth, P. & Sniezek, J.A. (1997). 'The Social Influence of Confidence in Group Decision Making'. *Journal of Experimental Social Psychology*, *33*(4), 345–366.
11. Penrod, S. & Cutler, B. (1995). 'Witness confidence and witness accuracy: Assessing their forensic relation'. *Psychology, Public Policy, and Law*, *1*(4), 817.
12. Sporer, S.L., Penrod, S., Read, D. & Cutler, B. (1995). 'Choosing, Confidence, and Accuracy: A Meta-Analysis of the Confidence-Accuracy Relation in Eyewitness Identification Studies'. *Psychological Bulletin*, *118*(3), 315–327
13. Shamir, B., House, R. & Arthur, M. (1993). 'The Motivational Effects of Charismatic Leadership: A Self-Concept Based Theory'. *Organization Science*, *4*(4), 577–594.
14. Kahneman, D. (2011). *Thinking, fast and slow*. Farrar, Straus and Giroux, New York.
15. Conger, J.A. & Kanungo, R.N. (1987). 'Toward a behavioral theory of charismatic leadership in organizational settings'. *Academy of management review*, *12*(4), 637–647.
16. Buunk, B.P., Dijkstra, P., Fetchenhauer, D. & Kenrick, D.T. (2002). 'Age and Gender Differences Inmate Selection Criteria for Various Involvement Levels'. *Personal Relationships*, *9*, 271–278.
17. Moscovici, S. & Lage, E. (1976). 'Studies in social influence III: Majority versus minority influence in a group'. *European Journal of Social Psychology*, *6*(2), 149–174.
18. Stasser, G. & Davis, J.H. (1981). 'Group decision making and social influence: A social interaction sequence model'. *Psychological Review*, *88*(6), 523.
19. Barrick, M.R., Shaffer, J.A. & DeGrassi, S.W. (2009). 'What You See May Not Be What You Get: Relationships Among Self-Presentation Tactics and Ratings of Interview and Job Performance'. *Journal of Applied Psychology*, *94*(6), 1394–1411.
20. Patel, D., Fleming, S.M. & Kilner, J.M. (2012). 'Inferring subjective

states through the observation of actions'. Proceedings of the Royal Society B: Biological Sciences. 279(1748), 4853–4860.

21. Marshall, J.A.R., Brown, G. & Radford, A.N. (2017). 'Individual Confidence-Weighting and Group Decision-Making'. *Trends in Ecology and Evolution*, *32*(9), 636–645.
22. Krause, J., Ruxton, G.D. & Krause, S. (2010). 'Swarm intelligence in animals and humans'. *Trends in Ecology & Evolution*, *25*(1), 28–34.
23. 'Ask the Audience', Who Wants to Be a Millionaire Wiki, https://millionaire.fandom.com/wiki/Ask_the_Audience.
24. Kempe, M. & Mesoudi, A. (2014). 'Experimental and theoretical models of human cultural evolution'. *Wiley Interdisciplinary Reviews: Cognitive Science*, *5*(3), 317–326.
25. 'Ask the Audience', Who Wants to Be a Millionaire Wiki, https://millionaire.fandom.com/wiki/Ask_the_Audience.
26. Marshall, J.A.R., Brown, G. & Radford, A.N. (2017). 'Individual Confidence-Weighting and Group Decision-Making'. *Trends in Ecology and Evolution*, *32*(9), 636–645.
27. Koriat, A. (2012). 'When are two heads better than one and why?' *Science*, *336*(April), 20–22.
28. Bang, D., Fusaroli, R., Tylén, K., Olsen, K., Latham, P.E., Lau, J.Y.F., Roepstorff, A., Rees, G., Frith, C.D. & Bahrami, B. (2014). 'Does interaction matter? Testing whether a confidence heuristic can replace interaction in collective decision-making'. *Consciousness and Cognition*, *26*(1), 13–23.
29. Yaniv, I. (2004). 'Receiving other people's advice: Influence and benefit'. *Organizational Behavior and Human Decision Processes*, *93*(1), 1–13.
30. Sah, S., Moore, D.A. & MacCoun, R.J. (2013). 'Cheap talk and credibility: The consequences of confidence and accuracy on advisor credibility and persuasiveness'. *Organizational Behavior and Human Decision Processes*, *121*(2), 246–255.
31. Penrod, S. & Cutler, B. (1995). 'Witness confidence and witness accuracy: Assessing their forensic relation'. *Psychology, Public Policy, and Law*, *1*(4), 817.
32. Cutler, B.L., Penrod, S.D. & Stuve, T.E. (1988). 'Juror decision making in eyewitness identification cases'. *Law and Human Behavior*, *12*(1), 41–55.
33. Sporer, S.L., Penrod, S., Read, D. & Cutler, B. (1995). 'Choosing, Confidence, and Accuracy: A Meta-Analysis of the Confidence-Accuracy Relation in Eyewitness Identification Studies'. *Psychological Bulletin*, *118*(3), 315–327.
34. Tenney, E.R., MacCoun, R.J., Spellman, B.A. & Hastie, R. (2007).

'Calibration trumps confidence as a basis for witness credibility'. *Psychological Science*, *18*(1), 46–50.

35. Tenney, E.R., MacCoun, R.J., Spellman, B.A. & Hastie, R. (2007). 'Calibration trumps confidence as a basis for witness credibility'. *Psychological Science*, *18*(1), 46–50.
36. Tenney, E.R., Spellman, B.A. & MacCoun, R.J. (2008). 'The benefits of knowing what you know (and what you don't): How calibration affects credibility'. *Journal of Experimental Social Psychology*, *44*(5), 1368–1375.
37. Tenney, E.R., Small, J.E., Kondrad, R.L., Jaswal, V.K. & Spellman, B.A. (2011). 'Accuracy, Confidence, and Calibration: How Young Children and Adults Assess Credibility'. *Developmental Psychology*, *47*(4), 1065–1077.
38. Tenney, E.R., Small, J.E., Kondrad, R.L., Jaswal, V.K. & Spellman, B.A. (2011). 'Accuracy, Confidence, and Calibration: How Young Children and Adults Assess Credibility'. *Developmental Psychology*, *47*(4), 1065–1077.
39. Tenney, E.R., Spellman, B.A. & MacCoun, R.J. (2008). 'The benefits of knowing what you know (and what you don't): How calibration affects credibility'. *Journal of Experimental Social Psychology*, *44*(5), 1368–1375.
40. Vullioud, C., Clément, F., Scott-Phillips, T. & Mercier, H. (2017). 'Confidence as an expression of commitment: why misplaced expressions of confidence backfire'. *Evolution and Human Behavior*, *38*(1), 9–17.
41. Zarnoth, P. & Sniezek, J.A. (1997). 'The Social Influence of Confidence in Group Decision Making'. *Journal of Experimental Social Psychology*, *33*(4), 345–366.
42. Mercier, H. (2020). *Not Born Yesterday*. Princeton University Press, Princeton.
43. Sah, S., Moore, D.A. & MacCoun, R.J. (2013). 'Cheap talk and credibility: The consequences of confidence and accuracy on advisor credibility and persuasiveness'. *Organizational Behavior and Human Decision Processes*, *121*(2), 246–255.
44. Altay, S. & Mercier, H. (2020). 'Relevance Is Socially Rewarded, But Not at the Price of Accuracy'. *Evolutionary Psychology*, *18*(1), 1–7.
45. A recent study showed that people were more likely to share stories that would be interesting if true: Altay, S., De Araujo, E. & Mercier, H. (2022). '"If this account is true, it is most enormously wonderful": Interestingness-if-true and the sharing of true and false news'. *Digital Journalism*, *10*(3), 373–394.

46. Or when our incentives align with them. See Mercier, H. (2020). *Not Born Yesterday*. Princeton University Press, Princeton.

3. SMARTER THAN THE AVERAGE BEAR

1. 'Nobody Knows More Than Trump About Anything: A Supercut', NowThis News, https://www.youtube.com/watch?v=sR3f95BGIiA.
2. Alicke, M.D. & Govorun, O. (2005). 'The better-than-average effect'. In Alicke, M.D., Dunning, D.A. & Krueger, J. (Eds) *The Self in Social Judgment*. Psychology Press, New York, 85–106.
3. Mercier, H. (2020). *Not Born Yesterday*. Princeton University Press, Princeton.
4. Sah, S., Moore, D.A. & MacCoun, R.J. (2013). 'Cheap talk and credibility: The consequences of confidence and accuracy on advisor credibility and persuasiveness'. *Organizational Behavior and Human Decision Processes*, *121*(2), 246–255.
5. Moore, D.A. & Healy, P.J. (2008).' The Trouble With Overconfidence'. *Psychological Review*, *115*(2), 502–517.
6. Paulhus, D.L., Harms, P.D., Bruce, M.N. & Lysy, D.C. (2003). 'The Over-Claiming Technique: Measuring Self-Enhancement Independent of Ability'. *Journal of Personality and Social Psychology*, *84*(4), 890–904.
7. As cited in Alicke, M.D. & Govorun, O. (2005). 'The better-than-average effect'. In Alicke, M.D., Dunning, D.A. & Krueger, J. (Eds) *The Self in Social Judgment*. Psychology Press, New York, 85–106.
8. Merkle, C. & Weber, M. (2011). 'True overconfidence: The inability of rational information processing to account for apparent overconfidence'. *Organizational Behavior and Human Decision Processes*, *116*(2), 262–271.
9. Cross, K.P. (1977). 'Not can, but will college teaching be improved?'. *New Directions for Higher Education*, *1977*(17), 1–15.
10. Zenger, T.R. (1992). 'Why do employers only reward extreme performance? Examining the relationships among performance, pay, and turnover'. *Administrative Science Quarterly*, 198–219.
11. Benoit, J.P., Dubra, J. & Moore, D.A. (2015). 'Does the better-than-average effect show that people are overconfident?: Two experiments'. *Journal of the European Economic Association*, *13*(2), 293–329.
12. See citations in Epley, N. & Dunning, D. (2000). 'Feeling "holier than thou": Are self-serving assessments produced by errors in self-or social prediction?'. *Journal of personality and social psychology*, *79*(6), 861.
13. Pronin, E., Lin, D.Y. & Ross, L. (2002). 'The Bias Blind Spot: Perceptions

of Bias in Self Versus Others'. *Personality and Social Psychology Bulletin*, *28*(3), 369–381.

14. Shepperd, J.A., Waters, E.A., Weinstein, N.D. & Klein, W.M.P. (2015). 'A Primer on Unrealistic Optimism'. *Current Directions in Psychological Science*, *24*(3), 232–237.
15. Weinstein, N.D. (1980). 'Unrealistic optimism about future life events'. *Journal of Personality and Social Psychology*, *39*(5), 806–820.
16. Weinstein, N.D. (1987). 'Unrealistic optimism about susceptibility to health'. *Journal of Behavioral Medicine*, *10*(5), 481–500.
17. Weinstein, N.D. (1980). 'Unrealistic optimism about future life events'. *Journal of Personality and Social Psychology*, *39*(5), 806–820.
18. Bass, B.M. & Yammarino, F.J. (1991). 'Congruence of self and others' leadership ratings of naval officers for understanding successful performance'. *Applied psychology*, *40*(4), 437–454.
19. MacDonald, T.K. & Ross, M. (1999). 'Assessing the accuracy of predictions about dating relationships: How and why do lovers' predictions differ from those made by observers?'. *Personality and Social Psychology Bulletin*, *25*(11), 1417–1429.
20. Harris, M.M. & Schaubroeck, J. (1988). 'A meta-analysis of self-supervisor, self-peer, and peer-supervisor ratings'. *Personnel psychology*, *41*(1), 43–62.
21. John, O.P. & Robins, R.W. (1994). 'Accuracy and bias in self-perception: individual differences in self-enhancement and the role of narcissism'. *Journal of Personality and Social Psychology*, 66(1), 206.
22. Kruger, J. (1999). 'Lake Wobegon be gone! The "below-average effect" and the egocentric nature of comparative ability judgements'. *Journal of Personality and Social Psychology*, 77(2), 221–232.
23. Hoelzl, E. & Rustichini, A. (2005). 'Overconfident: Do you put your money on it?'. *The Economic Journal*, *115*(503), 305–318.
24. Glaser, M., Langer, T. & Weber, M. (2013). 'True overconfidence in interval estimates: Evidence based on a new measure of miscalibration'. *Journal of Behavioral Decision Making*, *26*(5), 405–417.
25. Krawczyk, M., & Wilamowski, M. (2019). 'Task difficulty and overconfidence: Evidence from distance running'. *Journal of Economic Psychology*, 75, 102128.
26. Alicke, M.D. & Govorun, O. (2005). 'The better-than-average effect'. In Alicke, M.D., Dunning, D.A. & Krueger, J. (Eds.) *The Self in Social Judgment*. Psychology Press, New York, 85–106.
27. Sparks, P. & Shepherd, R. (1994). 'Public perceptions of the potential hazards associated with food production and food consumption: an empirical study'. *Risk analysis*, *14*(5), 799–806.

28. Alicke, M.D., Klotz, M.L., Breitenbecher, D.L., Yurak, T.J. & Vredenburg, D.S. (1995). 'Personal Contact, Individuation, and the Better-Than-Average Effect'. *Journal of Personality and Social Psychology*, *68*(5), 804–825.
29. 'Our story: Jørn Utzon AC, Sydney Opera House, https://www.sydneyoperahouse.com/our-story/jorn-utzon.
30. Buehler, R., Griffin, D. & Ross, M. (2002). 'Inside the planning fallacy: The causes and consequences of optimistic time predictions'. In Gilovich, T., Griffin D. & Kahneman, D. (Eds), *Heuristics and Biases: The Psychology of Intuitive Judgment*. Cambridge University Press, 250–270.
31. Buehler, R., Griffin, D. & Ross, M. (1994). 'Exploring the "planning fallacy": Why people underestimate their task completion times'. *Journal of Personality and Social Psychology*, *67*(3), 366.
32. Topham, Gwyn. 'HS2 to be delayed by up to five years as cost spirals to up to £88bn'. *The Guardian*, 3 September 2019.
33. Finch, Hannah. 'What is the route of HS2, what's the cost and will it ever get finished?'. *Business Live*, 5 April 2021.
34. *Oakervee Review*, available at: https://assets.publishing.service.gov.uk/government/uploads/system/uploads/attachment_data/file/870092/oakervee-review.pdf.
35. Syal, Rajeev and Topham, Gwyn. 'HS2 late and billions over budget due to Tory failures, report finds', *The Guardian*, 24 January 2020.
36. 'HS2 "needs realistic timetable" say MPs'. *BBC News*, 14 September 2016.
37. Topham, Gwyn. 'HS2 to be delayed by two more years due to soaring costs'. *The Guardian*, 9 March 2023.
38. M. Naveen, 'Cost and & time overrun marks Bengaluru metro phase-I', *The Economic Times*, 9 March 2017.
39. Epley, N. & Dunning, D. (2000). 'Feeling "holier than thou": Are self-serving assessments produced by errors in self—or social prediction?'. *Journal of Personality and Social Psychology*, *79*(6), 861–875.
40. Epley, N. & Whitchurch, E. (2008). 'Mirror, mirror on the wall: Enhancement in self-recognition'. *Personality and Social Psychology Bulletin*, *34*(9), 1159–1170.
41. For an excellent review, see Dunning, D., Heath, C. & Suls, J.M. (2004). 'Flawed self-assessment implications for health, education, and the workplace'. *Psychological Science in the Public Interest*, *5*(3), 69–106.
42. Loftus, E.F. & Wagenaar, W.A. (1988). 'Lawyers' predictions of success'. In Krivoshey, R.M. (Ed.) *Instructions, Verdicts, and Judicial Behavior*. Routledge, New York, 213–229.

43. Krawczyk, M. & Wilamowski, M. (2018). 'Task difficulty and overconfidence. Evidence from distance running'. *Journal of Economic Psychology*, 75, 102128.
44. Oskam, J., Kingma, J. & Klasen, H.J. (2000). 'Clinicians' recognition of 10 different types of distal radial fractures'. *Perceptual and Motor Skills*, *91*(3), 917–924.
45. Cambridge, R.M. & Shreckengost, R.C. (1978). *Are You Sure?: The Subjective Probability Assessment Test*. Information Science Center, Office of Training, Central Intelligence Agency—as cited in Dunning, D., Heath, C. & Suls, J.M. (2004). 'Flawed self-assessment implications for health, education, and the workplace'. *Psychological Science in the Public Interest, 5*(3), 69–106.
46. Clark, J. & Friesen, L. (2009). 'Overconfidence in forecasts of own performance: An experimental study'. *Economic Journal*, *119*(534), 229–251.
47. For a good review, read Shepperd, J.A., Waters, E.A., Weinstein, N.D. & Klein, W.M.P. (2015). 'A Primer on Unrealistic Optimism'. *Current Directions in Psychological Science*, *24*(3), 232–237.
48. Weinstein, N.D. & Lyon, J.E. (1999). 'Mindset, optimistic bias about personal risk and health-protective behaviour'. *British Journal of Health Psychology*, *4*(4), 289–300.
49. Rothman, A.J., Klein, W.M. & Weinstein, N.D. (1996). 'Absolute and relative biases in estimations of personal risk 1'. *Journal of Applied Social Psychology*, *26*(14), 1213–1236.
50. Yang, S., Markoczy, L. & Qi, M. (2007). 'Unrealistic optimism in consumer credit card adoption'. *Journal of Economic Psychology*, *28*(2), 170–185.
51. Moore, D.A. & Cain, D.M. (2007). 'Overconfidence and underconfidence: When and why people underestimate (and overestimate) the competition'. *Organizational Behavior and Human Decision Processes*, *103*(2), 197–213.
52. Moore, D.A., Tenney, E.R. & Haran, U. (2015). 'Overprecision in Judgment'. *The Wiley Blackwell Handbook of Judgment and Decision Making*, 2, 182–209.
53. Alpert, M. & Raiffa, H. (1982). 'A progress report on the training of probability assessors'. In Kahneman, D., Slovic, P. & Tversky, A. (Eds.) *Judgment under Uncertainty: Heuristics and Biases*. Cambridge University Press, Cambridge, 294–305.
54. Gigerenzer, G. & Hoffrage, U. (1995). 'How to improve Bayesian reasoning without instruction: Frequency formats'. *Psychological Review*, *102*(4), 684–704.

55. Gigerenzer, G., Hoffrage, U. & Kleinbfilting, H. (1991). 'Probabilistic Mental Models: A Brunswikian Theory of Confidence'. *Psychological Review*, *98*(4) 506–528.
56. Vullioud, C., Clément, F., Scott-Phillips, T. & Mercier, H. (2017). 'Confidence as an expression of commitment: why misplaced expressions of confidence backfire'. *Evolution and Human Behavior*, *38*(1), 9–17.
57. Yaniv, I. & Foster, D.P. (1995). 'Graininess of judgment under uncertainty: An accuracy-informativeness trade-off'. *Journal of Experimental Psychology: General*, *124*(4), 424–432.
58. Dunning, D., Heath, C. & Suls, J.M. (2004). 'Flawed self-assessment implications for health, education, and the workplace'. *Psychological Science in the Public Interest, Supplement*, *5*(3), 69–106.
59. Svenson, O. (1981). 'Are we all less risky and more skillful than our fellow drivers?'. *Acta Psychologica*, *47*(2), 143–148.
60. White, M.J., Cunningham, L.C. & Titchener, K. (2011). 'Young drivers' optimism bias for accident risk and driving skill: Accountability and insight experience manipulations'. *Accident Analysis and Prevention*, *43*(4), 1309–1315.
61. DeJoy, D.M. (1989). 'The optimism bias and traffic accident risk perception'. *Accident Analysis & Prevention*, *21*(4), 333–340.
62. McCormick, I. A., Walkey, F.H. & Green, D.E. (1986). 'Comparative perceptions of driver ability—A confirmation and expansion'. *Accident Analysis and Prevention*, *18*(3), 205–208.
63. Preston, C.E. & Harris, S. (1965). 'Psychology of drivers in traffic accidents'. *Journal of Applied Psychology*, *49*(4), 284.
64. Dunning, D., Heath, C. & Suls, J.M. (2004). 'Flawed Self-Assessment Implications for Health, Education, and the Workplace'. *Psychological Science in the Public Interest*, *5*(3), 69–106.
65. Chemers, M.M., Hu, L.T. & Garcia, B.F. (2001). 'Academic self-efficacy and first year college student performance and adjustment'. *Journal of Educational Psychology*, *93*(1), 55.
66. Hansford, B.C. & Hattie, J.A. (1982). 'The relationship between self and achievement/performance measures'. *Review of Educational Research*, *52*(1), 123–142.
67. Falchikov, N. & Boud, D. (1989). 'Student self-assessment in higher education: A meta-analysis'. *Review of Educational Research*, *59*(4), 395–430.
68. For an excellent and more complete review read: Dunning, D., Heath, C. & Suls, J.M. (2004). 'Flawed Self-Assessment Implications for

Health, Education, and the Workplace'. *Psychological Science in the Public Interest*, *5*(3), 69–106.

69. Crosby, R.A. & Yarber, W.L. (2001). 'Perceived versus actual knowledge about correct condom use among US adolescents: Results from a national study'. *Journal of Adolescent Health*, *28*(5), 415–420.
70. Hoorens, V. & Harris, P.P.R.P. (1998). 'Distortions in reports of health behaviors: The time span effect and illusory superiority'. *Psychology & Health*, *13*(3), 451–466.
71. Weinstein, N.D. (1984). 'Why it won't happen to me: perceptions of risk factors and susceptibility'. *Health psychology*, *3*(5), 431.
72. Hoorens, V. & Harris, P. (1998). 'Distortions in reports of health behaviors: The time span effect and illusory superiority'. *Psychology and Health*, *13*(3), 451–466.
73. Lima de Miranda, K., Detlefsen, L. & Stolpe, M. (2020). 'Overconfidence and hygiene non-compliance in hospitals'. Kiel Working Paper, No. 2156.
74. Bushuven, S., Juenger, J., Moeltner, A. & Dettenkofer, M. (2018). 'Overconfidence in infection control proficiency'. *American Journal of Infection Control*, *47*(5), 545–550.
75. Marteau, T.M., Johnston, M., Wynne, G. & Evans, T.R. (1989). 'Cognitive factors in the explanation of the mismatch between confidence and competence in performing basic life support'. *Psychology and Health*, *3*(3), 173–182.
76. Risucci, D.A., Tortolani, A.J. & Ward, R.J. (1989). 'Ratings of surgical residents by self, supervisors and peers'. *Surgery, Gynecology & Obstetrics*, *169*(6), 519–526.
77. Christensen-Szalanski, J.J. & Bushyhead, J.B. (1981). 'Physicians' use of probabilistic information in a real clinical setting'. *Journal of Experimental Psychology: Human Perception and Performance*, *7*(4), 928.
78. Sheer, V.C. & Cline, R.J. (1994). 'The development and validation of a model explaining sexual behavior among college students: Implications for AIDS communication campaigns'. *Human Communication Research*, *21*(2), 280–304.
79. Burger, J.M. & Burns, L. (1988). 'The illusion of unique invulnerability and the use of effective contraception'. *Personality and Social Psychology Bulletin*, *14*(2), 264–270.
80. Dillard, A.J., Midboe, A.M. & Klein, W.M. (2009). 'The dark side of optimism: Unrealistic optimism about problems with alcohol predicts subsequent negative event experiences'. *Personality and social psychology bulletin*, *35*(11), 1540–1550.

81. Larwood, L. (1978). 'Swine flu: A field study of self-serving biases'. *Journal of Applied Social Psychology*, *8*(3), 283–289.

4. A BIASED WORLD

1. Rebecca Solnit, 'Men Explain Things to Me'. *Guernica*, 20 August 2012.
2. Solnit, R. (2014). *Men Explain Things to Me*. Haymarket Books, Chicago.
3. Henrich, J., Heine, S.J. & Norenzayan, A. (2010). 'The weirdest people in the world?'. *Behavioral and Brain Sciences*, *33*(2-3), 61–83.
4. Henrich, J., Heine, S. J. & Norenzayan, A. (2010). 'Most people are not WEIRD'. *Nature*, *466*(7302), 29.
5. Matthew Smith. 'International survey: globalisation is still seen as a force for good in the world'. *YouGov*, 17 November 2016.
6. YouGov Survey Results, October 2016, https://d25d2506sfb94s.cloudfront.net/cumulus_uploads/document/71wl1vs4ii/International%20toplines_W.pdf.
7. 'Understanding the Perspectives of Young People Around the World'. *Ipsos*, 24 September 2018, https://www.ipsos.com/en-us/news-polls/Gates-goalkeepers-youth-optimism.
8. Rebecca Ratcliffe and Carmen Aguillar. '"Our time is now": World youth poll reveals unexpected optimism'. *The Guardian*, 24 September 2018.
9. 'Our tomorrows: Teenagers around the world share their fears and dreams'. https://www.youtube.com/watch?v=IgmFn-suAi4&t=5s.
10. Deaton, A. (2018). 'What do self-reports of wellbeing say about life-cycle theory and policy?'. *Journal of Public Economics*, *162*, 18–25.
11. Isaacs, J.B. (2008). 'International comparisons of economic mobility'. In Haskins R., Isaacs, J.B. & Sawhill, I.V. (Eds) *Getting Ahead or Losing Ground: Economic Mobility in America*. Washington, D.C., Brookings and Pew Economic Mobility Project, 37–46.
12. Julia B. Isaacs. 'International Comparisons of Economic Mobility'. The Brookings Institution. https://www.brookings.edu/wp-content/uploads/2016/07/02_economic_mobility_sawhill_ch3.pdf.
13. 'Americans overestimate social mobility in their country'. *The Economist*, 14 February 2018.
14. Alesina, A., Stantcheva, S. & Teso, E. (2018). 'Intergenerational mobility and preferences for redistribution'. *American Economic Review*, *108*(2), 521–554.
15. Kuwar Singh. 'Indians are the biggest believers in the rags-to-riches fairytale'. *Quartz*, 21 January 2019.

16. Ranjan Ray, 'The Unrealistic Optimism of Indians on Prospects of Upward Social Mobility'. *The Wire*, 14 June 2019.
17. Asher, S., Novosad, P. & Rafkin, C. (2022). 'Intergenerational mobility in India: New methods and estimates across time, space, and communities'. Unpublished manuscript. Available at: https:// paulnovosad. com/pdf/anr-india-mobility. pdf.
18. Singh, Kuwar. 'Indians are the biggest believers in the rags-to-riches fairytale'. *Quartz*, 21 January 2019.
19. Kapur, Devesh, Sircar, Neelanjan & Vaishnav, Milan. 'It's not ideology but aspiration that drives India's middle class—politicians take note'. *Quartz*, 4 December 2017.
20. Barsbai, T., Schmidt, U. & Zirpel, U. (2022). 'Overconfidence and Risk Taking in the Field: Evidence from Ethiopian Farmers'. *Economic Development and Cultural Change*, *70*(3), 1065–1102.
21. Morony, S., Kleitman, S., Lee, Y.P. & Stankov, L. (2013). 'Predicting achievement: Confidence vs self-efficacy, anxiety, and self-concept in Confucian and European countries'. *International Journal of Educational Research*, *58*, 79–96.
22. Stankov, L. & Lee, J. (2014). 'Overconfidence across world regions'. *Journal of Cross-Cultural Psychology*, *45*(5), 821–837.
23. Heine, S.J. & Hamamura, T. (2007). 'In search of East Asian self-enhancement'. *Personality and Social Psychology Review*, *11*(1), 4–27.
24. Mezulis, A.H., Abramson, L.Y., Hyde, J.S. & Hankin, B.L. (2004). 'Is there a universal positivity bias in attributions? A meta-analytic review of individual, developmental, and cultural differences in the self-serving attributional bias'. *Psychological Bulletin*, *130*(5), 711–747.
25. Yates, J.F., Lee, J.W. & Shinotsuka, H. (1996). 'Beliefs about overconfidence, including its cross-national variation'. *Organizational Behavior and Human Decision Processes*, *65*(2), 138–147.
26 Moore, D.A., Dev, A.S. & Goncharova, E.Y. (2018). 'Overconfidence Across Cultures'. *Collabra: Psychology*, *4*(1), 1–37.
27. Sedikides, C., Gaertner, L. & Vevea, J.L. (2005). 'Pancultural self-enhancement reloaded: A meta-analytic reply to Heine' (2005). *Journal of Personality and Social Psychology*, *89*(4), 539–551.
28. Sedikides, C., Gaertner, L. & Toguchi, Y. (2003). 'Pancultural Self-Enhancement'. *Journal of Personality and Social Psychology*, *84*(1), 60–79.
29. Gaertner, L., Sedikides, C. & Chang, K. (2008). 'On Pancultural Self-Enhancement Well-Adjusted Taiwanese Self-Enhance on Personally Valued Traits'. *Journal of Cross-Cultural Psychology*, *39*(4), 463–477.
30. Muthukrishna, M., Henrich, J., Toyokawa, W., Hamamura, T., Kameda,

T. & Heine, S.J. (2018). 'Overconfidence is universal? Elicitation of genuine overconfidence (EGO) procedure reveals systematic differences across domain, task knowledge, and incentives in four populations'. *PLoS One*, *13*(8), 1–30.

31. Sedikides, C., Gaertner, L. & Toguchi, Y. (2003). 'Pancultural self-enhancement'. *Journal of Personality and Social Psychology*, *84*(1), 60.
32. Stuhlmacher, A.F. & Walters, A.E. (1999). 'Gender differences in negotiation outcome: A meta-analysis'. *Personnel Psychology*, *52*(3), 653–677.
33. Bosquet, C., Combes, P.P. & García-Peñalosa, C. (2019). 'Gender and promotions: Evidence from academic economists in France'. *The Scandinavian Journal of Economics*, *121*(3), 1020–1053.
34. Furnham, A., Hosoe, T. & Tang, T.L.P. (2002). 'Male hubris and female humility? A cross-cultural study of ratings of self, parental, and sibling multiple intelligence in America, Britain, and Japan'. *Intelligence*, *30*(1), 101–115.
35. Benson, A., Li, D. & Shue, K. (2021). '"Potential" and the gender promotion gap'. Working paper. Available at SSRN.
36. Somers, Meredith. 'Women are less likely than men to be promoted. Here's one reason why'. MIT Sloan, 12 April 2022.
37. Thomas, Tobi. 'Women who ask for pay rise less successful than men, UK poll reveals'. *The Guardian*, 3 April 2022.
38. Krawczyk, M. & Wilamowski, M. (2019). 'Task difficulty and overconfidence. Evidence from distance running'. *Journal of Economic Psychology*, *75*, 102128.
39. Deaner, R.O., Carter, R.E., Joyner, M.J. & Hunter, S.K. (2015). 'Men are more likely than women to slow in the marathon'. *Medicine and Science in Sports and Exercise*, *47*(3), 607.
40. Nekby, L., Thoursie, P.S. & Vahtrik, L. (2008). 'Gender and self-selection into a competitive environment: Are women more overconfident than men?'. *Economics Letters*, *100*(3), 405–407.
41. Cao, Q., Li, J. & Niu, X. (2019). 'The Role of Overconfidence in Overweighting Private Information: Does gender matter?'. ZBW-Leibniz Information Centre for Economics, No. 203448.
42. Perilloux, C., Easton, J.A. & Buss, D.M. (2012). 'The misperception of sexual interest'. *Psychological Science*, *23*(2), 146–151.
43. Williams, Rhiannon. 'Men more than twice as likely to fall for romance scams than women, new study reveals'. iNews, 12 February 2021.
44. Moore, D.A., Dev, A.S. & Goncharova, E.Y. (2018). 'Overconfidence across cultures'. *Collabra: Psychology*, *4*(1).
45. Muthukrishna, M., Henrich, J., Toyokawa, W., Hamamura, T., Kameda,

T. & Heine, S.J. (2018). 'Overconfidence is universal? Elicitation of Genuine Overconfidence (EGO) procedure reveals systematic differences across domain, task knowledge, and incentives in four populations'. *PloS One*, *13*(8), e0202288.

46. Dracup, K., Moser, D.K., Eisenberg, M., Meischke, H., Alonzo, A.A. & Braslow, A. (1995). 'Causes of delay in seeking treatment for heart attack symptoms'. *Social Science & Medicine*, *40*(3), 379–392.
47. Svenson, O. (1981). 'Are we all less risky and more skillful than our fellow drivers?'. *Acta Psychologica*, *47*(2), 143–148.
48. Prims, J.P. & Moore, D.A. (2017). 'Overconfidence over the lifespan'. *Judgment and Decision Making*, *12*(1), 29–41.
49. See summary and references in Moore, D.A., Tenney, E.R. & Haran, U. (2015). 'Overprecision in Judgment'. In Keren, G.,Wu, G. (Eds), *Blackwell Handbook of Judgment and Decision Making*, Wiley, New York, 182–212.
50. Schulz, J.F. & Thöni, C. (2016). 'Overconfidence and Career Choice'. *PloS One*, *11*(1), e0145126.
51. Twenge, J.M. & Campbell, S.M. (2008). 'Generational differences in psychological traits and their impact on the workplace'. *Journal of Managerial Psychology*, *23*(8), 862–877.
52. Twenge, J.M. & Foster, J.D. (2010). 'Birth Cohort Increases in Narcissistic Personality Traits Among American College Students, 1982-2009'. *Social Psychological and Personality Science*, *1*(1), 99–106.
53. Twenge, J.M. & Campbell, S.M. (2008). 'Generational differences in psychological traits and their impact on the workplace'. *Journal of Managerial Psychology*, *23*(8), 862–877.
54. Twenge, J.M., Konrath, S., Foster, J.D., Campbell, W.K. & Bushman, B.J. (2008). 'Egos inflating over time: A cross-temporal meta-analysis of the narcissistic personality inventory'. *Journal of Personality*, *76*(4), 875–902.
55. Smits, I.A.M., Dolan, C.V., Vorst, H.C.M., Wicherts, J.M. & Timmerman, M.E. (2011). 'Cohort differences in big five personality factors over a period of 25 years'. *Journal of Personality and Social Psychology*, *100*(6), 1124–1138.
56. Twenge, J.M. & Campbell, S.M. (2008). 'Generational differences in psychological traits and their impact on the workplace'. *Journal of Managerial Psychology*, *23*(8), 862–877.
57. Ackerman, R.A., Witt, E.A., Donnellan, M.B., Trzesniewski, K.H., Robins, R.W. & Kashy, D.A. (2011). 'What does the narcissistic personality inventory really measure?'. *Assessment*, *18*(1), 67–87.

58. Trzesniewski, K.H., Donnellan, M.B. & Robins, R.W. (2008). 'Do Today's Young People Really Think They Are So Extraordinary?'. *Psychological Science*, *19*(2), 181–188.
59. Trzesniewski, K.H. & Donnellan, M.B. (2010). 'Rethinking "generation me": A study of cohort effects from 1976-2006'. *Perspectives on Psychological Science*, *5*(1), 58–75.
60. Schrager, Alison. 'The financial crisis may have scarred a generation for life'. *Quartz*, 15 September 2018.

5. THE EXPERTS AND US

1. 'Why some people believe the Earth is flat'. *BBC Earth*, https://www.bbcearth.com/news/why-some-people-believe-the-earth-is-flat. Also see: 'How the ancient Greeks proved Earth was round over 2,000 years ago'. *Independent*, 28 December 2017.
2. Shastry, Vyasa. 'How Aryabhata got the earth's circumference right'. *Mint*, 15 February 2018.
3. Kennedy, Brian, Tyson, Alec & Funk, Cary, 'Americans' Trust in Scientists, Other Groups Declines'. Pew Research Center, https://www.pewresearch.org/science/2022/02/15/americans-trust-in-scientists-other-groups-declines/.
4. Ipsos Veracity Index: Trust in the police drops for the second year in a row, https://www.ipsos.com/en-uk/ipsos-veracity-index-trust-police-drops-second-year-row. ('The Ipsos Veracity Index is the longest-running poll on trust in professions in Britain, having been asked consistently since 1983.')
5. Mercier, H. (2020). 'Not born yesterday'. In *Not Born Yesterday*. Princeton University Press, Princeton.
6 Langseth, T. (2012). 'B.A.S.E. jumping—Beyond the thrills'. *European Journal for Sport and Society*, *9*(3), 155–176.
7. Kruger, J. & Dunning, D. (1999). 'Unskilled and Unaware of It: How Difficulties in Recognizing One's Own Incompetence Lead to Inflated Self-Assessments'. *Journal of Personality and Social Psychology*, *77*(6), 1121–1134.
8. Sanchez, C. & Dunning, D. (2018). 'Overconfidence among beginners: Is a little learning a dangerous thing?'. *Journal of Personality and Social Psychology*, *114*(1), 10–28.
9. Stankov, L. & Lee, J. (2014). 'Overconfidence Across World Regions'. *Journal of Cross-Cultural Psychology*, *45*(5), 821–837.
10. Mahase, Elisabeth (2019). 'Measles cases rise 300% globally in first few months of 2019'. *The BMJ*, 365:l1810.

11. Ellis-Petersen, Hannah. 'Measles outbreak in Philippines kills 70, with vaccine fearmongering blamed'. *The Guardian*, 12 February 2019.
12. 'Measles Cases and Outbreaks'. CDC, https://www.cdc.gov/measles/cases-outbreaks.html.
13. Newman, D., Lewandowsky, S. & Mayo, R. (2022). 'Believing in nothing and believing in everything: The underlying cognitive paradox of anti-COVID-19 vaccine attitudes'. *Personality and Individual Differences, 189*.
14. For the full story, read this book review: Omer, Saad B. 'The discredited doctor hailed by the anti-vaccine movement', *Nature*, 27 October 2020.
15. Motta, M., Callaghan, T. & Sylvester, S. (2018). 'Knowing less but presuming more: Dunning-Kruger effects and the endorsement of anti-vaccine policy attitudes'. *Social Science & Medicine*, *211*, 274–281.
16. Pennycook, G., Ross, R.M., Koehler, D.J. & Fugelsang, J.A. (2017). 'Dunning–Kruger effects in reasoning: Theoretical implications of the failure to recognize incompetence'. *Psychonomic Bulletin and Review*, *24*(6), 1774–1784.
17. Dunning, D. (2011). 'The Dunning–Kruger Effect: On Being Ignorant of One's Own Ignorance'. In *Advances in Experimental Social Psychology*, *44*, 247–296.
18. Burson, K.A., Larrick, R.P. & Klayman, J. (2006). 'Skilled or Unskilled, but Still Unaware of It : How Perceptions of Difficulty Drive Miscalibration in Relative Comparisons'. *Journal of Personality and Social Psychology*, *90*(1), 60–77.
19. Gignac, G.E. & Zajenkowski, M. (2020). 'The Dunning-Kruger effect is (mostly) a statistical artefact: Valid approaches to testing the hypothesis with individual differences data'. *Intelligence*, *80*(March).
20. Ackerman, P.L., Beier, M.E. & Bowen, K.R. (2002). 'What we really know about our abilities and our knowledge'. *Personality and individual differences*, *33*(4), 587–605.
21. Summarised in Dunning, D. (2011). 'The Dunning–Kruger Effect: On Being Ignorant of One's Own Ignorance'. In Advances in Experimental Social Psychology, *44*, 247–296.
22. Feld, J., Sauermann, J. & de Grip, A. (2017). 'Estimating the relationship between skill and overconfidence'. *Journal of Behavioral and Experimental Economics*, *68*(10611), 18–24.
23. Ehrlinger, J., Johnson, K., Banner, M., Dunning, D. & Kruger, J. (2008). 'Why the unskilled are unaware: Further explorations of (absent) self-insight among the incompetent'. *Organizational Behavior and Human Decision Processes*, *105*, 98–121.

24. Krajč, M. & Ortmann, A. (2008). 'Are the unskilled really that unaware? An alternative explanation'. *Journal of Economic Psychology*, *29*(5), 724–738.
25. Mazor, M. & Fleming, S.M. (2021). 'The Dunning-Kruger effect revisited'. *Nature Human Behaviour*, *5*(6), 677–678.
26. Jansen, R.A., Rafferty, A.N. & Griffiths, T.L. (2021). 'A rational model of the Dunning–Kruger effect supports insensitivity to evidence in low performers'. *Nature Human Behaviour*, *5*(6), 756–763.
27. McIntosh, R.D., Fowler, E.A., Lyu, T. & Sala, S. Della. (2019). 'Wise Up: Clarifying the Role of Metacognition in the Dunning-Kruger Effect'. *Journal of Experimental Psychology: General*, *148*(11), 1882–1897.
28. Liu, J., Zhang, W., Zhan, Y., Song, L., Guan, P. & Kang, D. (2019). 'The Effect of Negative Feedback on Positive Beliefs in Self-Deception'. *Frontiers in Psychology*, *10*(April), 1–12.
29. Ryvkin, D., Krajč, M. & Ortmann, A. (2012). 'Are the unskilled doomed to remain unaware?'. *Journal of Economic Psychology*, *33*(5), 1012–1031.
30. Weisberg, D.S., Landrum, A.R., Metz, S.E. & Weisberg, M. (2018). 'No missing link: Knowledge predicts acceptance of evolution in the United States'. *BioScience*, *68*(3), 212–222.
31. Montanez, Amanda. 'People Who Understand Evolution Are More Likely to Accept It'. *Scientific American*, 1 May 2018.
32. Hoogeveen, S., Sarafoglou, A. & Wagenmakers, E.J. (2020). 'Laypeople can predict which social-science studies will be replicated successfully'. *Advances in Methods and Practices in Psychological Science*, *3*(3), 267–285.
33. Önkal, D., Yates, J.F., Simga-Mugan, C. & Öztin, Ş. (2003). 'Professional vs. amateur judgment accuracy: The case of foreign exchange rates'. *Organizational Behavior and Human Decision Processes*, *91*(2), 169–185.
34. McKenzie, C.R., Liersch, M.J. & Yaniv, I. (2008). 'Overconfidence in interval estimates: What does expertise buy you?'. *Organizational Behavior and Human Decision Processes*, *107*(2), 179–191.
35. Sturgis, P. & Allum, N. (2004). 'Science in society: re-evaluating the deficit model of public attitudes'. *Public Understanding of Science*, *13*(1), 55–74.
36. Nyhan, B., Reifler, J., Richey, S. & Freed, G.L. (2014). 'Effective messages in vaccine promotion: a randomized trial'. *Pediatrics*, *133*(4), e835-e842.
37. Lemaitre, T., Carrier, N., Farrands, A., Gosselin, V., Petit, G. & Gagneur, A. (2019). 'Impact of a vaccination promotion intervention using

motivational interview techniques on long-term vaccine coverage: the PromoVac strategy'. *Human Vaccines & Immunotherapeutics*, *15*(3), 732–739.

6. BUILDING A LIE

1. Viscusi, W.K. (1990). 'Do smokers underestimate risks?'. *Journal of Political Economy*, *98*(6), 1253–1269.
2. Lerner, J.S., Gonzalez, R.M., Small, D.A. & Fischhoff, B. (2003). 'Effects of fear and anger on perceived risks of terrorism: A national field experiment'. *Psychological Science*, *14*(2), 144–150.
3. Khomami, Nadia, 'London garden bridge project collapses in acrimony after £37m spent'. *The Guardian*, 14 August 2017.
4. Klayman, J. (1995). 'Varieties of Confirmation Bias'. *Psychology of Learning and Motivation*, *32*, 385–418.
5. Klayman, J. (1995). 'Varieties of Confirmation Bias'. *Psychology of Learning and Motivation*, *32*, 385–418.
6. Oswald, M.E. & Grosjean, S. (2004). 'Confirmation bias'. In Pohl, R.F. Ed. *Cognitive Illusions: A Handbook on Fallacies and Biases in Thinking, Judgement and Memory*, Psychology Press, London, 79–96.
7. Nickerson, R.S. (1998). 'Confirmation bias: A ubiquitous phenomenon in many guises'. *Review of General Psychology*, *2*(2), 175–220.
8. Lockwood, B. (2017). 'Confirmation bias and electoral accountability'. *Political Science*, *11*, 471–501.
9. Gilead, M., Sela, M. & Maril, A. (2019). 'That's My Truth: Evidence for Involuntary Opinion Confirmation'. *Social Psychological and Personality Science*, *10*(3), 393–401.
10. Rajsic, J., Wilson, D.E. & Pratt, J. (2015). 'Confirmation bias in visual search'. *Journal of Experimental Psychology: Human Perception and Performance*, *41*(5), 1353–1364.
11. Bastone, Nick. 'Jeff Bezos: Today's internet is a 'confirmation bias machine' that could help autocratic regimes'. *Business Insider*, 16 October 2018.
12. Lelkes, Y., Sood, G. & Iyengar, S. (2017). 'The Hostile Audience: The Effect of Access to Broadband Internet on Partisan Affect'. *American Journal of Political Science*, *61*(1), 5–20.
13. Brady, W.J., Wills, J.A., Jost, J.T., Tucker, J.A., van Bavel, J.J. & Fiske, S.T. (2017). 'Emotion shapes the diffusion of moralized content in social networks'. *Proceedings of the National Academy of Sciences of the United States of America*, *114*(28), 7313–7318.
14. Knobloch-Westerwick, S., Johnson, B. K., & Westerwick, A. (2015). 'Confirmation bias in online searches: Impacts of selective exposure

before an election on political attitude strength and shifts'. *Journal of Computer-Mediated Communication*, *20*(2), 171–187.

15. Pennycook, G. & Rand, D.G. (2019). 'Lazy, not biased: Susceptibility to partisan fake news is better explained by lack of reasoning than by motivated reasoning'. *Cognition*, *188*, 39–50.
16. Sjastad, H., Skard, S., Thorbjornsen, H. & Norman, E. (2019). 'Self-serving optimism in hedonic prediction: People believe in a bright future for themselves and their friends, but not for their enemies'. *Psyarxiv*, *262675*, 1–11.
17. Kunda, Z. (1990). 'The case for Motivated Reasoning'. *Psychological Bulletin*, *108*(3), 480–498.
18. Kunda, Z. (1987). 'Motivated Inference: Self-Serving Generation and Evaluation of Causal Theories'. *Journal of Personality and Social Psychology*, *53*(4), 636–647.
19. Kunda, Z. (1987). 'Motivated Inference: Self-Serving Generation and Evaluation of Causal Theories'. *Journal of Personality and Social Psychology*, *53*(4), 636–647.
20. Friedman, S., O'Brien, D. & McDonald, I. (2021). 'Deflecting privilege: Class identity and the intergenerational self'. *Sociology*, *55*(4), 716–733.
21. Friedman, Sam. 'Why do so many professional, middle-class Brits insist they're working class?'. *The Guardian*, 18 January 2021.
22. Berscheid, E., Graziano, W., Monson, T. & Dermer, M. (1976). 'Outcome dependency: Attention, attribution, and attraction'. *Journal of Personality and Social Psychology*, *34*(5), 978–989.
23. Kunda, Z. (1987). 'Motivated Inference: Self-Serving Generation and Evaluation of Causal Theories'. *Journal of Personality and Social Psychology*, *53*(4), 636–647.
24. Kunda, Z. (1987). 'Motivated Inference: Self-Serving Generation and Evaluation of Causal Theories'. *Journal of Personality and Social Psychology*, *53*(4), 636–647.
25. See a review of the evidence in Kunda, Z. (1990). 'The case for Motivated Reasoning'. *Psychological Bulletin*, *108*(3), 480–498.
26. Kassarjian, H.H. & Cohen, J.B. (1965). 'Cognitive dissonance and consumer behavior'. *California Management Review*, *8*(1), 55–64.
27. Kunda, Z. (1987). 'Motivated Inference: Self-Serving Generation and Evaluation of Causal Theories'. *Journal of Personality and Social Psychology*, *53*(4), 636–647.
28. Epley, N. & Dunning, D. (2006). 'The mixed blessings of self-knowledge in behavioral prediction: Enhanced discrimination but exacerbated bias'. *Personality and Social Psychology Bulletin*, *32*(5), 641–655.

29. Logg, J.M., Haran, U. & Moore, D.A. (2018). 'Is overconfidence a motivated bias? Experimental evidence'. *Journal of Experimental Psychology: General*, *147*(10), 1445–1465.
30. Baekgaard, M., Christensen, J., Dahlmann, C.M., Mathiasen, A. & Petersen, N.B.G. (2017). 'The Role of Evidence in Politics: Motivated Reasoning and Persuasion among Politicians'. *British Journal of Political Science*, 1–24.
31. von Hippel, W. & Trivers, R. (2011). 'The evolution and psychology of self-deception'. *Behavioral and Brain Sciences*, *34*(1), 1–16; discussion 16–56.
32. Trivers, R. (2012). *Deceit and Self-Deception: Fooling Yourself the Better to Fool Others*. Penguin Books, London.
33. Trivers, R. (2000). 'The elements of a scientific theory of self-deception'. *Annals of the New York Academy of Sciences*, *907*, 114–131.
34. Sloman, S.A., Fernbach, P.M. & Hagmayer, Y. (2010). 'Self-deception requires vagueness'. *Cognition*, *115*(2), 268–281.
35. Brilon, S., Grassi, S., Grieder, M. & Schulz, J.F. (2024). 'Strategic competition and self-confidence'. *Management Science*, 70(1), 507–525.
36. Chance, Z., Norton, M.I., Gino, F. & Ariely, D. (2011). 'Temporal view of the costs and benefits of self-deception'. *Proceedings of the National Academy of Sciences*, *108*, 15655–15659.
37. Herranz-Zarzoso, N., & Sabater-Grande, G. (2018). 'Monetary incentives and self-chosen goals in academic performance: An experimental study'. *International Review of Economics Education, 27*, 34–44..
38. Golman, R., Hagmann, D. & Loewenstein, G. (2017). 'Information avoidance'. *Journal of economic literature*, *55*(1), 96–135.
39. Williams, D. (2020). 'Socially adaptive belief'. *Mind and Language*, July 2019, 1–22.
40. Williams, D. (2020). 'Motivated ignorance, rationality, and democratic politics'. *Synthese*. 198(8), 7807–7827.
41. Sharot, T. (2012). The Optimism Bias: Why we're wired to look on the bright side. Pantheon Books, New York.
42. Koellinger, P. & Treffers, T. (2015). 'Joy leads to overconfidence, and a simple countermeasure'. *PLoS One*, *10*(12), e0143263.
43. Kress, L. & Aue, T. (2017). 'The link between optimism bias and attention bias: A neurocognitive perspective'. *Neuroscience and Biobehavioral Reviews*, *80*(May), 688–702.
44. Sharot, T., Riccardi, A.M., Raio, C.M. & Phelps, E.A. (2007). 'Neural mechanisms mediating optimism bias'. *Nature*, *450*(7166), 102–105.

45. Sharot, T., Korn, C.W. & Dolan, R.J. (2011). 'How unrealistic optimism is maintained in the face of reality'. *Nature Neuroscience*, *14*(11), 1475–1479.
46. Rollwage, M., Loosen, A., Hauser, T.U., Moran, R., Dolan, R.J. & Fleming, S.M. (2020). 'Confidence drives a neural confirmation bias'. *Nature Communications*, *11*(1): 2634.
47. Sharot, T., Guitart-Masip, M., Korn, C.W., Chowdhury, R. & Dolan, R.J. (2012). 'How dopamine enhances an optimism bias in humans'. *Current Biology*, *22*(16), 1477–1481.
48. Sharot, T., Guitart-Masip, M., Korn, C.W., Chowdhury, R. & Dolan, R.J. (2012). 'How dopamine enhances an optimism bias in humans'. *Current Biology*, *22*(16), 1477–1481.
49. Koole, S.L., Dijksterhuis, A. & Van Knippenberg, A. (2001). 'What's in a name: implicit self-esteem and the automatic self'. *Journal of personality and social psychology*, *80*(4), 669.
50. Spalding, L.R. & Hardin, C.D. (1999). 'Unconscious unease and self-handicapping: Behavioral consequences of individual differences in implicit and explicit self-esteem'. *Psychological Science*, *10*(6), 535–539.
51. Mezulis, A.H., Abramson, L.Y., Hyde, J.S. & Hankin, B.L. (2004). 'Is there a universal positivity bias in attributions? A meta-analytic review of individual, developmental, and cultural differences in the self-serving attributional bias'. *Psychological Bulletin*, *130*(5), 711–747.
52. van de Rijt, A., Kang, S.M., Restivo, M. & Patil, A. (2014). 'Field experiments of success-breeds-success dynamics'. *Proceedings of the National Academy of Sciences*, *111*(19), 6934–6939.
53. Ehrlinger, J., Mitchum, A. L., & Dweck, C. S. (2016). 'Understanding overconfidence: Theories of intelligence, preferential attention, and distorted self-assessment'. *Journal of Experimental Social Psychology*, 63, 94-100.
54. Dasgupta, U., Mani, S., Sharma, S. & Singhal, S. (2023). 'Social identity, behavior, and personality: evidence from India'. *The Journal of Development Studies, 59*(4), 472–489..
55. Ehrlinger, J. & Dunning, D. (2003). 'How Chronic Self-views Influence (and Potentially Mislead) Estimates of Performance'. *Journal of Personality and Social Psychology*, *84*(1), 5–17.
56. Epley, N. & Dunning, D. (2000). 'Feeling "holier than thou": Are self-serving assessments produced by errors in self—or social prediction?'. *Journal of Personality and Social Psychology*, *79*(6), 861–875.
57. Littrell, S., Risko, E.F. & Fugelsang, J.A. (2021). '"You can't bullshit a bullshitter" (or can you?): Bullshitting frequency predicts receptivity

to various types of misleading information'. *British Journal of Social Psychology, 60*(4), 1484–1505..

58. Wyness, Gill. *Rules of the Game*. Sutton Trust, https://www.suttontrust.com/our-research/rules-of-the-game-university-admissions/.
59. Weale, Sally. 'Disadvantaged students given lower predicted A-level grades, report says'. *The Guardian*, 19 December 2017.
60. Reeves, Richard V., Howard, Kimberly. *The Glass Floor: Education, Downward Mobility, and Opportunity Hoarding*. The Brookings Institution, https://www.brookings.edu/articles/the-glass-floor-education-downward-mobility-and-opportunity-hoarding/.
61. Fast, N.J., Sivanathan, N., Mayer, N.D. & Galinsky, A.D. (2012). 'Power and overconfident decision-making'. *Organizational Behavior and Human Decision Processes, 117*(2), 249–260.
62. Macenczak, L.A., Campbell, S., Henley, A.B. & Campbell, W.K. (2016). 'Direct and interactive effects of narcissism and power on overconfidence'. *Personality and Individual Differences, 91*, 113–122.
63. Proeger, T. & Meub, L. (2014). 'Overconfidence as a social bias: Experimental evidence'. *Economics Letters, 122*(2), 203–207.
64. Heidhues, P., Kőszegi, B. & Strack, P. (2019). 'Overconfidence and prejudice'. *arXiv preprint arXiv:1909.08497*.
65. Ng, H.W. (2020). 'Overconfidence and Elitism'. Working Paper, https://drive.google.com/file/d/1uV4g8r24Tp2l_u1KYPkdnGrPikRAbVUJ/view.
66. Ng, H.W. & Semenov, O. (2020). 'Overconfidence and In-Group Effects in Preferences for Redistribution: An Experimental Study'. Working Paper, https://drive.google.com/file/d/1tjNCgVqaBAgRsAICMi6deDbRETk1Q6vp/view.
67. Buser, T., Grimalda, G., Putterman, L. & van der Weele, J. (2020). 'Overconfidence and gender gaps in redistributive preferences: Cross-country experimental evidence'. *Journal of Economic Behavior & Organization, 178*, 267–286.
68. Kishishita, D., Yamagishi, A., & Matsumoto, T. (2023). 'Overconfidence, income-ability gap, and preferences for income equality'. *European Journal of Political Economy*, 77, 102279.
69. Williams, D. (2020). 'Socially adaptive belief'. *Mind and Language*, July 2019, 1–22.
70. West, K. & Eaton, A.A. (2019). 'Prejudiced and unaware of it: Evidence for the Dunning-Kruger model in the domains of racism and sexism'. *Personality and Individual Differences, 146*(December 2018), 111–119.
71. Dunning, D., Leuenberger, A. & Sherman, D.A. (1995). 'A New Look

at Motivated Inference: Are Self-Serving Theories of Success a Product of Motivational Forces?'. *Journal of Personality and Social Psychology, 69*(1), 58–68.

72. Alicke, M.D., LoSchiavo, F.M., Zerbst, J. & Zhang, S. (1997). 'The person who out performs me is a genius: Maintaining perceived competence in upward social comparison'. *Journal of Personality and Social Psychology, 73*(4), 781–789.
73. Fein, S. & Spencer, S.J. (1997). 'Prejudice as Self-Image Maintenance: Affirming the Self Through Derogating Others'. *Journal of Personality and Social Psychology, 73*(1), 31–44.
74. Roese, N.J. & Olson, J.M. (2007). 'Better, Stronger, Faster Self-Serving Judgment, Affect Regulation, and the Optimal Vigilance Hypothesis'. *Perspectives on Psychological Science, 2*(2), 124–141.
75. Mercier, H. & Sperber, D. (2017). *The Enigma of Reason.* Harvard University Press, Cambridge, Massachusetts.
76. Haselton, M.G., Nettle, D. & Andrews, P.W. (2005). 'The Evolution of Cognitive Bias'. In D. Buss (Ed.), *The Handbook of Evolutionary Psychology*. John Wiley & Sons Inc., Hoboken, NJ, 724–746.
77. Haselton, M.G. & Nettle, D. (2006). 'The paranoid optimist: An integrative evolutionary model of cognitive biases'. *Personality and Social Psychology Review, 10*(1), 47–66.
78. Kahneman, D. (2011). *Thinking, Fast and Slow.* Farrar, Straus and Giroux, New York.

7. THE ADVANTAGES OF IGNORANCE

1. Graham, Bryan Armen. 'Mayweather retires after picking apart Conor McGregor in 10 rounds'. *The Guardian*, 27 August 2017.
2. Bunce, Steve. 'Floyd Mayweather vs Conor McGregor: A genius boxer against a carnival showman—but it is a truly thrilling circus'. *The Independent*, 15 June 2017.
3. Bysouth, Alex. 'For the love of boxing: Why fighters still compete in the "toughest of sports"'. *BBC*, 3 November 2016.
4. Graham, Bryan Armen. 'Mayweather retires after picking apart Conor McGregor in 10 rounds'. *The Guardian*, 27 August 2017.
5. von Hippel, W. & Trivers, R. (2011). 'The evolution and psychology of self-deception'. *Behavioral and Brain Sciences, 34*(1), 1–16; discussion 16–56.
6. Trivers, R. (2011). *Deceit and Self-deception: Fooling Yourself the Better to Fool Others*. Penguin, London.
7. DePaulo, B.M., Lindsay, J.J., Malone, B.E., Muhlenbruck, L., Charlton,

K. & Cooper, H. (2003). 'Cues to deception'. *Psychological Bulletin, 129*(1), 74–118.

8. Byrne, C.C. & Kurland, J.A. (2001). 'Self-deception in an evolutionary game'. *Journal of Theoretical Biology, 212*(4), 457–480.
9. Ramírez, J.C. & Marshall, J.A.R. (2015). 'Self-deception can evolve under appropriate costs'. *Current Zoology, 61*(2), 382–396.
10. Lamba, S. & Nityananda, V. (2014). 'Self-deceived individuals are better at deceiving others'. *PloS One, 9*(8), e104562.
11. Schwardmann, P., & Van der Weele, J. (2019). 'Deception and self-deception'. *Nature Human Behaviour, 3*(10), 1055–1061.
12. Smith, M.K., Trivers, R. & von Hippel, W. (2017). 'Self-deception facilitates interpersonal persuasion'. *Journal of Economic Psychology, February*.
13. Anderson, C., Brion, S., Moore, D.A. & Kennedy, J.A. (2012). 'A status-enhancement account of overconfidence'. *Journal of Personality and Social Psychology, 103*, 718–735.
14. Kennedy, J.A., Anderson, C. & Moore, D.A. (2013). 'When overconfidence is revealed to others: Testing the status-enhancement theory of overconfidence'. *Organizational Behavior and Human Decision Processes, 122*(2), 266–279.
15. Lu, H.J. & Chang, L. (2014). 'Deceiving Yourself to Better Deceive High-Status Compared to Equal-Status Others'. *Evolutionary Psychology, 12*(3), 635–654.
16. Jerrim, J., Parker, P.D. & Shure, N. (2023). 'The big-fish-little-pond effect and overclaiming'. *International Journal of Educational Research*, 121, 102215..
17. Vullioud, C., Clément, F., Scott-Phillips, T. & Mercier, H. (2017). 'Confidence as an expression of commitment: why misplaced expressions of confidence backfire'. *Evolution and Human Behavior, 38*(1), 9–17.
18. Williams, D. (2020). 'Socially adaptive belief'. *Mind and Language, July 2019*, 1–22.
19. Kahan, Dan M. (2017). 'Misconceptions, Misinformation, and the Logic of Identity-Protective Cognition'. Cultural Cognition Project Working Paper Series No. 164, Yale Law School, Public Law Research Paper No. 605, Yale Law & Economics Research Paper No. 575.
20. Kahan, Dan M., Ellen Peters, Erica Cantrell Dawson & Paul Slovic (2017). 'Motivated numeracy and enlightened self-government'. *Behavioural Public Policy* 1, No. 1: 54-86.
21. Op-ed. 'Changing Sides in the Debate on Iraq'. *NPR*, 10 April 2006.

22. Podcast. 'How to Change Your Mind (Update)'. Freakonomics.com, 16 March 2022.
23. Johnson, D.P. & Fowler, J.H. (2011). 'The evolution of overconfidence'. *Nature*, *477*(7364), 317–320.
24. Johnson, D.P. & Fowler, J.H. (2013). 'Complexity and simplicity in the evolution of decision-making biases'. *Trends in Ecology and Evolution*, *28*(8), 446–447.
25. Li, K., Szolnoki, A., Cong, R. & Wang, L. (2016). 'The coevolution of overconfidence and bluffing in the resource competition game'. *Scientific Reports*, *6*, 1–9.
26. Li, K., Cong, R., Wu, T. & Wang, L. (2014). 'Bluffing promotes overconfidence on social networks'. *Scientific Reports*, *4*, 1–7.
27. Tenney, E.R., Logg, J.M. & Moore, D.A. (2015). '(Too) optimistic about optimism: The belief that optimism improves performance'. *Journal of Personality and Social Psychology*, *108*(3), 377.
28. Finn, B. & Metcalfe, J. (2014). 'Overconfidence in children's multi-trial judgments of learning'. *Learning and Instruction*, *32*, 1–9.
29. Schneider, W. (1998). 'Performance prediction in young children: Effects of skill, metacognition and wishful thinking'. *Developmental Science*, *1985*, 291–297.
30. Stipek, D. & Iver, D.M. (1989). 'Developmental Change in Children's Assessment of Intellectual Competence'. *Child Development*, *60*(3), 521–538.
31. Bjorklund, D.F., Gaultney, J.F. & Green, B.L. (1993). '"I watch therefore I can do": The development of metaimitation over the preschool years and the advantage of optimism in one's imitative skills'. *Emerging Themes in Cognitive Development*, 2, 79–102.
32. Shin, H.E., Bjorklund, D.F. & Beck, E.F. (2007). 'The adaptive nature of children's overestimation in a strategic memory task'. *Cognitive Development*, *22*(2), 197–212.
33. Chen, S. & Schildberg-Hörisch, H. (2019). 'Looking at the bright side: The motivational value of confidence'. *European Economic Review*, *120*, 103302.
34. Kaniel, R., Massey, C. & Robinson, D.T. (2014). 'The Importance of Being an Optimist: Evidence from Labor Markets'. Working Paper 16328, September 2010, National Bureau of Economic Research.
35. Editorial, 'Many junior scientists need to take a hard look at their job prospects'. *Nature*, 26 October 2017.
36. Maher, B. & Anfres, M.S. 'Young scientists under pressure: what the data show'. *Nature*, 26 October 2016.
37. Ghaffarzadegan, N., Hawley, J., Larson, R. & Xue, Y. (2015). 'A note

on PhD population growth in biomedical sciences'. *Systems Research and Behavioral Science*, *32*(3), 402–405.

38. Bothwell, E. 'Career impact on relationships "worst for junior academics"'. *Times Higher Education News*, 8 February 2018.
39. Woolston, C. 'Graduate survey: A love–hurt relationship'. *Nature*, 26 October 2017.
40. Woolston, C. 'Graduate survey: A love–hurt relationship'. *Nature*, 26 October 2017.
41. Acton, S.E., Bell, A.J.D., Toseland, C.P. & Twelvetrees, A. (2019) 'Research Culture: A survey of new PIs in the UK', eLife 8:e46827.
42. Afonso, A. 'How Academia Resembles a Drug Gang', Impact of Social Sciences: LSE Blog, 11 December 2013.
43. Taylor, S.E. & Brown, J.D. (1988). 'Illusion and Well-Being: A Social Psychological Perspective on Mental Health'. *Psychological Bulletin*, *103*(2), 193–210.
44. Sedikides, C., Rudich, E.A., Gregg, A.P., Kumashiro, M. & Rusbult, C. (2004). 'Are normal narcissists psychologically healthy?: Self-esteem matters'. *Journal of Personality and Social Psychology*, *87*(3), 400–416.
45. Lee, L.O., James, P., Zevon, E.S., Kim, E.S., Trudel-Fitzgerald, C., Spiro, A., Grodstein, F. & Kubzansky, L.D. (2019). 'Optimism is associated with exceptional longevity in 2 epidemiologic cohorts of men and women'. *Proceedings of the National Academy of Sciences*, *116*(37), 18357–18362.
46. Sharot, T. (2011). 'The optimism bias'. *Current Biology*, *21*(23), R941-5.
47. Hrgović, J. & Hromatko, I. (2019). 'Self-deception as a function of social status'. *Evolutionary Behavioral Sciences*, *13*(3), 223.
48. Moore, M.T. & Fresco, D.M. (2012). 'Depressive realism: A meta-analytic review'. *Clinical psychology review*, *32*(6), 496–509.
49. Alloy, L.B. & Abramson, L.Y. (1988). 'Depressive realism: Four theoretical perspectives'. In L.B. Alloy (Ed.), *Cognitive processes in depression*. The Guilford Press, New York, 223–265.
50. Seidel, E.M., Satterthwaite, T.D., Eickhoff, S.B., Schneider, F., Gur, R.C., Wolf, D.H., Habel, U. & Derntl, B. (2012). 'Neural correlates of depressive realism—An fMRI study on causal attribution in depression'. *Journal of affective disorders*, *138*(3), 268–276.
51. Murphy, S.C., Barlow, F.K. & von Hippel, W. (2017). 'A Longitudinal Test of Three Theories of Overconfidence'. *Social Psychological and Personality Science*, *9*(3), 194855061769925.
52. Charness, G., Rustichini, A. & van de Ven, J. (2018). 'Self-confidence and strategic behavior'. *Experimental Economics*, *21*(1), 72–98.

53. Ewers, M. & Zimmermann, F. (2015). 'Image and misreporting'. *Journal of the European Economic Association*, *13*(2), 363–380.
54. Houston, A.I., Trimmer, P.C., Fawcett, T.W., Higginson, A.D., Marshall, J.A.R. & McNamara, J.M. (2012). 'Is optimism optimal? Functional causes of apparent behavioural biases'. *Behavioural Processes*, *89*(2), 172–178.
55. Marshall, J.A.R., Trimmer, P. C., Houston, A.I. & McNamara, J.M. (2013). 'On evolutionary explanations of cognitive biases'. *Trends in Ecology & Evolution*, *28*(8), 1–5.
56. Johnson, D.P., Blumstein, D.T., Fowler, J.H. & Haselton, M.G. (2013). 'The evolution of error: error management, cognitive constraints, and adaptive decision-making biases'. *Trends in Ecology & Evolution*, *28*(8), 474–481.
57. Langseth, T. (2012). 'B . A . S . E . Jumping—Beyond the Thrills'. *European Journal for Sport and Society*, *9*(3), 155–176.
58. Robins, R.W. & Beer, J.S. (2001). 'Positive illusions about the self: short-term benefits and long-term costs'. *Journal of Personality and Social Psychology*, *80*(2), 340–352.
59. Tenney, E.R., Vazire, S. & Mehl, M.R. (2013). 'This Examined Life: The Upside of Self-Knowledge for Interpersonal Relationships'. *PLoS One*, *8*(7).
60. Heck, P.R. & Krueger, J.I. (2016). 'Social perception of self-enhancement bias and error'. *Social Psychology*, *47*(6), 327–339.
61. Heck, P.R. & Krueger, J.I. (2016). 'Social perception of self-enhancement bias and error'. *Social Psychology*, *47*(6), 327–339.
62. Lamba, S. & Nityananda, V. (2014). 'Self-deceived individuals are better at deceiving others'. *PloS One*, *9*(8), e104562.
63. Littrell, S., & Fugelsang, J. A. (2023). 'Bullshit blind spots: The roles of miscalibration and information processing in bullshit detection'. *Thinking & Reasoning*, Advance online publication.
64. Zaragoza, M.S., Payment, K.E., Ackil, J.K., Drivdahl, S.B. & Beck, M. (2001). 'Interviewing Witnesses: Forced Confabulation and Confirmatory Feedback Increase False Memories'. *Psychological Science*, *12*(6), 473–477.
65. Vo, T.V.A., Gunderson, C.A. & Ten Brinke, L. (2022). 'How deception and believability feedback affect recall'. *Memory*, *30*(6), 706–714.

8. UNDERDOGS AND IMPOSTORS

1. Muthukrishna, M., Henrich, J., Toyokawa, W., Hamamura, T., Kameda, T. & Heine, S.J. (2018). 'Overconfidence is universal? Elicitation of genuine overconfidence (EGO) procedure reveals systematic differences

across domain, task knowledge, and incentives in four populations'. *PLoS One*, *13*(8), 1–30.

2. Luciana Maia Campos Machado, C. & Yoshinaga, E. (2018). 'Self-assessment Accuracy, Overconfidence and Student Performance'. *The New Educational Review*.
3. Stankov, L. & Lee, J. (2014). 'Overconfidence Across World Regions'. *Journal of Cross-Cultural Psychology*, *45*(5), 821–837.
4. Kruger, J. (1999). 'Lake Wobegon be gone! The "below-average effect" and the egocentric nature of comparative ability judgments'. In *Journal of Personality and Social Psychology*, *77*(2), 221–232.
5. Burson, K.A., Larrick, R.P. & Klayman, J. (2006). 'Skilled or Unskilled, but Still Unaware of It: How Perceptions of Difficulty Drive Miscalibration in Relative Comparisons'. *Journal of Personality and Social Psychology*, *90*(1), 60–77.
6. Moore, D.A. & Cain, D.M. (2007). 'Overconfidence and Underconfidence: When and Why People Underestimate (and Overestimate) the Competition'. *Organizational Behavior and Human Decision Processes*, *103*, 197–213.
7. Lerner, J.S., Gonzalez, R.M., Small, D.A. & Fischhoff, B. (2003). 'Effects of fear and anger on perceived risks of terrorism: A national field experiment'. *Psychological Science*, *14*(2), 144–150.
8. Ji, L.J., Zhang, Z., Usborne, E. & Guan, Y. (2004). 'Optimism across cultures: In response to the severe acute respiratory syndrome outbreak'. *Asian Journal of Social Psychology*, *7*(1), 25–34.
9. Viscusi, W.K. (1990). 'Do smokers underestimate risks?'. *Journal of Political Economy*, *98*(6), 1253–1269.
10. Woloshin, S., Schwartz, L.M., Black, W.C. & Welch, H.G. (1999). 'Women's perceptions of breast cancer risk: how you ask matters'. *Medical Decision Making*, *19*(3), 221–229.
11. Moore, D.A. & Cain, D.M. (2007). 'Overconfidence and Underconfidence: When and Why People Underestimate (and Overestimate) the Competition'. *Organizational Behavior and Human Decision Processes*, *103*, 197–213.
12. Clance, P.R. & Imes, S.A. (1978). 'The imposter phenomenon in high achieving women: Dynamics and therapeutic intervention'. *Psychotherapy: Theory, Research & Practice*, *15*(3), 241–247.
13. Dudău, D.P. (2014). 'The Relation between Perfectionism and Impostor Phenomenon'. *Procedia—Social and Behavioral Sciences*, *127*, 129–133.
14. Egwurugwu, J.N., Ugwuezumba, P.C., Ohamaeme, M.C., Dike, E.I., Eberendu, I., Egwurugwu, E.N.A., Ohamaeme, R.C. & Egwurugwu U.F. (2018). 'Relationship between Self-Esteem and Impostor Syndrome

among Undergraduate Medical Students in a Nigerian University'. *International Journal of Brain and Cognitive Sciences, 7*(1), 9–16.

15. 'Oprah Talks to Meryl Streep, Nicole Kidman and Julianne Moore', https://www.oprah.com/omagazine/oprah-interviews-meryl-streep-nicole-kidman-and-julianne-moore/all.
16. Dudău, D.P. (2014). 'The Relation between Perfectionism and Impostor Phenomenon'. *Procedia—Social and Behavioral Sciences, 127*, 129–133.
17. Langford, J. & Clance, P.R. (1993). 'The impostor phenomenon: Recent research findings regarding dynamics, personality and family patterns and their implications for treatment'. *Psychotherapy, 30*(3), 495–501.
18. Sakulku, J. & Alexander, J. (2011). 'The Impostor Phenomenon'. *International Journal of Behavioural Science, 6*(1), 73–92.
19. Thompson, T., Davis, H. & Davidson, J. (1998). 'Attributional and affective responses of impostors to academic success and failure outcomes'. *Personality and Individual Differences, 25*(2), 381–396.
20. Egwurugwu, J.N., Ugwuezumba, P.C., Ohamaeme, M.C., Dike, E.I., Eberendu, I., Egwurugwu, E.N.A., Ohamaeme, R.C. & Egwurugwu U.F. (2018). 'Relationship between Self-Esteem and Impostor Syndrome among Undergraduate Medical Students in a Nigerian University'. *International Journal of Brain and Cognitive Sciences, 7*(1), 9–16.
21. Langford, J. & Clance, P.R. (1993). 'The impostor phenomenon: Recent research findings regarding dynamics, personality and family patterns and their implications for treatment'. *Psychotherapy, 30*(3), 495–501.
22. Sakulku, J. & Alexander, J. (2011). 'The Impostor Phenomenon'. *International Journal of Behavioural Science, 6*(1), 73–92.
23. Dahlbom, L., Jakobsson, A., Jakobsson, N. & Kotsadam, A. (2011). 'Gender and overconfidence: Are girls really overconfident?'. *Applied Economics Letters, 18*(4), 325–327.
24. Jakobsson, N., Levin, M. & Kotsadam, A. (2013). 'Gender and Overconfidence: Effects of Context, Gendered Stereotypes, and Peer Group'. *Advances in Applied Sociology, 03*(02), 137–141.
25. Jakobsson, N. (2012). 'Gender and confidence: Are women underconfident?'. *Applied Economics Letters, 19*(11), 1057–1059.
26. Lundeberg, M.A., Fox, P.W. & Punćcohař, J. (1994). 'Highly Confident, but Wrong: Gender Differences and Similarities in Confidence Judgments'. *Journal of Educational Psychology, 86*(1), 114–121.
27. Beyer, S. & Bowden, E.M. (1997). 'Gender differences in self-perceptions: Convergent evidence from three measures of accuracy and bias'. *Personality and Social Psychology Bulletin, 23*(2), 157–172.
28. Hardies, K., Breesch, D. & Branson, J. (2013). 'Gender differences in

overconfidence and risk taking: Do self-selection and socialization matter?' *Economics Letters*, *118*(3), 442–444.

29. Syzmanowicz, A. & Furnham, A. (2011). 'Gender differences in self-estimates of general, mathematical, spatial and verbal intelligence: Four meta analyses'. *Learning and Individual Differences*, *21*(5), 493–504.
30. Niederle, M. & Vesterlund, L. (2007). 'Do women shy away from competition? Do men compete too much?'. *Quarterly Journal of Economics*, *122*(3), 1067–1101.
31. Brilon, S., Grassi, S., Grieder, M. & Schulz, J.F. (2024). 'Strategic competition and self-confidence'. *Management Science*, *70*(1), 507–525..
32. Ehrlinger, J. & Dunning, D. (2003). 'How Chronic Self-views Influence (and Potentially Mislead) Estimates of Performance'. *Journal of Personality and Social Psychology*, *84*(1), 5–17.
33. Roel van Veldhuizen (2022). 'Gender Differences in Tournament Choices: Risk Preferences, Overconfidence, or Competitiveness?'. *Journal of the European Economic Association*, *20*(4) 1595–1618.
34. Charness, G., Rustichini, A. & van de Ven, J. (2018). 'Self-confidence and strategic behavior'. *Experimental Economics*, *21*(1), 72–98.
35. Kay, K. & Shipman, C. 'The Confidence Gap'. *The Atlantic*, May 2014.
36. Shipman, C. & Kay, K. (2009). *Womenomics: Write your own rules for success*. Harper Collins, New York.
37. Reuben, E., Rey-Biel, P., Sapienza, P. & Zingales, L. (2012). 'The emergence of male leadership in competitive environments'. *Journal of Economic Behavior and Organization*, *83*(1), 111–117.
38. Gneezy, U., Leonard, K.L. & List, J.A. (2009). 'Gender Differences in Competition: Evidence From a Matrilineal and a Patriarchal Society'. *Econometrica*, *77*(5), 1637–1664.
39. Palacios-Huerta I. (2022). 'Competitiveness among Nandi female husbands'. *Proceedings of the National Academy of Sciences USA*. Apr 26;119(17):e2117454119.
40. Thoma, C. (2016). 'Under-versus overconfidence: an experiment on how others perceive a biased self-assessment'. *Experimental Economics*, *19*, 218–239.
41. Whillans, A.V., Jordan, A.H. & Chen, F.S. (2020). 'The upside to feeling worse than average (WTA): A conceptual framework to understand when, how, and for whom WTA beliefs have long-term benefits'. *Frontiers in Psychology*, *11*, 642.
42. Gadsby, Stephen (2022). 'Imposter syndrome and self-deception'. *Australasian Journal of Philosophy*, 100, No. 2: 247–261.
43. Whillans, A.V., Christie, C.D., Cheung, S., Jordan, A.H. & Chen, F.S. (2017). 'From misperception to social connection: Correlates

and consequences of overestimating others' social connectedness'. *Personality and Social Psychology Bulletin*, *43*(12), 1696–1711.

44. Leary, M.R., Patton, K.M., Orlando, A.E. & Funk, W.W. (2000). 'The impostor phenomenon: self-perceptions, reflected appraisals, and interpersonal strategies'. *Journal of Personality*, *68*(August 2000), 725–756.
45. Lamba, S. & Nityananda, V. (2014). 'Self-deceived individuals are better at deceiving others'. *PloS One*, *9*(8), e104562.
46. Trivers, R. (2011). *Deceit and Self-deception: Fooling Yourself the Better to Fool Others*. Penguin, London.
47. Thoma, C. (2016). 'Under- versus overconfidence: an experiment on how others perceive a biased self-assessment'. *Experimental Economics*, *19*(1), 218–239.
48. Whillans, A.V., Jordan, A.H. & Chen, F.S. (2020). 'The Upside to Feeling Worse Than Average (WTA): A Conceptual Framework to Understand When, How, and for Whom WTA Beliefs Have Long-Term Benefits'. *Frontiers in Psychology*, *11*.
49. Kumar, V., 'For Rohith Vemula, who wanted to learn, but ended up taking his own life; and for Savarnas who are too good to learn', *Firstpost*, 25 January 2019.

9. VERY SMART PEOPLE WITH A LOT OF MONEY

1. Chen, W., Mrkaic, M. & Nabar, M. 'Lasting Effects: The Global Economic Recovery 10 Years After the Crisis', IMF Blog, 3 October 2018.
2. 'The impact of the global financial crisis: What does this tell us about state capacity and political incentives to respond to shocks and manage risks? Literature review. Part 1: The effects of the global financial crisis on developing countries'. Department for International Development, 1 January 2012, https://www.gov.uk/research-for-development-outputs/the-impact-of-the-global-financial-crisis-what-does-this-tell-us-about-state-capacity-and-political-incentives-to-respond-to-shocks-and-manage-risks-literature-review-part-1-the-effects-of-the-global-financial-crisis.
3. Chen, W., Mrkaic, M. & Nabar, M. 'Lasting Effects: The Global Economic Recovery 10 Years After the Crisis', IMF Blog, 3 October 2018.
4. Rajan, R.G. (2006). 'Has finance made the world riskier?'. *European financial management*, *12*(4), 499–533.
5. Podcast, 'This Economist Predicted the Last Crisis. What's the Next One?'. *Freakonomics.com*, 6 February 2019.

6. Roll, R. (1986). The hubris hypothesis of corporate takeovers. *Journal of Business*, *59*(2), 197–216.
7. Malmendier, U. & Tate, G. (2005). 'CEO overconfidence and corporate investment'. *Journal of Finance*, *60*(6), 2661–2700.
8. Malmendier, U. & Tate, G. (2005). 'Does overconfidence affect corporate investment? CEO overconfidence measures revisited'. *European Financial Management*, *11*(5), 649–659.
9. Qasim, M., Hussain, R.Y., Mehboob, I. & Arshad, M. (2019). 'Impact of herding behavior and overconfidence bias on investors' decision-making in Pakistan'. *Accounting*, *5*, 1–10.
10. Arifin, Z. & Soleha, E. (2019). 'Overconfidence, Attitude Toward Risk, and Financial Literacy: A Case in Indonesia Stock Exchange'. *Review of Integrative Business and Economics Research*, *8*(4), 144–153.
11. Boujedra, F. & Ismaliia, F. (2019). 'Overconfidence and trading volume: the case of the Tunisian stock market'. *Journal of Accounting and Finance*, *19*(2), 11–16.
12. Liu, L., Le, H. & Thompson, S. (2022). 'CEO overconfidence and bank systemic risk: Evidence from US bank holding companies'. *International Journal of Finance & Economics*, *27*(3), 2977–2996.
13. Malmendier, U. & Tate, G. (2005). 'CEO overconfidence and corporate investment'. *The Journal of Finance*, *60*(6), 2661–2700.
14. Malmendier, U. & Tate, G. (2008). 'Who makes acquisitions? CEO overconfidence and the market's reaction'. *Journal of Financial Economics*, *89*(1), 20–43.
15. Ferris, S.P., Jayaraman, N. & Sabherwal, S. (2013). 'CEO Overconfidence and International Merger and Acquisition Activity'. *Journal of Financial and Quantitative Analysis*, *48*(01), 137–164.
16. Hayward, M.L. & Hambrick, D.C. (1997). 'Explaining the premiums paid for large acquisitions: Evidence of CEO hubris'. *Administrative science quarterly*, 103–127.
17. Dunning, D., Heath, C. & Suls, J.M. (2004). 'Flawed Self-Assessment Implications for Health, Education, and the Workplace'. *Psychological Science in the Public Interest*, *5*(3), 69–106.
18. Li, Y. 'GameStop mania explained: How the Reddit retail trading crowd ran over Wall Street pros'. *CNBC*, 27 January 2021.
19. Orland, K. 'Gaming the system: How GameStop stock surged 1,500% in nine months'. *Ars Technica*, 19 January 2021.
20. Pound, J. 'GameStop stock drops by 40% in 25 minutes'. *CNBC*, 10 March 2021.
21. Schwarz, J. 'Here's How Much Money You've Lost If You Took Matt Damon's Crypto Advice One Year Ago'. *The Intercept*, 26 October 2022.

22. Gura, D. '2022 was the year crypto came crashing down to Earth'. *NPR*, 29 December 2022.
23. Schwarz, J. 'Here's How Much Money You've Lost If You Took Matt Damon's Crypto Advice One Year Ago'. *The Intercept*, 26 October 2022.
24. Cunningham, K. 'Matt Damon's Viral Crypto Ad Is an Embarrassing Cash Grab'. *Daily Beast*, 3 January 2022.
25. Merkle, C. (2017). 'Financial overconfidence over time: Foresight, hindsight, and insight of investors'. *Journal of Banking and Finance*, *84*, 68–87.
26. Malmendier, U. & Tate, G. (2015). 'Behavioral CEOs: The role of managerial overconfidence'. *Journal of Economic Perspectives*, *29*(4), 37–60.
27. Pikulina, E., Renneboog, L. & Tobler, P.N. (2017). 'Overconfidence and investment: An experimental approach'. *Journal of Corporate Finance*, *43*, 175–192.
28. Merkle, C. (2017). 'Financial overconfidence over time: Foresight, hindsight, and insight of investors'. *Journal of Banking and Finance*, *84*, 68–87.
29. Barber, B.M. & Odean, T. (2001). 'Boys will be boys: gender, overconfidence, and common stock investment'. *The Quarterly Journal of Economics*, *116*(February 2001), 261–292.
30. 'Are Women Better Investors? Stash Data Flips Gender Stereotypes'. *Stash*, 6 September 2018.
31. Fessler, L. 'A new study suggests male investors are prone to panic, while women play it smart'. *Quartz*, 18 September 2018.
32. Deaves, R., Lüders, E. & Luo, G.Y. (2009). 'An experimental test of the impact of overconfidence and gender on trading activity'. *Review of Finance*, *13*(3), 555–575.
33. Cao, G. & Zhang, J. (2020). 'Guanxi, overconfidence and corporate fraud in China'. *Chinese Management Studies*, *15*(3), 501–556.
34. Gietl, D. & Kassner, B. (2020). 'Managerial Overconfidence and Bank Bailouts'. *Journal of Economic Behavior and Organization*, *179*, 202–222.
35. Kahneman, D. (2011). *Thinking, fast and slow*. Farrar, Straus and Giroux, New York.
36. Abbes, M.B. (2012). 'Does Overconfidence Bias Explain Volatility During the Global Financial Crisis?'. *Transition Studies Review*, *19*(3), 291–312.
37. Moosa, I. & Ramiah, V. (2017). 'Overconfidence and Self-Serving Bias'. *The Financial Consequences of Behavioural Biases*, 45–69.

38. 'Fuld criticises Fed for letting Lehman fail'. *Financial Times*, 2 September 2010.
39. La Roche, J. 'You're Going To Cringe When You Read Dick Fuld's Frat-Boy Language In His Emails'. *Business Insider*, 1 May 2012.
40. Gervais, S. & Odean, T. (2001). 'Learning to be overconfident'. *The Review of Financial Studies*, *14*(1), 1–27.
41. Billett, M.T. & Qian, Y. (2008). 'Are Overconfident CEOs Born or Made? Evidence of Self-Attribution Bias from Frequent Acquirers'. *Management Science*, *54*(6), 1037–1051.
42. Doukas, J.A. & Petmezas, D. (2007). 'Acquisitions, overconfident managers and self-attribution bias'. *European Financial Management*, *13*(3), 531–577.
43. Gao, H., Shi, D. & Zhao, B. (2021). 'Does good luck make people overconfident? Evidence from a natural experiment in the stock market'. *Journal of Corporate Finance*, *68*, 101933.
44. Gervais, S. & Odean, T. (2001). 'Learning to be overconfident'. *The Review of Financial Studies*, *14*(1), 1–27.
45. Huffman, D., Raymond, C. & Shvets, J. (2022). 'Persistent overconfidence and biased memory: Evidence from managers'. *American Economic Review*, *112*(10), 3141-75.
46. Walters, D.J. & Fernbach, P.M. (2021). 'Investor memory of past performance is positively biased and predicts overconfidence'. *Proceedings of the National Academy of Sciences of the United States of America*, *118*(36), 1–8.
47. Ou, A.Y., Waldman, D.A. & Peterson, S.J. (2018). 'Do Humble CEOs Matter? An Examination of CEO Humility and Firm Outcomes'. *Journal of Management*, *44*(3), 1147–1173.
48. Huang, J. & Kisgen, D. J. (2013). 'Gender and corporate finance: Are male executives overconfident relative to female executives?'. *Journal of financial Economics*, *108*(3), 822–839.
49. La Rocca, M., Neha Neha & La Rocca, T. (2020). 'Female management, overconfidence and debt maturity: European evidence'. *Journal of Management and Governance*, *24*(3), 713–747.
50. Chen, J., Leung, W.S., Song, W. &Goergen, M., (2017). 'Why female board representation matters: The role of female directors in reducing male CEO overconfidence in corporate decisions'. *Journal of Empirical Finance*, *53*, 70–90.
51. Shekhar, D.J, 'Women Hold 17% Of Board Positions In Corporate India, But Only 11% Leadership Roles'. *Forbes India*, 8 December 2020.
52. Chen, J., Leung, W.S., Song, W. & Goergen, M., (2017). 'Why female

board representation matters: The role of female directors in reducing male CEO overconfidence in corporate decisions'. *Journal of Empirical Finance*, *53*, 70–90.

53. Chen, J., Leung, W.S., Song, W. & Goergen, M. (2019). 'Why female board representation matters: The role of female directors in reducing male CEO overconfidence;. *Journal of Empirical Finance*, *53*, 70–90.
54. 'Women on boards in financial services worldwide from 2016 to 2021'. *Statista*.
55. Shekhar, D.J, 'Women Hold 17% Of Board Positions In Corporate India, But Only 11% Leadership Roles'. *Forbes India*, 8 December 2020.
56. Hirshleifer, D. & Luo, G.Y. (2001). 'On the survival of overconfident traders in a competitive securities market'. *Journal of Financial Markets*, *4*(1), 73–84.
57. Mundi, H.S. & Kaur, P. (2019). 'Impact of CEO Overconfidence on Firm Performance: An Evidence from S&P BSE 200'. *Vision*, *23*(3), 234–243.
58. Hirshleifer, D., Low, A. & Teoh, S.H. (2012). 'Are Overconfident CEOs Better Innovators?'. *Journal of Finance*, *67*(4), 1457–1498.
59. Englmaier, F. (2004). 'A strategic rationale for having overconfident managers'. *32nd Conference of the European Association for Research in Industrial Economics*.
60. Goel, A.M. & Thakor, A.V. (2008). 'Overconfidence, CEO selection, and corporate governance'. *The Journal of Finance*, *63*(6), 2737–2784.
61. Gervais, S. & Goldstein, I. (2007). 'The positive effects of biased self-perceptions in firms'. *Review of Finance*, *11*(3), 453–496.
62. Hirshleifer, D. & Luo, G.Y. (2001). 'On the survival of overconfident traders in a competitive securities market'. *Journal of Financial Markets*, *4*(1), 73–84.
63. Gervais, S., Heaton, J.B. & Odean, T. (2011). 'Overconfidence, Compensation Contracts, and Capital Budgeting'. *Journal of Finance*, *66*(5), 1735–1777.
64. Sautmann, A. (2013). 'Contracts for Agents with Biased Beliefs: Some Theory and an Experiment'. *American Economic Journal: Microeconomics*, *5*(3), 124–156.
65. Hirshleifer, D., Low, A. & Teoh, S.H. (2012). 'Are Overconfident CEOs Better Innovators?'. *Journal of Finance*, *67*(4), 1457–1498.
66. Dunning, D., Heath, C. & Suls, J.M. (2004). 'Flawed Self-Assessment Implications for Health, Education, and the Workplace'. *Psychological Science in the Public Interest*, *5*(3), 69–106.
67. Cooper, A.C., Woo, C.Y. & Dunkelberg, W.C. (1988). 'Entrepreneurs'

perceived chances for success'. *Journal of business venturing*, *3*(2), 97–108.

68. Camerer, C. & Lovallo, D. (1999). 'Overconfidence and excess entry: An experimental approach'. *American Economic Review*, *89*(1), 306–318.
69. Koellinger, P., Minniti, M. & Schade, C. (2007). '"I think I can, I think I can": Overconfidence and entrepreneurial behavior'. *Journal of Economic Psychology*, *28*(4), 502–527.
70. Moore, D.A. & Cain, D.M. (2007). 'Overconfidence and underconfidence: When and why people underestimate (and overestimate) the competition'. *Organizational Behavior and Human Decision Processes*, *103*(2), 197–213.
71. Cain, D.M., Moore, D.A. & Haran, U. (2015). 'Making sense of overconfidence in market entry'. *Strategic Management Journal*, *36*(1), 1–18.
72. Gonzalez, G. & Ruffo, H. (2019). 'Entrepreneurial Overconfidence: Evidence from a Public Program'. *Journal of Economic and Business Studies*, 2(5), 1–17.
73. Schrage, A. 'The financial crisis may have scarred a generation for life'. *Quartz*, 15 September 2018.
74. Landier, A. & Thesmar, D. (2009). 'Financial contracting with optimistic entrepreneurs'. *The Review of Financial Studies*, *22*(1), 117–150.
75. Koellinger, P., Minniti, M. & Schade, C. (2007). '"I think I can, I think I can": Overconfidence and entrepreneurial behavior'. *Journal of Economic Psychology*, *28*(4), 502–527.
76. Busenitz, L.W. & Barney, J.B. (1997). 'Differences between entrepreneurs and managers in large organizations: Biases and heuristics in strategic decision-making'. *Journal of business venturing*, *12*(1), 9–30.
77. Landier, A. & Thesmar, D. (2009). 'Financial contracting with optimistic entrepreneurs'. *The Review of Financial Studies*, 22(1), 117–150.
78. Kollewe, J. 'Twitter makes first quarterly profit in its history'. *The Guardian*, 8 February 2018.
79. Griswold, A. 'Lyft warns it may never make any money'. *Quartz*, 2 March 2019.
80. Griswold, A. 'Lyft stock starts trading on the Nasdaq in $24 billion IPO', *Quartz*, 29 March 2019.
81. 'Uber lost over $5bn in the second quarter'. *The Economist*, 9 August 2019.
82. Sherman, L. 'Why Can't Uber Make Money?'. *Forbes*, 14 December 2019.
83. Landier, A. & Thesmar, D. (2003). 'Financial contracting with optimistic entrepreneurs: theory and evidence'. Discussion Paper No. 3971, www.cepr.org.

84. Yang, S., Markoczy, L. & Qi, M. (2007). 'Unrealistic optimism in consumer credit card adoption'. *Journal of Economic Psychology*, *28*(2), 170–185.
85. Shiller, R.J. (2015). *Irrational exuberance*. Princeton University Press, Princeton.
86. Abbes, M.B. (2012). 'Does Overconfidence Bias Explain Volatility During the Global Financial Crisis?'. *Transition Studies Review*, *19*(3), 291–312.
87. Lee, J.P., Lin, E.M.H., Lin, J.J. & Zhao, Y. (2020). 'Bank systemic risk and CEO overconfidence'. *North American Journal of Economics and Finance*, *54*.
88. Liu, L., Le, H. & Thompson, S. (2022). 'CEO overconfidence and bank systemic risk: Evidence from U.S. bank holding companies'. *International Journal of Finance and Economics*, *27*(3), 2977–2996.
89. Ho, P.H., Huang, C.W., Lin, C.Y. & Yen, J.F. (2016). 'CEO overconfidence and financial crisis: Evidence from bank lending and leverage'. *Journal of Financial Economics*, *120*(1), 194–209.
90. Fahlenbrach, R., Prilmeier, R. & Stulz, R.M. (2012). 'This Time Is the Same: Using Bank Performance in 1998 to Explain Bank Performance during the Recent Financial Crisis'. *Journal of Finance*, *67*(6), 2139–2185.
91. Ho, P.H., Huang, C.W., Lin, C.Y. & Yen, J.F. (2016). 'CEO overconfidence and financial crisis: Evidence from bank lending and leverage'. *Journal of Financial Economics*, *120*(1), 194–209.
92. Liu, L., Le, H. & Thompson, S. (2022). 'CEO overconfidence and bank systemic risk: Evidence from U.S. bank holding companies'. *International Journal of Finance and Economics*, *27*(3), 2977–2996.
93. Liu, L., Le, H. & Thompson, S. (2022). 'CEO overconfidence and bank systemic risk: Evidence from U.S. bank holding companies'. *International Journal of Finance and Economics*, *27*(3), 2977–2996.

10. WARS OF ERROR

1. Tzŭ, Sun. *The Art of War*. https://www.gutenberg.org/files/132/132-h/132-h.htm.
2. Farrell, Henry. 'Thomas Schelling has died. His ideas shaped the Cold War and the world'. *The Washington Post*, 13 December 2016.
3. Wright, Tom. 'Schelling helped stop the cold war turning very hot'. *The Irish Times*, 15 October 2005.
4. Wrangham, R. (1999). Is military incompetence adaptive?. *Evolution and Human Behavior*, *20*(1), 3–17.

5. Tzu, Chuang. *Mystic, Moralist, and Social Reformer*. https://www.gutenberg.org/ebooks/59709.
6. Johnson, D.D.P., Weidmann, N.B., Cederman, L.E. (2011). 'Fortune Favours the Bold: An Agent-Based Model Reveals Adaptive Advantages of Overconfidence in War'. *PloS One*, 6(6): e20851.
7. Johnson, D.D., McDermott, R., Barrett, E.S., Cowden, J., Wrangham, R., McIntyre, M.H. & Peter Rosen, S. (2006). 'Overconfidence in wargames: experimental evidence on expectations, aggression, gender and testosterone'. *Proceedings of the Royal Society B: Biological Sciences*, *273*(1600), 2513–2520.
8. Khamsi, Roxanne. 'Overconfidence is a disadvantage in war, finds study'. *New Scientist*, 21 June 2006.
9. Greenspan, Jesse. 'Why Napoleon's Invasion of Russia Was the Beginning of the End'. *History.com*, 22 June 2012.
10. As I learnt in Robert Graves's book: Graves, R. (1989). *Claudius the God: And His Wife Messalina*. Vintage, New York.
11. Gaur, Vatsala, 'Dharam Vir: The unsung hero of famous "Battle of Longewala"', *The Economic Times*, 2 December 2023. Also see: Shah, Zameer Uddin, 'The 1971 Battle of Longewala: A night of confusion, Sam Manekshaw's order, Pakistan's folly'. *The Print*, 3 December 2019.
12. Johnson, D.D. (2004). *Overconfidence and War: The Havoc and Glory of Positive Illusions*. Harvard University Press, Cambridge, Massachusetts.
13. Tuchman, B.W. (1985). *The March of Folly: From Troy to Vietnam*. Random House Trade Paperbacks, New York.
14. Ganguly, S. (2002). *Conflict Unending: India-Pakistan Tensions Since 1947*. Columbia University Press, New York.
15. Beaumont, Peter. 'Lawrence Freedman: "Autocracies tend to make catastrophic decisions. That's the case with Putin"'. *The Guardian*, 21 August 2022.
16. Menuet, M. & Sekeris, P.G. (2021). Overconfidence and conflict. *Economic Inquiry*, *59*(4), 1483–1499.
17. Johnson, D.D. (2004). *Overconfidence and War: The Havoc and Glory of Positive Illusions*. Harvard University Press, Cambridge, Massachusetts.
18. Johnson, D.D. (2004). *Overconfidence and War: The Havoc and Glory of Positive Illusions*. Harvard University Press, Cambridge, Massachusetts.
19. Rush, Julian. 'Downing St dossier plagiarised'. *Channel 4 News*, 6 February 2003.
20. 'Timeline: The 45-minute claim'. BBC, 13 October 2004.

21. Frankopan, P. (2015). *The Silk Roads: A New History of the World.* Bloomsbury Publishing, London.
22. Igielnik, Ruth & Parker, Kim. 'Majorities of U.S. veterans, public say the wars in Iraq and Afghanistan were not worth fighting'. Pew Research Center, 10 July 2019.
23. Smith, Matthew. 'Jeremy Corbyn is on the right side of public opinion on foreign policy: except for the Falklands'. *YouGov.co.uk*, 30 May 2017.
24. Dahlgreen, Will. 'Memories of Iraq: did we ever support the war?'. *YouGov.co.uk*, 3 June 2015.
25. 'Iraq'. UK Polling Report, https://pollingreport.uk/articles/iraq.
26. Dahlgreen, Will. 'Memories of Iraq: did we ever support the war?'. *YouGov.co.uk*, 3 June 2015.
27. Fallows, James. 'The Fifty-First State?'. *The Atlantic*, November 2002.
28. Antoon, Sinan. 'Fifteen Years Ago, America Destroyed My Country'. *The New York Times*, 19 March 2018.
29. von Hippel, W. & Trivers, R. (2011). 'The evolution and psychology of self-deception'. *Behavioral and Brain Sciences*, *34*(1), 1–16; discussion 16–56.
30. Fallows, James. 'Blind Into Baghdad'. *The Atlantic*, February 2004.
31. Fallows, J. (2006). *Blind into Baghdad: America's War in Iraq*. Vintage, New York.
32. Cunningham, D.E., Gleditsch, K.S. & Salehyan, I. (2009). 'It takes two: A dyadic analysis of civil war duration and outcome'. *Journal of Conflict Resolution*, *53*(4), 570–597.
33. Wucherpfennig, J., Metternich, N.W., Cederman, L.E. & Gleditsch, K.S. (2012). 'Ethnicity, the state, and the duration of civil war'. *World Politics*, *64*(1), 79–115.
34. Caprioli, M. & Boyer, M.A. (2001). 'Gender, violence, and international crisis'. *Journal of Conflict Resolution*, *45*(4), 503–518.
35. Dube, O. & Harish, S.P. (2020). 'Queens'. *Journal of Political Economy*, *128*(7), 2579–2652.
36. 'Who gets into more wars, kings or queens?'. *The Economist*, 1 June 2017.
37. Guildford, Gwyn. 'Throughout history, women rulers were more likely to wage war than men'. *Quartz*, 26 April 2017.
38. Malhotra, I. (2014). *Indira Gandhi: A Personal and Political Biography*. Hay House, Carlsbad, California.
39. Horowitz, J.M., Igielnik, R. & Parker, K. 'Women and Leadership 2018'. Pew Reserch Center, 20 September 2018.

40. Englund, Will. 'How stereotypes of women as weak push female politicians to be hawkish'. *The Washington Post*, 28 October 2016.
41. MacAskill, Ewen. 'George Bush: "God told me to end the tyranny in Iraq"'. *The Guardian*, 7 October 2005.

11. PANDEMICS DON'T BLUFF

1. Griffin, Andrew. 'Hurricane Fish: Deadly storm would still not have been predicted with today's supercomputers, study finds'. *The Independent*, 11 October 2017.
2. 'That Turn To Pascagoula'. Cautionary Tales with Tim Harford, podcast, *Omny.fm*, 10 July 2020.
3. Labib, A. & Read, M. (2013). 'Not just rearranging the deckchairs on the Titanic: Learning from failures through Risk and Reliability Analysis'. *Safety Science*, *51*(1), 397–413.
4. Gregory, Andy. 'What really happened at Chernobyl? How the world's worst nuclear accident happened'. *The Independent*, 2 May 2023.
5. Beer, Daniel. '*Chernobyl: History of a Tragedy* by Serhii Plokhy review—Europe nearly became uninhabitable'. *The Guardian*, 9 May 2018.
6. Labib, A. & Read, M. (2013). 'Not just rearranging the deckchairs on the Titanic: Learning from failures through Risk and Reliability Analysis'. *Safety Science*, *51*(1), 397–413.
7. Trivers, R. (2011). *Deceit and Self-deception: Fooling Yourself the Better to Fool Others*. Penguin UK, London.
8. Trivers, R.L. & Newton, H.P. (1982). 'The crash of Flight 90: doomed by self-deception'. *Science Digest*, *111*(Nov), 66–67.
9. Labib, A. & Read, M. (2013). 'Not just rearranging the deckchairs on the Titanic: Learning from failures through Risk and Reliability Analysis'. *Safety Science*, *51*(1), 397–413.
10. Yong, Ed. 'How the Pandemic Defeated America'. *The Atlantic*, September 2020.
11. Calvert, J., Arbuthnott, G. & Leake, J. 'Coronavirus: 38 days when Britain sleepwalked into disaster'. *The Times*, 19 April 2020.
12. Voce, A., Clarke, S., Barr, C., McIntyre, N. & Duncan, P. 'Coronavirus excess deaths: UK has one of highest levels in Europe'. *The Guardian*, 29 May 2020.
13. Burn-Murdoch, J. & Giles, C. 'UK suffers second-highest death rate from coronavirus'. *Financial Times*, 28 May 2020.
14. Flaxman, S., Mishra, S., Gandy, A. et al. (2020) 'Estimating the effects of non-pharmaceutical interventions on COVID-19 in Europe'. *Nature*, 584, 257–261.

15. Fazio, R.H., Ruisch, B.C., Moore, C.A., Granados Samayoa, J.A., Boggs, S.T. & Ladanyi, J.T. (2021). 'Social distancing decreases an individual's likelihood of contracting COVID-19'. *Proceedings of the National Academy of Sciences*, *118*(8), e2023131118.
16. Hsiang, S., Allen, D., Annan-Phan, S., Bell, K., Bolliger, I., Chong, T. & Wu, T. (2020). 'The effect of large-scale anti-contagion policies on the COVID-19 pandemic'. *Nature*, *584*(7820), 262–267.
17. Vogel, G. '"It's been so, so surreal". Critics of Sweden's lax pandemic policies face fierce backlash'. Science, 6 October 2020. https://www.science.org/content/article/it-s-been-so-so-surreal-critics-sweden-s-lax-pandemic-policies-face-fierce-backlash.
18. 'Sweden records highest death tally in 150 years in first half of 2020'. *The Guardian*, 19 August 2020.
19. Goodman, P.S. 'Sweden Has Become the World's Cautionary Tale'. *The New York Times*, 7 July 2020.
20. GDP growth (annual%) of Sweden, World Bank, https://data.worldbank.org/indicator/NY.GDP.MKTP.KD.ZG?locations=SE.
21. GDP growth (annual%) of Norway, World Bank, https://data.worldbank.org/indicator/NY.GDP.MKTP.KD.ZG?locations=NO.
22. GDP growth (annual%) of Denmark, World Bank, https://data.worldbank.org/indicator/NY.GDP.MKTP.KD.ZG?locations=DK.
23. Correia, S., Luck, S. & Verner, E. (2022). 'Pandemics depress the economy, public health interventions do not: Evidence from the 1918 flu'. *The Journal of Economic History*, *82*(4), 917–957.
24. Wolf, M. 'What the world can learn from the Covid-19 pandemic'. *Financial Times*, 24 November 2020.
25. Alvelda, P., Ferguson, T. & Mallery, J.C. 'To Save the Economy, Save People First'. Institute for New Economic Thinking, 18 November 2020.
26. Calvert, J., Arbuthnott, G. & Leake, J. 'Coronavirus: 38 days when Britain sleepwalked into disaster'. *The Times*, 19 April 2020.
27. Merrick, J. 'Coronavirus testing: UK missed "critical moment" to stop Covid-19 as MPs attack "pivotal" decision to cut back testing'. *iNews*, 19 May 2020.
28. Sridhar, D. 'Britain had a head start on Covid-19, but our leaders squandered it'. *The Guardian*, 23 March 2020.
29. Clark, P., Cookson, C. & Hughes, L. 'How the UK got coronavirus testing wrong'. *Financial Times*, 27 March 2020.
30. Evans-Pritchard, A. 'The handling of COVID-19 has led to a very British disaster'. *The Age*, 14 May 2020.

31. Pilkington, E. 'Anger grows at Trump administration's coronavirus testing failures'. *The Guardian*, 12 March 2020.
32. Shesgreen, D. 'Senegal's quiet COVID success: Test results in 24 hours, temperature checks at every store, no fights over masks'. *USA Today*, 6 September 2020.
33. Drexler, M. 'Bhutan Is the World's Unlikeliest Pandemic Success Story'. *The Atlantic*, 10 February 2021.
34. Jones, A. 'Coronavirus: How "overreaction" made Vietnam a virus success'. *BBC News*, 15 May 2020.
35. Sebenius, I. & Sebenius, J.K. 'How many needless Covid-19 deaths were caused by delays in responding? Most of them'. *Stat*, 19 June 2020.
36. Pilkington, E. 'Anger grows at Trump administration's coronavirus testing failures'. *The Guardian*, 12 March 2020.
37. Lewis, D. 'Why the WHO took two years to say COVID is airborne'. *Nature*, 6 April 2022.
38. World Health Organization, 29 March 2020. https://twitter.com/who/status/1243972193169616898.
39. '"Hero who told the truth": Chinese rage over coronavirus death of whistleblower doctor'. *The Guardian*, 7 February 2020.
40. Graham-Harrison. 'The whistleblower doctor who fell victim to China's coronavirus'. *The Guardian*, 6 February 2020.
41. Richard McGregor. 'The coronavirus outbreak has exposed the deep flaws of Xi's autocracy'. *The Guardian*, 9 February 2020.
42. 'Democracies contain epidemics most effectively'. *The Economist*, 6 June 2020.
43. Londoño, E., Andreoni, M. & Casado, L. 'President Bolsonaro of Brazil Tests Positive for Coronavirus'. *The New York Times*, 7 July 2020.
44. 'The Guardian view on Jair Bolsonaro: A danger to Brazilians'. *The Guardian*, 31 March 2020.
45. Phillips, T. 'Bolsonaro "led Brazilian people into a canyon", says ex-health minister'. *The Guardian*, 15 August 2020.
46. Saxena, S. & Costa, F. 'Bolsonaro's Colossal Negligence Sparks 'Genocide' Debate in Brazil', *The Wire*, 20 July 2020.
47. Mano, A. 'Brazil takes down COVID-19 data, hiding soaring death toll'. *Reuters*, 8 June 2020.
48. '"I shook hands with everybody," says Boris Johnson weeks before coronavirus diagnosis'. *The Guardian*, video, 27 March 2020.
49. Stephen, P. 'How politics thwarted the UK's Covid-19 response'. *Financial Times*, 23 April 2020.
50. Lipton, E., Sanger, D.E., Haberman, M., Shear, M.D., Mazzetti, M. &

Barnes, J.E. 'He Could Have Seen What Was Coming: Behind Trump's Failure on the Virus'. *The New York Times*, 11 April 2020.

51. Patel, N. & Rao A. 'Doctors have been whistleblowers throughout history. They've also been silenced'. *The Guardian*, 8 April 2020.
52. Lloyd, G. '"Trump is killing his own supporters"—even White House insiders know it'. *The Guardian*, 5 April 2020.
53. Mander, H. 'What govt could have done differently to deal with the pandemic, what it can still do now'. *The Indian Express*, 13 June 2020.
54. 'India Covid-19: PM Modi "did not consult" before lockdown'. *BBC*, 29 March 2021.
55. Editorial, 'India's COVID-19 emergency', *The Lancet*, 8 May 2021.
56. Safi, M. '"We are not special": how triumphalism led India to Covid-19 disaster'. *The Guardian*, 29 April 2021.
57. India's second Covid wave undermines herd immunity theory | Financial Times, 25 March 2021.
58. Thomas, S.A. 'Out of Oxygen'. *London Review of Books*, 30 April 2021.
59. Sharma, H. 'April, November last year: Officials, House panel flagged oxygen need, shortage'. *The Indian Express*, 23 April 2021.
60. Safi, M. '"We are not special": how triumphalism led India to Covid-19 disaster'. *The Guardian*, 29 April 2021.
61. Biswas, S. 'Covid-19: How India failed to prevent a deadly second wave'. *BBC*, 19 April 2021.
62. 'India's devastating second wave: "It is much worse this time"'. *Financial Times*, 21 April 2021.
63. Ellis-Petersen, H. '"We're burning pyres all day": India accused of undercounting deaths'. *The Guardian*, 1 May 2021.
64. Srivastava, P. 'Covid: Yogi orders crack down on hospitals flagging oxygen shortage'. *Telegraph*, 27 April 2021.
65. Jaiswal, S. 'BJP fired ex-Uttarakhand chief minister TS Rawat for restricting Kumbh gatherings'. *The Caravan*, 8 May 2021.
66. Tharoor, I. 'Coronavirus pandemic: Trump joins the world's "ostrich" leaders with their heads in the sand'. *The Washington Post*, 20 April 2020.
67. Wittenberg-Cox, A. 'What Do Countries With The Best Coronavirus Responses Have In Common? Women Leaders'. *Forbes*, 13 April 2020.
68. Garikipati, S. & Kambhampati, U. (2021). 'Leading the fight against the pandemic: Does gender really matter?' *Feminist Economics*, 27(1-2), 401–418.
69. Garikipati, S. & Kambhampati, U. 'Women leaders are better at fighting the pandemic'. The Centre for Economic Policy Research, 21 June 2020.

70. Henley, J. 'Female-led countries handled coronavirus better, study suggests'. *The Guardian*, 18 August 2020.
71. Purkayastha, S., Salvatore, M. & Mukherjee, B. (2020). 'Are women leaders significantly better at controlling the contagion during the COVID-19 pandemic?'. *Journal of Health and Social Sciences*, *5*(2), 231.
72. Lincoln, M. 'Study the role of hubris in nations' COVID-19 response', *Nature*, 15 September 2020.
73. Gelfand, M.J., Jackson, J.C., Pan, X., Nau, D., Pieper, D., Denison, E. & Wang, M. (2021). 'The relationship between cultural tightness–looseness and COVID-19 cases and deaths: a global analysis'. *The Lancet Planetary Health*, *5*(3), e135-e144.
74. van Bavel, J.J., Cichocka, A., Capraro, V., Sjåstad, H., Nezlek, J.B., Pavlović, T., Alfano, M., Gelfand, M.J., Azevedo, F., Birtel, M.D., Cislak, A., Lockwood, P.L., Ross, R.M., Abts, K., Agadullina, E., Aruta, J.J.B., Besharati, S.N., Bor, A., Choma, B.L., Boggio, P.S. (2022). 'National identity predicts public health support during a global pandemic'. *Nature Communications*, *13*(1).
75. Dodwell, D. 'The science is clear: women-led countries are doing better in the pandemic'. *South China Morning Post*, 22 August 2020.

12. POLITICIANS AND PARTISANS

1. Hagerty, J.A. 'Republican Sway in House Indicated in 24-State Survey; Lesser Margin Held Possible. However, After Study of Disputed Areas National Trend a Factor. Dewey Victory Outlook Seen as at Least 27 States and 333 Electoral Votes Survey Indicates Continued Republican Control in the Next House of Representatives'. *The New York Times*, 18 October 1948.
2. A famous cartoon captures the mood of the polling: https://www.archives.gov/exhibits/running-for-office/index.php?page=45.
3. 'The Election of 1948', Harry S. Truman Library and Museum.
4. 'The Press: Study of a Failure'. *Time*, 15 November 1948.
5. See headline 26 here: Zender, M. '26 Schlagzeilen, die besser sind, als alles, was du heute lesen wirst'. *Buzzfeed*, 4 June 2021.
6. Biswas, S. 'How India's elections were won and lost'. *BBC News*, 13 May 2004.
7. John, T. 'These Brexit Voters Think They Have Made a Horrible Mistake'. *Time*, 24 June 2016, https://time.com/4381464/vote-leave-regret-referendum/.
8. Dovere, E.I., 'How Clinton lost Michigan—and blew the election'. *Politico*, 14 December 2016.

9. Kakutani, M., '"Shattered" Charts Hillary Clinton's Course Into the Iceberg'. *The New York Times*, 17 April 2017.
10. Smith, A., 'Hillary Clinton disputes one of the most common critiques of her campaign in her new book'. *Business Insider*, 13 September 2017.
11. Enos, R.D. & Hersh, E.D. (2017). Campaign Perceptions of Electoral Closeness: Uncertainty, Fear and Over-Confidence. *British Journal of Political Science*, *47*(3), 501–519.
12. Rogers, T. & Moore, D. (2015). 'It's Close But We're Losing: The Motivating Power of Under-Confidence'. *Academy of Management Proceedings 2015*(1), 15338.
13. Anderson, C., Brion, S., Moore, D.A. & Kennedy, J.A. (2012). 'A status-enhancement account of overconfidence'. *Journal of Personality and Social Psychology*, *103*, 718–735.
14. Brunell, A.B., Gentry, W.A., Campbell, W.K., Hoffman, B.J., Kuhnert, K.W. & Demarree, K.G. (2008). Leader emergence: The case of the narcissistic leader. *Personality and Social Psychology Bulletin*, *34*(12), 1663–1676.
15. Reuben, E., Rey-Biel, P., Sapienza, P. & Zingales, L. (2012). 'The emergence of male leadership in competitive environments'. *Journal of Economic Behavior & Organization*, *83*(1), 111–117.
16. Grijalva, E., Newman, D.A., Tay, L., Donnellan, M.B., Harms, P.D., Robins, R.W. & Yan, T. (2015). 'Gender differences in narcissism: a meta-analytic review'. *Psychological Bulletin*, *141*(2), 261.
17. 'Women's representation in Lok Sabha rises to a record at 14.4%'. *The Hindu*, 25 May 2019.
18. Ronay, R., Oostrom, J.K., Lehmann-Willenbrock, N., Mayoral, S. & Rusch, H. (2019). 'Playing the trump card: Why we select overconfident leaders and why it matters'. *The Leadership Quarterly*, *30*(6), 101316.
19. Costa, R. & Goldstein, A. 'Trump vows "insurance for everybody" in Obamacare replacement plan'. *The Washington Post*, 15 January 2017.
20. Liptak, K. 'Trump: "Nobody knew health care could be so complicated"'. *CNN Politics*, 28 February 2017.
21. 'How Popular Is Donald Trump?'. *FiveThirtyEight*, 20 January 2021.
22. Helm, T. 'Brexit has completely failed for UK, say clear majority of Britons—poll'. *The Guardian*, 30 December 2023.
23. McDonnell, A. 'Where do Scots stand on independence in 2022?'. *YouGov*, 14 June 2022.
24. Wood, V. 'No-deal Brexit to trigger civil unrest and food shortages, councils across UK warn'. *The Independent*, 14 September 2019.

25. Major, K. 'Why are we so surprised that Boris Johnson lied when he's been sacked for lying twice before?'. *The Independent*, 27 June 2016.
26. Ball, J. 'All the times Boris Johnson flat-out lied'. *iNews*, 9 July 2018.
27. Moore, R. 'An absurd vanity project for our age—Boris Johnson's garden bridge'. *The Guardian*, 17 February 2019.
28. For a good discussion see: Moore, D.A., Tenney, E.R. & Haran, U. (2015). 'Overprecision in judgment'. *The Wiley Blackwell Handbook of Judgment and Decision Making*, 2, 182–209.
29. Shipman, A.S. & Mumford, M.D. (2011). 'When confidence is detrimental: Influence of overconfidence on leadership effectiveness'. *Leadership Quarterly*, *22*(4), 649–665.
30. Sheffer, L. & Loewen, P. (2017). 'Electoral Confidence, Overconfidence, and Risky Behavior: Evidence from a Study with Elected Politicians'. *Political Behavior*, 31–51.
31. Baekgaard, M., Christensen, J., Dahlmann, C.M., Mathiasen, A. & Petersen, N.B.G. (2019). 'The Role of Evidence in Politics: Motivated Reasoning and Persuasion among Politicians'. *British Journal of Political Science*, *49*(3), 1117–1140.
32. Fast, N.J., Sivanathan, N., Mayer, N.D. & Galinsky, A.D. (2012). 'Power and overconfident decision-making'. *Organizational Behavior and Human Decision Processes*, *117*(2), 249–260.
33. Macenczak, L.A., Campbell, S., Henley, A.B. & Campbell, W.K. (2016). 'Direct and interactive effects of narcissism and power on overconfidence'. *Personality and Individual Differences*, *91*, 113–122.
34. Tost, L.P., Gino, F. & Larrick, R.P. (2012). 'Power, competitiveness, and advice taking: Why the powerful don't listen'. *Organizational Behavior and Human Decision Processes*, *117*(1), 53–65.
35. See, K.E., Morrison, E.W., Rothman, N.B. & Soll, J.B. (2011). 'The detrimental effects of power on confidence, advice taking, and accuracy'. *Organizational Behavior and Human Decision Processes*, *116*(2), 272–285.
36. Ronay, R., Oostrom, J.K., Lehmann-Willenbrock, N. & van Vugt, M. (2017). 'Pride before the fall: (Over)confidence predicts escalation of public commitment'. *Journal of Experimental Social Psychology*, *69*, 13–22.
37. Menon, R. 'Demonetisation: Zimbabwe, Myanmar, and USSR have been there, done that, and screwed themselves over', *Quartz*, 25 November 2016, https://qz.com/india/845803/demonetisation-zimbabwe-myanmar-and-ussr-have-been-there-done-that-and-screwed-themselves-over.

38. 'Made it clear to government that demonetisation was not a good idea: Raghuram Rajan'. *The Hindu*, 12 April 2018.
39. Chakravarty, P. 'Six years on, demonetisation must be seen as independent India's greatest economic folly'. *The Indian Express*, 8 November 2022.
40. Moharkan, F. & Goel, S. 'Consumption slowdown started with note ban: RBI data'. *Deccan Herald*, 7 September 2019.
41. Daniyal, S. 'History revisited: How Tughlaq's currency change led to chaos in 14th century India'. *Scroll*, 15 November 2016.
42. Boseley, S. 'Mbeki Aids denial 'caused 300,000 deaths''. *The Guardian*, 26 November 2008.
43 Hambling, D. 'Weatherwatch: Hitler's plan for intuitive meteorologists'. *The Guardian*, 12 October 2020.
44. Hotez, P.J. 'Anti-science kills: From Soviet embrace of pseudoscience to accelerated attacks on US biomedicine'. *PLOS Biology*, 28 January 2021.
45. Dugatkin, L.A. 'The Botanist Who Defied Stalin'. *Nautilus*, 21 April 2021.
46. Dikötter, F. 'Mao's Great Leap to Famine'. *The New York Times*, 15 December 2010.
47. For a critical analysis of this idea read: Massing, M. 'Does Democracy Avert Famine?'. *The New York Times*, 1 March 2003.
48. Menon, S. & Sirilal, R. 'Why is there a food emergency in Sri Lanka?'. *BBC News*, 20 September 2021.
49. 'Did organic farming cause Sri Lanka's collapse?'. *BBC World Service, The Inquiry*, 17 July 2022.
50. Son, B. 'Is eroding democracy bad for the economy? What Venezuela, Hungary and Turkey suggest'. *Scroll.in*, 6 February 2019.
51. Robinson, J.A. & Acemoglu, D. (2012). *Why nations fail: The origins of power, prosperity and poverty*. Profile Books, London.
52. Varieties of Democracy keeps track of autocratic politics worldwide and produces reports discussing their effects. See for example: Boese-Schlosser, V.A., Alizada, N., Lundstedt, M., Morisson, K., Natsika, N., Sato, Y., Tai, H. & Lindberg, S.I. 'Autocratization Changing Nature?' *Democracy Report 2022*, Varieties of Democracy Institute, March 1 2022.
53. 'Breaking Down Putin's Latest Move to Consolidate Power In Russia'. *NPR*, 17 January 2020.
54. 'Ipsos Perils of Perception'. *Ipsos UK*, 6 December 2018, https://www.slideshare.net/IpsosMORI/ipsos-perils-of-perception-2018-125172179.
55. Ortoleva, P. & Snowberg, E. (2018). 'Overconfidence in political behavior'. *The American Economic Review*, *105*(2), 504–535.

56. Bond, S. 'Just 12 People Are Behind Most Vaccine Hoaxes On Social Media, Research Shows'. *NPR*, 14 May 2021.
57. 'Political Polarization in the American Public'. *Pew Research Center*, 12 June 2014.
58. Ahler, D.J. & Sood, G. (2017). 'The Parties in our Heads: Misperceptions About Party Composition and Their Consequences'. *The Journal of Politics*, 94.
59. van Bavel, J.J. & Pereira, A. (2017). 'The partisan brain: An Identity-based model of political belief'. *Trends in Cognitive Sciences*.
60. Bavel, J.V. 'Partisan Brain'. 30 June 2018, https://www.slideshare.net/JayVanBavel/partisan-brain.
61. Blais, A., Gidengil, E. & Kilibarda, A. (2017). 'Partisanship, information, and perceptions of government corruption'. *International Journal of Public Opinion Research*, *29*(1), 95–110.
62. Lyons, J. & Jaeger, W.P. (2014). 'Who do voters blame for policy failure? Information and the partisan assignment of blame'. *State Politics and Policy Quarterly*, *14*(3), 321–341.
63. 'A Sampling of Public Opinion in India'. *Pew Research Center*, 25 March 2019.
64. Ecker, U.K.H. & Ang, L.C. (2019). 'Political Attitudes and the Processing of Misinformation Corrections'. *Political Psychology*, *40*(2), 241–260.
65. Jones, P.E. (2020). 'Partisanship, Political Awareness, and Retrospective Evaluations, 1956–2016'. *Political Behavior*, *42*(4), 1295–1317.
66. Taber, C.S. & Lodge, M. (2006). 'Motivated skepticism in the evaluation of political beliefs'. *American Journal of Political Science*, *50*(3), 755–769.
67. Thibodeau, P., Peebles, M.M., Grodner, D.J. & Durgin, F.H. (2015). 'The Wished-For Always Wins Until the Winner Was Inevitable All Along: Motivated Reasoning and Belief Bias Regulate Emotion During Elections'. *Political Psychology*, *36*(4), 431–448.
68. Jerit, J. & Barabas, J. (2012). 'Partisan perceptual bias and the information environment'. *Journal of Politics*, *74*(3), 672–684.
69. Kahan, D.M., Peters, E., Dawson, E.C. & Paul Slovic (2017). 'Motivated numeracy and enlightened self-government'. *Behavioural Public Policy, 1*(1), 54-86.
70. Kahan, D.M. (2017). 'Misconceptions, Misinformation, and the Logic of Identity-Protective Cognition'. Cultural Cognition Project Working Paper Series No. 164, Yale Law School, Public Law Research Paper No. 605 & Yale Law & Economics Research Paper No. 575.
71. Rollwage, M., Dolan, J. & Fleming, S.M. (2018). 'Metacognitive failure as a feature of those holding radical political beliefs'. *Current Biology*, *344*(24), 4014–4021.

72. Gollwitzer, A., Martel, C., Brady, W.J., Pärnamets, P., Freedman, I.G., Knowles, E.D. & van Bavel, J.J. (2020). 'Partisan differences in physical distancing are linked to health outcomes during the COVID-19 pandemic'. *Nature Human Behaviour*, *4*(11), 1186–1197.
73. Yong, E. 'How the Pandemic Defeated America'. *The Atlantic*, 4 August 2020.
74. 'Pandemic fears are boosting demand for trustworthy news'. *The Economist*, 29 July 2020.
75. 'People "fly to quality" news on social sites when faced with uncertainty'. *University of Michigan School of Information*, 22 July 2020.
76. Bullock, J.G., Gerber, A.S., Hill, S.J. & Huber, G.A. (2013). 'Partisan Bias in Factual Beliefs about Politics'. *Quarterly Journal of Political Science*, *10*(4), 519–578.
77. Khanna, K. & Sood, G. (2017). 'Motivated Responding in Studies of Factual Learning'. *Political Behavior*, *40*(1), 1–23.
78. 'Ipsos MORI State of the Nation 2018'. *Ipsos UK*, 20 December 2018, https://www.slideshare.net/IpsosMORI/ipsos-mori-state-of-the-nation-2018-126344104.
79. Mounk, Y. & Kyle, J. 'What 46 Populist Leaders Did to Democracy'. *The Atlantic*, 26 December 2018.
80. Traub, J. 'The Pandemic Is the World's Long Overdue Reality Check'. *Foreign Policy*, 1 July 2020.

13. OVERCOMING OVERCONFIDENCE

1. For summaries of the causes of overconfidence and strategies for dealing with it, see Russo, J.E. & Schoemaker, P.J. (1992). 'Managing overconfidence'. *Sloan Management Review*, *33*(2), 7-17. Also, Dunning, D., Heath, C. & Suls, J.M. (2004). 'Flawed self-assessment: Implications for health, education, and the workplace'. *Psychological Science in the Public Interest*, *5*(3), 69–106.
2. 'Guide to developing the project business case'. *HM Treasury*, 2018.
3. As highlighted in Kahneman, D. (2011). *Thinking, Fast and Slow*. Farrar, Straus and Giroux, New York.
4. Silver, N. 'There Really Was A Liberal Media Bubble'. *FiveThirtyEight*, 10 March 2017.
5. Russo, J.E. & Schoemaker, P.J. (1992). 'Managing overconfidence'. *Sloan Management Review*, *33*(2), 7–17.
6. Malmendier, U. & Tate, G. (2008). 'Who makes acquisitions? CEO overconfidence and the market's reaction'. *Journal of Financial Economics*, *89*(1), 20–43.

7. Anderson, E. 'Red teaming 101: What is red teaming?'. *IBM*, 19 July 2023, https://www.ibm.com/blog/red-teaming-101-w.
8. Kahneman, D. (2011). *Thinking, Fast and Slow*. Farrar, Straus and Giroux, New York.
9. Again, summarised well in Kahneman, D. (2011). *Thinking, Fast and Slow*. Farrar, Straus and Giroux, New York.
10. Obermeyer, Z., Powers, B., Vogeli, C. & Mullainathan, S. (2019). 'Dissecting racial bias in an algorithm used to manage the health of populations'. *Science*, *366*(6464), 447–453.
11. 'Amazon scrapped "sexist AI" tool'. *BBC News*, 10 October 2018.
12. Martin, K. (2019). 'Ethical implications and accountability of algorithms'. *Journal of business ethics*, *160*, 835–850.
13. For a good discussion, see Dunning, D., Heath, C. & Suls, J.M. (2004). 'Flawed Self-Assessment Implications for Health, Education, and the Workplace'. *Psychological Science in the Public Interest*, *5*(3), 69–106.
14. Kreuter, M.W. & Strecher, V.J. (1995). 'Changing inaccurate perceptions of health risk: results from a randomized trial'. *Health Psychology*, *14*(1), 56.
15. Lamba, S. & Nityananda, V. (2014). 'Self-deceived individuals are better at deceiving others'. *PloS One*, *9*(8), e104562.
16. Baranski, J.V. & Petrusic, W.M. (1994). 'The calibration and resolution of confidence in perceptual judgments'. *Perception & Psychophysics*, *55*(4), 412–428.
17. Swire, B., Berinsky, A.J., Lewandowsky, S. & Ecker, U.K. (2017). 'Processing political misinformation: Comprehending the Trump phenomenon'. *Royal Society Open Science*, *4*(3), 160802.
18. Aird, M.J., Ecker, U.K.H., Swire, B., Berinsky, A.J. & Lewandowsky, S. (2019). 'Does truth matter to voters? The effects of correcting political misinformation in an Australian sample'. *Royal Society Open Science*, *5*(12), 180593.
19. Swire-Thompson, B., Ecker, U.K., Lewandowsky, S. & Berinsky, A.J. (2020). 'They might be a liar but they're my liar: Source evaluation and the prevalence of misinformation'. *Political Psychology*, *41*(1), 21–34.
20. Koriat, A., Lichtenstein, S. & Fischhoff, B. (1980). 'Reasons for confidence'. *Journal of Experimental Psychology: Human Learning and Memory*, 6(2), 107.
21. Ahler, D.J. & Sood, G. (2017). 'The Parties in our Heads: Misperceptions About Party Composition and Their Consequences'. *The Journal of Politics*,, 94.
22. Dunning, D., Heath, C. & Suls, J.M. (2018). 'Reflections on self-reflection: Contemplating flawed self-judgments in the clinic, classroom,

and office cubicle'. *Perspectives on Psychological Science*, *13*(2), 185–189.

23. Hansen, W.B. & Graham, J.W. (1991). 'Preventing alcohol, marijuana, and cigarette use among adolescents: Peer pressure resistance training versus establishing conservative norms'. *Preventive Medicine*, *20*(3), 414–430.
24. Kruger, J. & Dunning, D. (1999). 'Unskilled and unaware of it: how difficulties in recognizing one's own incompetence lead to inflated self-assessments'. *Journal of Personality and Social Psychology*, *77*(6), 1121.
25. Pennycook, G. & Rand, D.G. (2019). 'Lazy, not biased: Susceptibility to partisan fake news is better explained by lack of reasoning than by motivated reasoning'. *Cognition*, *188*(September 2017), 39–50.
26. Pennycook, G. & Rand, D.G. (2021). 'The Psychology of Fake News'. *Trends in Cognitive Sciences*, *25*(5), 388–402.
27. Pennycook, G. & Rand, D.G. (2021). 'The Psychology of Fake News'. *Trends in Cognitive Sciences*, *25*(5), 388–402.
28. Ehrlinger, J., Mitchum, A.L. & Dweck, C.S. (2016). 'Understanding overconfidence: Theories of intelligence, preferential attention, and distorted self-assessment'. *Journal of Experimental Social Psychology*, *63*, 94–100.
29. Gregersen, N.P. (1996). 'Young drivers' overestimation of their own skill—an experiment on the relation between training strategy and skill'. *Accident Analysis & Prevention*, *28*(2), 243–250.
30. As discussed in Benoit, J.P., Dubra, J. & Moore, D.A. (2015). 'Does the better-than-average effect show that people are overconfident?: Two experiments'. *Journal of the European Economic Association*, *13*(2), 293–329.
31. Yagil, D., Reuveni, Y. & Segal-Karpas, D. (2020). 'Physicians' cognitive strategies for avoiding overconfidence'. *Evaluation in Clinical Practice*, *May*, 1–7.
32. Lemaitre, T., Carrier, N., Farrands, A., Gosselin, V., Petit, G. & Gagneur, A. (2019). 'Impact of a vaccination promotion intervention using motivational interview techniques on long-term vaccine coverage: the PromoVac strategy'. *Human Vaccines & Immunotherapeutics*, *15*(3), 732–739.
33. Gigerenzer, G., Hoffrage, U. & Kleinbölting, H. (1991). 'Probabilistic mental models: a Brunswikian theory of confidence'. *Psychological Review*, *98*(4), 506.
34. Falchikov, N. & Boud, D. (1989). 'Student self-assessment in higher education: A meta-analysis'. *Review of Educational Research*, *59*(4), 395–430.

35. Khanna, K. & Sood, G. (2017). 'Motivated Responding in Studies of Factual Learning'. *Political Behavior*, *40*(1), 1–23.
36. Gietl, D. & Kassner, B. (2020). 'Managerial overconfidence and bank bailouts'. *Journal of Economic Behavior & Organization*, *179*, 202–222.
37. Discussed in Leeper, T.J. & Slothuus, R. (2014). 'Political parties, motivated reasoning, and public opinion formation'. *Political Psychology*, *35*, 129–156.
38. Tetlock, P.E. (1983). 'Accountability and complexity of thought'. *Journal of Personality and Social Psychology*, *45*(1), 74.
39. Badrinathan, S. & Chauchard, S. (2023). '"I Don't Think That's True, Bro!" Social Corrections of Misinformation in India'. *The International Journal of Press/Politics*, *29*(2), 394–416.
40. Pennycook, G., Epstein, Z., Mosleh, M., Arechar, A.A., Eckles, D. & Rand, D.G. (2021). 'Shifting attention to accuracy can reduce misinformation online'. *Nature*, *592*(7855), 590–595.
41. Lyons, B.A., Montgomery, J.M., Guess, A.M., Nyhan, B. & Reifler, J. (2021). 'Overconfidence in news judgments is associated with false news susceptibility'. *Proceedings of the National Academy of Sciences of the United States of America*, *118*(23), e2019527118.
42. Pronin, E., Lin, D.Y. & Ross, L. (2002). 'The Bias Blind Spot : Perceptions of Bias in Self Versus Others'. *Personality and Social Psychology Bulletin*, *28*(3), 369–381.
43. Ecker, U.K.H. & Ang, L.C. (2018). 'Political Attitudes and the Processing of Misinformation Corrections'. *Political Psychology*, *40*(2), 241–260.
44. Cook, J., Lewandowsky, S. & Ecker, U.K. (2017). 'Neutralizing misinformation through inoculation: Exposing misleading argumentation techniques reduces their influence'. *PloS One*, *12*(5), e0175799.
45. Roozenbeek, J., Van Der Linden, S., Goldberg, B., Rathje, S. & Lewandowsky, S. (2022). 'Psychological inoculation improves resilience against misinformation on social media'. *Science Advances*, *8*(34), eabo6254.
46. Kahan, Dan M. (2017). 'Misconceptions, Misinformation, and the Logic of Identity-Protective Cognition'. Cultural Cognition Project Working Paper Series No. 164, Yale Law School, Public Law Research Paper No. 605 & Yale Law & Economics Research Paper No. 575.
47. Nyhan, B. & Reifler, J. (2010). 'When corrections fail: The persistence of political misperceptions'. *Political Behavior*, *32*(2), 303–330.
48. Bail, C.A., Argyle, L.P., Brown, T. W., Bumpus, J.P., Chen, H., Fallin Hunzaker, M.B., Lee, J., Mann, M., Merhout, F. & Volfovsky, A. (2018).

'Exposure to opposing views on social media can increase political polarization'. *Proceedings of the National Academy of Sciences of the United States of America*, *115*(37), 9216–9221.

49. Badrinathan, S. (2021). 'Educative interventions to combat misinformation: Evidence from a field experiment in India'. *American Political Science Review*, *115*(4), 1325–1341.
50. Cook, J. & Lewandowsky, S. (2016). 'Rational irrationality: Modeling climate change belief polarization using Bayesian networks'. *Topics in Cognitive Science*, *8*(1), 160–179.
51. Cook, J., Lewandowsky, S. & Ecker, U.K. (2017). 'Neutralizing misinformation through inoculation: Exposing misleading argumentation techniques reduces their influence'. *PloS One*, *12*(5), e0175799.
52. Wood, T. & Porter, E. (2018). 'The Elusive Backfire Effect: Mass Attitudes' Steadfast Factual Adherence'. *Political Behavior*, 1–29.
53. Kubin, E., Puryear, C., Schein, C. & Gray, K. (2021). Personal experiences bridge moral and political divides better than facts. *Proceedings of the National Academy of Sciences*, *118*(6), e2008389118.
54. Kahan, D.M., Landrum, A., Carpenter, K., Helft, L. & Hall Jamieson, K. (2017). 'Science curiosity and political information processing'. *Political Psychology*, *38*, 179–199.
55. Altay, S., Schwartz, M., Hacquin, A.S., Allard, A., Blancke, S. & Mercier, H. (2022). 'Scaling up interactive argumentation by providing counterarguments with a chatbot'. *Nature Human Behaviour*, *6*(4), 579–592.
56. Brand, C.O. & Stafford, T. (2022). 'Using dialogues to increase positive attitudes towards COVID-19 vaccines in a vaccine-hesitant UK population'. *Royal Society Open Science*, *9*(10), 220366.
57. Johnson, D.D. & Fowler, J.H. (2011). 'The evolution of overconfidence'. *Nature,* 477(7364), 317–320.

Index